PRAISE FOR *THE LEADERSHIP SECRETS OF NICK SABAN*

"This is a remarkable must-read book—an absolute masterpiece. John Talty has written an instant classic, one that grabs you on the first page and holds you breathlessly until its conclusion. The book takes you deep into the secret vault of college football's greatest coach with never-revealed stories and piercing analysis. Talty was already considered one of the sport's finest commentators and with this, he has cemented his legacy."
> —**Paul Finebaum, ESPN commentator and radio host**

"John Talty peels back the curtain on the greatest college football coach in the sport's history, giving us the rare inside look at Nick Saban's personality, tactics, and motivations. His book digs deep on a man few know well, offering an insightful, exciting, and revealing read, all in an effort to answer the mystery: *How's he done it?*"
> —**Ross Dellenger, *Sports Illustrated* national college football writer**

"I've spent my career teaching business leadership strategies. John Talty's new book, *The Leadership Secrets of Nick Saban*, just jumped to the top of my recommended reading list for my clients. It's an enjoyable and useful deep dive into what makes Saban tick, and how he creates a 'clear-eyed strategy' to building and maintaining a successful organization."
> —**Joe Calloway, author of *Be the Best at What Matters Most***

"I would recommend this book for everyone from Fortune 500 CEOs to my children, as they grow into leadership roles. John Talty's writing is so easy to read and accessible to all that anyone would benefit from reading this book."
> —**Sgt. Noah Galloway (retired), Purple Heart recipient and author of *Living with No Excuses: The Remarkable Rebirth of an American Soldier***

"John Talty has captured the key takeaways of Nick Saban's leadership excellence, and what he presents works—IF YOU DO IT. Get this book for everyone on your leadership team. Go through it together, hold each other accountable, and exponentially grow your organization. Success leaves clues. Learn from Saban and Talty."
> —**Dave Anderson, president of LearnToLead and author of *Intentional Mindset***

The
Leadership
Secrets *of*
Nick Saban

The
Leadership
Secrets *of*
Nick Saban

HOW ALABAMA'S COACH
BECAME THE GREATEST EVER

JOHN TALTY

Matt Holt Books
An Imprint of BenBella Books, Inc.
Dallas, TX

Matt Holt is an imprint of BenBella Books, Inc.
10440 N. Central Expressway
Suite 800
Dallas, TX 75231
benbellabooks.com
Send feedback to feedback@benbellabooks.com

BenBella and *Matt Holt* are federally registered trademarks.

Printed in the United States of America
10 9 8 7 6 5 4 3 2

Library of Congress Control Number: 2021062757
ISBN 9781637740835 (hardcover)
ISBN 9781637740842 (electronic)

Editing by Katie Dickman
Copyediting by Michael Fedison
Proofreading by Jenny Bridges and Doug Johnson
Indexing by Amy Murphy
Text design and composition by Aaron Edmiston
Cover design by Brigid Pearson
Cover image © AP Photo/Vasha Hunt
Printed by Lake Book Manufacturing

Special discounts for bulk sales are available.
Please contact bulkorders@benbellabooks.com.

For my son, Jack

Contents

Introduction 1

CHAPTER 1: The Turnaround Artist 7

CHAPTER 2: Build Your Team Framework 19

CHAPTER 3: Only Promise Opportunity 31

CHAPTER 4: You Can't Be the Only Leader 43

CHAPTER 5: Use Staff Turnover to Improve 57

CHAPTER 6: Give Distressed Assets Another Chance 73

CHAPTER 7: "The Process" 85

CHAPTER 8: Don't Let Outside Factors Impact Your Goals 95

CHAPTER 9: Pick Where You Can Win 105

CHAPTER 10: Delegation Is Good but Too Much Kills the Culture 117

CHAPTER 11: Preparation Is Everything 129

CHAPTER 12: Don't Waste a Failing 147

CHAPTER 13: Evaluate Yourself Constantly, Evolve When Necessary 159

CHAPTER 14: Honesty Is Hard but Critical 171

CHAPTER 15: "Rat Poison" and Other Lessons from the Podium 183

CHAPTER 16: Complacency Kills Future Success 195

CHAPTER 17: Be True to Yourself 205

CHAPTER 18: Applying Saban's Lessons Beyond Football 217

Acknowledgments 227

Index 229

Introduction

As Nick Saban raised the championship trophy above his head with confetti falling around him in Hard Rock Stadium, it solidified what many already knew to be true: he was college football's greatest coach ever.

His Alabama team easily defeated Ohio State on January 11, 2021, for his seventh national championship—his sixth while at Alabama—surpassing legendary Alabama coach Paul "Bear" Bryant for the most in the sport's history. Only moments after the game ended, there were already declarations that the 2020 Alabama team was the greatest in college football history.

That team highlighted so much of what makes Saban the greatest coach ever. The win over Ohio State showcased Saban's evolution as a coach, his refusal to accept complacency amid tremendous success, and his unmatched track record of hiring staff and recruiting players. Navigating Alabama to a national championship amid a global pandemic with daily coronavirus testing and "bubble" living required Saban's best coaching leadership yet.

It marked the culmination of a decades-long journey from an undersized football player in West Virginia whose father owned a local gas station to college football's highest-paid and most prominent coach. Nick Saban Sr. passed away when he was only forty-six years old—Nick Jr. was in college at the time—but his lessons and way of living carry the Alabama coach to this day. Growing up in a West Virginia mining town, Saban was taught that hard work was the only way to make it, and there were no shortcuts to success. Nick Sr. would tell his son, "If you don't have the time to do it right, where do you find the time to do it over? Because it's going to be done right." He learned that lesson over and over again when servicing cars at his dad's gas station as a teenager, lamenting when dark-colored cars came in, knowing his dad would make him wipe them down over and over again until there weren't any streaks left.

Big Nick, as he was known, was a tough, hardworking man who demanded perfection from his son in every aspect of his life. He loved his son but wasn't one to dole out praise easily. He was the type of parent who would point out his son's four turnovers after he led his basketball team to a win with 30 points. In his book, *How Good Do You Want to Be?*, Saban wrote that his father took him to the mines to send a message after he got a D in his eighth-grade music class. "When we reached the bottom, he turned to me, his face glowing red in the deep black. Is this what you want? You want to work down here the rest of your life? It scared me straight." His influence left a deep impression on a young Nick Saban, and set him on the path to always strive for more and never let success knock him off it.

"His father made him do things that on the outside looking in almost look like were too strong for a kid to have to do," says Darren Anderson, a member of the first team Saban led as head coach. "But it created a person who will never relent."

And that's who Saban is. He's a hard-charging leader who has never been satisfied with his personal success and has never stopped pushing his organizations to strive for more. The mentality his father instilled in him at an early age never went away as he became more famous and successful over his career.

In this book, we'll examine how that relentless attitude powered Saban's climb to college football's mountaintop and, most impressively, how he stayed atop it. It's not a biography but rather a leadership and business case study on the most successful coach and most successful college football program in history. It draws from hundreds of hours of interviews with Saban's former players, coaches, friends, rivals, and others who have come into his orbit over the years to offer never-before-heard stories that provide a window into Saban's success and a blueprint for how his approach can work in organizations everywhere. It examines how he finds and acquires the best players, what he looks for in the hiring process, his attention-to-detail preparations, and how he's been able to steer his organization clear of complacency amid tremendous success, among many other lessons.

It started in Fairmont, West Virginia, on Halloween 1951, when Nicholas Lou Saban Jr. entered this world. Many years later, Saban joked that his mother was still wondering whether she got a trick or a treat with him. As an adolescent, he played for his father's Pop Warner team, where he got early lessons about conditioning, getting what you demand, and the need for a relentless drive. His father was a demanding youth coach—more demanding than even Nick would be as a college coach—but the results spoke for themselves: the Idamay Black Diamonds had a thirty-nine-game winning streak at one point.

He played quarterback for Monongah High School and became known for getting the absolute most out of his abilities as the heady leader of the team. He wanted to play college football for his home school, West Virginia University, but when the school wasn't interested in a 5-foot-8 player with limited athleticism, he had to look elsewhere. He earned a scholarship offer to Kent State where he'd learn at the hand of Don James, a man who changed his life and became one of the most impactful mentors of his career. At Kent State, Saban switched to defensive back, a position he fell in love with, and became one of the leaders on a defense that included future NFL Hall of Fame linebacker Jack Lambert. "Nick was a hard worker, dedicated," says former teammate Gary Pinkel. "Really good player." When Saban's playing career at Kent State was over, James convinced him to spend a year as a defensive graduate assistant (GA). He had planned to go into the car business, but with his wife, Terry, needing to complete one more year of school, he accepted James' offer to get into the coaching business. He never looked back.

He became a coaching nomad, bouncing around from job to job every few years. After two years as a GA and two years as a linebackers coach at Kent State, he jumped to Syracuse to become Frank Maloney's outside linebackers coach. From there, an ambitious Saban returned home to coach at West Virginia for two years, then jumped to Ohio State for two seasons and then one at Navy. He slowed his job-jumping ways when he landed at Michigan State, enjoying the chance to learn program-building and defensive strategies under George Perles, a Chuck Noll disciple. While at Michigan State, he pursued the head coaching job at his alma mater but lost out to Dick Crum, a decision that crushed Saban. Kent State picked Crum over Saban not because the young Michigan State assistant wasn't good enough, but because the school's leaders believed the experienced Crum was less likely to screw up, according to Glen Mason, who preceded Crum at Kent State and personally recommended Saban for the job. That shortsighted decision-making stuck with Saban and informed later moves he made. He left Michigan State for the NFL, a world he'd return to multiple times, joining the Houston Oilers as Jerry Glanville's defensive backs coach.

After seventeen years as an assistant, he got his first head coaching opportunity at Toledo in 1989. His career really took off then as he became a coach worthy of a book like this. Four years with Bill Belichick in Cleveland. Five seasons as Michigan State's head coach. Five more at Louisiana State, where he won his first national championship. A two-year pit stop in the NFL as the Miami Dolphins' head coach and then back to college football, where he's reigned ever since. At Alabama, he's racked up nearly two hundred wins, six national championships, and put countless players into the NFL. After winning the 2021 national championship, Saban had so thoroughly dominated college football that *USA Today* had a story with the headline, "Alabama Is a College Football Monopoly. Is It Time to Break it Up?" which included suggestions on how to slow down the Tide dynasty. Saban left no doubt he was college football's greatest coach ever.

As a reporter and editor, I've spent years working to understand what makes Saban tick. I could understand it took hard work and dedication to have the success he did at Alabama, but I wanted to know what powered it and sustained it. I wasn't the only one searching for the recipe, either, as organizations collectively committed hundreds of millions of dollars hiring Saban's disciples hoping they'd bring a little of his magic with him.

I've covered Alabama national title victories and Alabama national title losses. I was there when national sportswriters declared the Alabama dynasty over, and when those same writers declared Saban the greatest ever. I've seen Saban laugh, yell, and cry. I've been witness to famous Saban rants. Over the years, I've talked to hundreds of people who know Saban.

I poured all that knowledge into this book, which will give you the blue-print Saban has used to build college football's greatest dynasty and truly one of the most successful organizations of the twenty-first century in any indus-try. But it'll also show you the complexities of a man who is much more than just a football coach. He is a man who cares what people think of him but is still willing to make the hard, unpopular decisions. He can bristle as much at positive stories about himself—that's rat poison—as he does of coverage that leans into the negative. He can be just as prone to yelling at an assistant coach during a game—in Saban's lexicon he calls those "ass chewings"—as he is to call in a job recommendation for a player who played for him twenty years ago.

Nick Saban can be abrasive and he can be charming. He can be gruff and he can be funny. He can be rude and he can be generous. He is a real human being, a man with strengths and weaknesses like the rest of us. This book isn't here to paint Saban as a perfect leader, because there's no such thing.

What he is, though, is an incredibly successful leader, and he didn't achieve that through luck or happenstance. He has developed a clear-eyed strategy to building and maintaining a successful organization that he's used to achieve unprecedented accomplishments.

Want to know how college football's greatest coach does it? It starts here.

CHAPTER 1

The Turnaround Artist

W hen a thirty-eight-year-old Nick Saban arrived at Toledo, it didn't take long for everyone to realize he meant business.

Toledo introduced him as its new head coach on December 22, 1989—however, at the time, he wasn't anything close to a known quantity. Players knew him only as some guy from the NFL.

His new team might not have known much about him when he walked in, but it quickly learned. When Saban addressed the group for the first time, there was no nervousness or long motivational speech about winning championships. It was short, to the point, and immediately established what his expectations were.

"Everybody sat up at attention," says safety Tim Caffey. "It was like, 'Whoa, this is different.' This is going to be a different culture from what we just went through last year."

Even as a young head coach, Saban knew what he wanted, and he wasn't going to wait to inform his new organization of his intentions. Inheriting a team that went 6-5 the previous two years, he didn't set up focus groups or waste months evaluating what did and didn't work under the previous head coach. For Saban, certain things were nonnegotiable and needed to happen immediately to build the winning culture he desired.

It started with a winter conditioning program that would prove to be a key ingredient to Saban's success throughout his career. Saban had a loyal lieutenant in strength and conditioning coach Ken Mannie, an energetic, high-powered coach who quickly made his presence felt. Mannie was like a pit bull who Saban let off his leash, barking at players and snarling at anyone who questioned his commands. He told the players he "pissed on all four corners of the building." Saban directed Mannie to turn what they inherited into a disciplined, tough football team with the stamina to outlast opponents on the field. To have any hope of achieving that in the first year, the work had to begin right away.

It's what Harvard Business School professor John Kotter calls instilling a "sense of urgency," a key first step in successfully leading change within an organization. It is critical to establish early on why an organization must change and the steps to do so to get the necessary buy-in to enact said change in an expeditious fashion. Kotter identified eight key steps in leading change at an organization, many of which Saban enacted years before the professor's best-selling book, *Leading Change*, came out in 1996. Kotter believes you have to:

1. Create a sense of urgency
2. Create a guiding coalition
3. Develop a vision and strategy
4. Communicate the change vision
5. Empower action
6. Generate short-term wins
7. Consolidate gains and empower more change
8. Anchor change in the culture

Before the first winter conditioning session, Saban was honest when he told his team, "This is going to be the hardest thing you ever do." He was very clear in setting and communicating expectations from the beginning about what it would take to succeed under his leadership. Initially, the players were skeptical about that proclamation. The returning players had been through winter conditioning before and thought they knew what to expect. They thought it was just a new coach trying to talk a big game.

They were wrong.

"Man, it was hard," says former linebacker Matt Eberflus. "The one thing that you recognized right away was you were going to move at his pace, and his pace was a championship pace. He was trying to toughen you up mentally as well as physically."

Saban held everyone to the same high standard, too. Before that first conditioning session, Saban met with his new staff and assigned each coach a different drill to run. He turned to L.C. Cole, his running backs coach, and asked him whether he could handle the jump rope drill. Cole felt confident he could.

The next day, Toledo players were stumbling around and struggling to do even basic tasks, including Cole's jump rope station. Saban, clad in a tie and blazer, walked around the basketball gym monitoring the sixteen stations and jotting down notes but saying very little. When the coaching staff met after the workout, Saban called out Cole for what he considered to be substandard jump rope techniques.

"L.C., what the hell are you doing?" Saban bellowed. "What is this, Suzy at the park? That ain't good enough."

He had similar critiques for the other coaches.

"He went around that whole table to every last coach and said, 'This is the way we want it done, and I don't want it done any other kind of way,'" Cole says. "So, in my mind, I said those jokers tomorrow are going to turn this rope. This rope is going to be turning."

Saban intended to establish that everything players and coaches did was to be done to a certain standard from the very first day. He laid out in clear terms what that standard was and communicated it to everyone in the building. One of Saban's favorite sayings is, "Mediocre people don't like high achievers, and high achievers don't like mediocre people." Saban believes it is of critical importance that everyone holds the same high standards if the organization has any chance of being successful, and those who are unwilling to do so need to look for opportunities elsewhere. When he didn't see it happening, he never hesitated to intervene and correct the behavior, as he did with Cole. Getting Cole wholly on board with his vision was important to getting his message reinforced with other members of the organization and to start building what Kotter calls a "guiding coalition" of other change agents. As you take over an organization, you need to identify and empower valuable allies who can carry out your change directives.

Not everyone embraced Saban's style. He faced the same challenges any leader faces when taking over a new organization. Whether it's football players or grocery store employees, when you inherit a group of people you didn't choose, there can be some early tension and resistance to accepting the new direction, especially when it is challenging. At Toledo, Saban took over a team accustomed to doing things a certain way. They had experienced moderate success to that point and enjoyed some of the perks of being a football player on a college campus. Players went out on Thursday nights, not worried about how it would impact them for their workouts the following morning. That didn't last under Saban.

"You didn't want any alcohol coming out of your system because he set up four trash cans and one in the middle," Caffey says. "He said, 'Don't ever throw up on my floor.' It happened one time, and that was it. That killed that mentality of 'I'm going to go out and kick it, and then work out.'"

Saban's extreme enforced culture change had players "dropping like flies," with six or seven players quitting the team before spring practice even started. Some of them were even players expected to have starting roles. Darren Anderson, a junior safety on the team, expected Saban to weed out the weak and then dial back the intensity once the team got settled. "But he pushes on the gas," Anderson says, "and he doesn't stop."

As a first-time head coach, Saban had a clear plan on what he wanted to do, but he was still rough around the edges. He used language that wouldn't exactly fly in a corporate boardroom. He was still trying to figure out the right buttons to push with his players, a process he'd work hard to perfect over the course of his career. He wanted to hold everyone to the same standard, but he'd learn later on there was a way to do that while still individualizing the system to best suit people with different needs and motivations. He struggled to understand why everyone didn't have the same hard-charging motivation as he did, and was especially flummoxed when veteran players quit the team rather than put in the work. He battled hard with defensive lineman Dan Williams, the best player on the team and a future NFL first-round pick, threatening to kick him off the team multiple times when he didn't listen to his coaches and put in the required effort.

Williams towered over his 5-foot-8 coach, but Saban let him know in no uncertain terms who was in charge. "He'd walk up on those big guys and get right in their faces," Cole says. "I'd think, 'Man, those guys are going to pound you.' But he'd be right up in their face talking to them. That's how he was."

Saban was prepared for the confrontations after coming off the most difficult years of his early coaching career. In his first foray into the NFL, Jerry Glanville handed him a rowdy group of players who seemed to relish making their stern position coach's life miserable. The Houston Oilers' defensive backs routinely cursed Saban out, turned their backs while he was talking, and questioned his directives. It was a culture shock for Saban, who had dealt with a far more obedient group at Michigan State. They seemed to take their cue from their renegade head coach, Glanville, who dressed in all black and would routinely leave tickets for deceased celebrities like Elvis Presley at the ticket office. "There's nobody there you'd want to take home to meet your family," Glanville told the *Houston Chronicle*. "We told [Saban] he was getting maybe the worst group in the history of football."

Saban didn't wilt under pressure. At times he reacted poorly to the disobedience—he and one player almost got into a fight during a film session—but he stuck to his plan. Eventually, the defensive backs' room bought into his vision when they realized he knew his stuff. "He didn't care if you were a ten-year veteran or a rookie; this is how we're going to do stuff," says former cornerback Cris Dishman, a rookie on that Oilers team. "There was no 'You're going to do it your way.' He would never give in and that's what you respect about him. He knew his way was the right way."

The methods weren't perfect but the results proved he was on to something. As players got faster and stronger through winter conditioning and spring practice, there was a palpable sense of buy-in from the team. He turned players like Anderson, who admits he was a little turned off by Saban's aggressive culture change, into converts. As you transform an organization, you have to give its members a reason to believe in you. Communicating a clear-eyed vision is of the utmost importance, but so is actually showing people you know what you're talking about in convincing them you can make them better. That last part is crucial, as an authentic desire to make everyone better for their gain as much as yours when enforcing change can be the difference between being a transformational leader and a toxic one. Saban excelled at that.

"He came into the defensive backs' room and started talking about stuff that just rang true. It just sounded so right," Anderson says. "As a cornerback, when you have someone who can come in and help you win the war, you just listen to him. He had me at hello."

That carried over to the season, when Toledo started the year 6-0 and ultimately won a share of a conference championship. In his first year as a head coach, Saban made Toledo into a champion. "For a lot of those guys, I can guarantee they're successful because of what we did that year," Caffey says. "It showed us what it takes to be a champion."

As Saban went on to have more and more success at every subsequent stop, the initial step after taking over an organization never changed. He needed to mold the culture to his satisfaction, and he did that through hard work.

When Saban got to Michigan State in 1995, he came with a reputation as one of the NFL's top defensive coordinators after four seasons of learning at the hand of Bill Belichick with the Cleveland Browns, one of the most impactful relationships of his career. That first Michigan State team meeting followed the same playbook as the one he conducted five years earlier in Toledo. "I remember it being all business," says former Michigan State tight end Josh Keur. "It was an immediate 180-degree turn of the entire ship. He was there to win and he made that clear to his staff."

Saban again brought Mannie with him to establish the culture he wanted. He was replacing his mentor, Perles, a man he spent five seasons working for in the mid-1980s. You can still see Perles' fingerprints on things Saban does at Alabama, as the Michigan State head coach was ahead of his time in many ways. But at the end of Perles' tenure at Michigan State, the standard Saban witnessed during his time working for him seemed to be slipping. Saban's "Fourth Quarter Program" conditioning regimen came from his time working under Perles, but the program went through three strength and conditioning coaches in three years, destroying any continuity for the players. By the time Saban arrived, players remember the offseason workout program consisting of little more than a weekly workout with occasional stretching. The Spartans didn't make a bowl game those final four seasons under Perles.

"A lot of guys weren't going in there lifting because they weren't held accountable," says former Michigan State defensive lineman Chris Smith. "The guys who really wanted to lift did and the guys who didn't wouldn't come."

Directly after the first team meeting, Saban put his new team through a conditioning session. There was no grace period to get to know the new boss; it was straight to work. The results were rough but they sent a message. Saban would tell his team, "Your toughness is a direct reflection of your conditioning."

"I don't know if 80 percent of the team didn't vomit following that team meeting," Keur says. "It was life-changing, and we all knew from that point forward there was a new sheriff in town and we were there to work. And if we weren't, it was time to go and seek life elsewhere."

It didn't stop after that first meeting. After hearing about guys hanging out and eating lunch in the weight room under the previous regime, Mannie ripped out the televisions and counters so there was no confusion about what was supposed to happen there. Smith said it took weeks to get used to Mannie's high-intensity style, and that multiple players quit because of it, but he grew to love it. He saw the culture changing right in front of his eyes and wanted to be a part of it. "You felt like you were going to die but I couldn't wait to continue it," Smith says. "I felt like we were finally working toward something."

At Michigan State, Saban had to shift what the organization valued the most. It is one thing to get people working hard toward a greater goal, but it is much harder to change what they believe. Perles might not have been winning as much at the end, but he was still beloved by his players. There is a unique challenge in replacing a popular boss and trying to shift the organization away from some of his beliefs without turning off all his supporters who remain. The worst thing you can do is come in and trash everything your well-liked predecessor did before you just because it isn't what you do.

It helped that Saban was very familiar with Perles' approach after working for him, but that didn't mean he shared all the same philosophies. "Perles was loyalty to the team no matter what; Saban was accountable to your teammates no matter what," Smith says. "That was the main difference that I saw right away."

Perles preached loyalty to your teammates, loyalty to your friends, and loyalty to the team. The concept made sense because it prompted an "us against the world" mentality to protect the organization at all costs, but it had downsides. Smith saw it go awry when players fell back on "loyalty" as a reason not to do the right thing when they saw their teammates do something wrong. There was plenty of resistance and frustration along the way. It's hard keeping other people accountable, and it's even harder to accept that as a new way of life after already buying into a different lifestyle.

By the time Saban got to Alabama, he was a known quantity. He had won a national championship at LSU and been an NFL head coach with the Miami Dolphins. He needed to establish a culture within an Alabama program beset by controversy, NCAA scandals, and mediocrity in the fifteen years since it had last won a national championship. Alabama went through four coaches in six years, including one (Mike Price) who never even coached a game and resigned over a stripper scandal. Alabama had the pedigree of a football blue blood but the more time went on, the more it looked like those days might be in the past. Once the Southeastern Conference's premier program, Alabama had been relegated to sideshow status. Saban wasn't inheriting anything close to a sure thing when he left the NFL for Tuscaloosa.

His predecessor, Mike Shula, had moderate success but lacked organization and consistency. Shula recruited some quality players who would play important roles for Saban, but his overall recruiting efforts were sloppy and uninspiring. Shula prioritized in-state kids over everyone else, which led to many happy high school coaches around the state but not the most talented team.

Taylor Pharr, who played at Alabama from 2006–2010, remembers never knowing what to expect at practice under Shula. Before some games, Shula had the team going all out in practices. In other weeks, it was primarily players in helmets and basketball shorts with little hitting going on. Saban established consistency, and that consistency was challenging. Mannie opted not to join him in Tuscaloosa, so Saban brought in Scott Cochran, a Tasmanian devil of a strength and conditioning coach who oozed high energy. That first Fourth Quarter Program was brutal, with Cochran having the team run dozens of 110-yard sprints, and if anyone bent over afterward, he had to rerun it. There was a clear goal behind the program: Saban wanted to know who would fight to persevere through the challenge and who would buckle and want to give up. No one had fun those first few training sessions, and as with many of his previous stops, there was plenty of vomiting as players got accustomed to Saban's expectations. More than anything, it was a clear message about what it would take to be successful.

"Everything was turned up," says Antoine Caldwell, an All-American offensive lineman at Alabama. "We worked very hard with Mike [Shula]; we worked very efficient with Nick. You'd knock out two hours of practice in forty-five minutes."

That first season at Alabama was hard for everyone involved. Like Perles, Shula was a beloved "player's coach" who might not have delivered enough wins but had the team's support. In came Saban with a drastically different style and delivery from what players had experienced previously, and it rubbed people the wrong way.

"I heard Shula raise his voice twice in one year," says former Alabama linebacker Alex Benson. "Whereas Saban, in the first five minutes of the first workout, dog-cussed every single one of us. It was night and day; that was obvious."

Saban knew what needed to be done but he faced resistance from some of the program's older players who didn't want to change everything they did in their final year. Benson says the program's top players under Shula were allowed to skip aspects of conditioning workouts while the third team and walk-ons were expected to do all of it. "The preferential treatment was crazy," he says. Saban stopped that right away, demanding everyone put in the same work, which, of course, prompted pushback. When one player, seemingly accustomed to what he could get away with under the previous regime, talked back to Saban during one early practice, the new coach was almost stunned by the audacity of it.

Caldwell, a junior starter on that 2007 team, remembers the internal battle within the team of players doing what they wanted versus what Saban wanted. There was a fear that a few veteran players' behaviors would pollute the younger, more impressionable players. It culminated in a series of losses Alabama could have avoided and an organization that seemed to be teetering at times.

"We had a few bad apples that weren't buying in 100 percent," Caldwell says. "Nick would say to us, 'We are going to keep working and doing what we do, but I need everyone to buy in.' Guys were used to doing things on and off the field, and when Nick came in and turned things around, a lot of guys revolted. I knew we were going to be good, but we had guys who didn't want to buy in and do things the right way, which is why we struggled a bit that first year."

Saban didn't crumble under the resistance he faced from some players on that team who would have preferred he wasn't their leader. One of the most critical challenges any leader faces is how to get buy-in from the rest of the organization, particularly when it's not willingly given from the outset. It can be frustrating, even demoralizing, when people aren't willing to endorse what you know in your heart is the right path forward for your organization. It's natural. But how you respond to that resistance can play a significant role in how much success you achieve.

"You may be the only one as the leader to see the way ahead, and you need to communicate that vision and set and enforce high standards," says Maj. Jordan Terry, an assistant professor of leadership at the U.S. Military Academy at West Point. "And then, over time, people get on board."

At Alabama, Saban worked tirelessly to get the necessary buy-in from the players and staffers he inherited from Shula. He worked hard to show them what they could accomplish together when they bought in and pointed out what they could do differently when things didn't go well. That first year was up and down, but it built the foundation for all the success that would later come.

"He was so well versed in how he wanted things, where he wanted to go, and what he wanted to do that I know the first year had to be brutal for him," says a former Alabama staffer. "He had some friends around him, but largely he was surrounded by strangers in a different environment. He knew where he wanted to take everything but he had to do it all over again with a lot of different people for the first time."

It's difficult to overstate just how important that first year is to establish a culture after taking over an organization. Saban wouldn't have won his first Alabama national championship in 2009 if he didn't do what he did in 2007. Those first days/weeks/months can be so crucial in shaping the long-term future. There will almost certainly be resistance, and you may have people leave rather than embrace the change and hard work that comes with it. But if you do it the right way, it'll have a lasting impact on not only the organization but also the people involved.

Eberflus, a linebacker on Saban's Toledo team, illustrates that point. He is now the head coach of the Chicago Bears, one of the NFL's most iconic and valuable organizations. He is expected to teach and guide grown men in the high-stakes NFL, where one minute you are a hot commodity and the next you are unemployed. But in 1990, Eberflus was just a young, tough linebacker who had to play for three different head coaches in as many years at Toledo. Thirty years later and Eberflus can still recall with great detail what it was like under Saban in those first few days at Toledo. He can still remember, in his first practice with Saban as a new head coach, pumping his fists and celebrating after making a perfect tackle. As Eberflus celebrated, Saban walked over and told him, "Don't worry about that play. Worry about the next play."

He learned an important lesson from his former college coach, one that stayed with him as he worked his way through the ranks before landing one of the most prestigious jobs in sports.

"You never get another chance to make a first impression," Eberflus says. "And on his first step on the stage as a head football coach, [Saban] certainly made a big impression on all of us."

CHAPTER 2

Build Your Team Framework

Nick Saban wanted everyone in the building to be at his first staff meeting.

He had just arrived at Alabama to a wild scene of fans greeting him at the airport. After years of Alabama wandering through the wilderness, Saban was hailed as the savior to get the Crimson Tide back on top. As Saban made his way through a throng of fans with loud "Roll Tide" cheers ringing out, one woman famously ran up and planted a kiss on his cheek. "It was like Michael Jordan arriving at O'Hare in his prime and walking through the airport," says Jon Gilbert, a former Alabama staffer. "It was a very surreal moment."

But first, Saban had to set the expectations for everyone working in his new football program. He told Todd Alles, one of his first hires as director of football operations, to gather everyone in the building—janitors, secretaries, anyone who worked in any capacity with the program—for a 3:00 p.m. meeting.

Saban walked in and delivered a message that has served as a crucial tenet to his Alabama success.

"Everything we do," Saban began, "is about recruiting. Everything we do."

Saban said if anyone walked into the building and the bathrooms were dirty, it would make the program look bad. Same if the floors weren't properly swept. "This place has to be show-ready 100 percent of the time," Saban said.

He then turned his attention to the secretaries. He explained how they were the first link to the football program, and they had to be ready to represent accordingly. How the secretaries answered the phone, Saban explained, is how the outside world would view Alabama football.

It was a masterclass in Saban's attention-to-detail prowess. Most importantly, it set the expectations for every person who went in and out of the building each day. From that day forward, no one had to guess what the top priority for the organization was. "He's direct and emphatic about how he wants things done," Alles says.

He'd directly use those established expectations as part of his recruiting pitch, too. "I heard him tell a parent in recruiting that anyone who is going to be in contact with your son—secretary, custodian, nutrition, trainer—everyone is being held to that standard," says former LSU assistant LeRoy Ryals. "If you're the custodian, you're going to dump the trash in that building to a certain standard."

In college football, there are all kinds of different sayings that speak to the importance of recruiting. Coaches call it the lifeblood of the sport. Some like to say, "It's not about the Xs and Os but the Jimmies and Joes."

But no coach has fully embraced the power of recruiting quite like Saban. After agreeing to leave the Miami Dolphins for Alabama, Saban jumped on a private plane with his wife, Terry, and his new boss, Alabama athletic director Mal Moore. Moore had just committed $32 million and his professional reputation to Saban having success in Tuscaloosa when his new football coach turned to him to assess what he had just done. "I just want you to know you've hired a horseshit football coach," Saban told Moore. "But nobody will out-recruit me."

Saban was greatly underrating his Xs and Os prowess—he's a terrific football tactician—but the primary reason he'll go down as college football's greatest coach is because of his sustained recruiting success. Saban realized early on that you can have the best game plan in the world, but if you don't have the right people to execute it, it won't work. If Saban was going to achieve what he wanted, he had to have not only the best players but also the right players.

Saban became the greatest college football coach ever because he focuses on recruiting every single day. Seriously, every single day.

The NCAA's draconian rule book limits what Saban can do, but he's maxing out those efforts every day. The NCAA even passed a "Saban rule" because rival coaches were mad about how much travel and effort he devoted to recruiting. When he's allowed to make phone calls, he's calling the top high school prospects and explaining why it would be mutually beneficial for them to come to Alabama. When he's able to hit the road, he's traversing the country meeting with high school coaches and families of players he thinks could bring value to his organization. It doesn't matter what else is going on at that moment; whether it's the middle of the season or the middle of the summer, Saban is making time to focus on recruiting.

Consider that for a moment. No matter what is going on, Saban is finding a way to spend time recruiting every day because he has determined it is critical to his organization's success. That means he's not skipping recruiting because a meeting or two ran long. Or saying he's too busy in the middle of the football season to worry about it. When you know when you wake up that you're going to be doing something regardless of that day's circumstances, it eliminates any potential excuse-making for why it didn't happen. And it's not like there weren't plenty of things involved with recruiting that would make the average person dread it. Most people who know Saban say he loves recruiting because he loves the competition, which is certainly true. But Bill Sheridan, who worked with Saban at Michigan State, believes, more than anything, it stemmed from Saban's discipline to do what needed to be done to benefit the organization.

"I always said there's only one thing that Nick disliked more than recruiting and that was playing with shitty players," says Sheridan. "If at any time because of injuries or whatever we had to have an inferior player in our lineup, Nick would be sick to his stomach. Because of that, he put the time and effort into recruitment. Driving all over the country, going in and out of airports, getting on the phone with kids during the season, it wasn't like he couldn't wait to do any of that stuff. But he understood it was necessary."

When Saban first landed at Alabama in 2007, he would watch ten to fifteen videos of prospective recruits each night. After Saban won his sixth national championship at Alabama in 2020, he was still doing the same thing.

That might seem outrageous to the average person—why would a man who has accomplished so much still feel the need to grind hours away watching football tapes of sixteen- and seventeen-year-old kids? For Saban, the answer is pretty simple. It took that level of commitment to get to the top, and if he wants to stay at that level, it's not going to get any easier. There will always be an upstart looking to challenge Alabama's supremacy, so Saban was never going to ease off the gas.

"When he would go on vacation, we'd load him up with like one hundred tapes," says Tyler Siskey, who served as his director of player personnel from 2013–2015. "He was watching every single day. He'd watch them, give them grades, and then watch them again. He's constantly going through the board and readjusting if we get new film in."

There was a system in place to get the tape onto Saban's desk, too. He wanted at least three people to look at it to vouch for the player's abilities before he'd watch the film. Saban trusted his assistants to find the right players, but as the leader of the organization, he wanted to have the final say before any new person joined it. "You have two or three guys on the staff saying this kid is an offer for us, most head coaches, just because of time constraints, they're fine with that," says Sheridan, who has also worked at Michigan and Notre Dame, among other schools. "He confirmed every offer. We never offered a kid until Nick looked at him."

It wasn't a formality, either. Even if three assistant coaches vouched for a player, there was no guarantee Saban would go along with it. "There were times he'd say, 'I don't know what the hell these guys are seeing, he's not that,'" says Louis LeBlanc, who worked as a recruiting graduate assistant at Alabama. Glen Mason, who worked with Saban at Ohio State, says Saban is the best talent evaluator he's ever been around. The former Minnesota head coach swallowed whatever ego he might have had and utilized Saban's prowess whenever he got a chance.

"There were a number of times [with] guys I was looking at that I couldn't make up my mind—do we want them or do we not want them? And I'd take the film and I'd say, 'Nick, what do you think?'" Mason says. "Not only was he right, but the feedback he gave me in his evaluation was far superior to what I had the ability to do. He saw things I never thought of or didn't see."

There are three major components to Saban's recruiting approach:

1. Have parameters for what you want to take the guesswork out.
2. Information is king.
3. Don't be afraid to adjust your opinion.

Saban takes as scientific an approach as possible when evaluating whether a prospective player would be a good fit in his organization. He has established critical factors for every position—quarterback, receiver, offensive lineman, you get the picture—that everyone on his staff is expected to follow. His approach is heavily influenced by his time working for Bill Belichick with the Cleveland Browns, though he's adjusted it in the years since to reflect the way the game has changed. Saban is exceptionally particular in what he wants for each position and tasks his staff with eliminating recruits who don't fit that.

There are hundreds of high school football players talented enough to play football at Alabama each year. But, for instance, if a defensive back isn't six feet tall with thirty-three-inch arms, Saban isn't going to pursue him heavily. It's as much for the player's benefit as Saban's knowing the type of player who has previously had success in his system.

"There has to be a specific purpose for every single player that you're recruiting and understanding, 'I'm bringing this guy here to do this job,'" says Trevor Hewett, who spent six years working in Alabama's recruiting department. "We had a critical-factors sheet that had each position and the ideal height, weight, that were the ideal physical parameters and mental parameters that you were looking for in a player."

The important lesson in Alabama's approach: don't fill your organization with people for whom you don't have a specific role in mind when you hire them. There are occasional exceptions when a player doesn't fit a specific mold, such as the slight DeVonta Smith, who didn't meet certain physical requisites yet possessed enough pure talent that Saban was willing to take a chance on him. It paid off when the 165-pound Smith won the Heisman Trophy in 2020 and went on to become a first-round NFL draft pick. Saban will move players around depending on needs, too—but Alabama isn't signing twenty-five wide receivers each year and saying, "We'll figure out what to do with them later." When you bring someone into your organization, you should already have a good sense of how that person fits into the structure and can be successful within it.

The "Saban sheets" allowed everyone to be more efficient. It eliminated the time-wasting politicking that typically happens in programs with assistant coaches pushing specific players for various reasons—geographic area, connection to that player's high school, "gut feeling," whatever. There was no freelancing, as it took power out of any one individual coach and put it into the system. There was accountability, too. After he wrapped up a recruiting cycle, Saban would save the evaluations of all the top players Alabama considered, both the ones it signed and those who got away. If an Alabama player struggled, Saban would refer back to the recruiting evaluation and assess where he went wrong. Same with a player Alabama didn't sign but was now experiencing success at another program. He wanted to know what he and his staff had missed in their evaluation so it wouldn't happen again. "We thought this was a bad trait," Saban would say, "but it was actually a good one."

It helped Saban when he first arrived at Alabama to find the right players to get a fallen dynasty back on track, and it helped him when every top player in the country had at least some interest in coming to Alabama. Success can change an organization's recruiting approach once a higher level of options is available. A perfect example is what happened to Villanova after it made a Final Four in 2009.

Jay Wright, the school's basketball coach, changed the type of player he brought into his organization. Wright told me when he first arrived at Villanova in 2001, he and his staff were very clear about what they wanted to build the program. But after the success, that clarity was missing. Wright started recruiting more highly ranked players now that Villanova was a program on the rise, but the pieces didn't fit well together. Something was missing. On paper, Villanova signed better players than it did early in Wright's tenure, but the results didn't follow. "We were getting good players, but I don't think I did a good job of structuring our roster," Wright says.

It took Villanova's program crashing down in 2011–2012 with a 13–19 record to make Wright realize just because he had access to a supposed higher-caliber player didn't mean said player was right for his organization's culture. He adjusted his approach to reflect what led to his early success, winning two national championships along the way.

Alabama faces a similar challenge. When you have access to everyone, it can feel like ordering off a Cheesecake Factory menu. Yes, there are lots of options, but you can have analysis paralysis with too many choices. Saban's critical-factors sheet is all about eliminating the players who don't fit into his system. The onus is then on everyone in the organization to determine if the players with the right physical attributes also have the mental and emotional ones to handle the intensity at Alabama. Siskey says when you recruit for Alabama, it almost comes with an inverse of the typical pitch: rather than selling players hard on coming to Alabama, the coaches would push each recruit to know and be comfortable with what he was signing up for.

When Pat Perles, son of former Michigan State coach George Perles, worked for Saban at Toledo, he remembers his boss imparting an essential lesson.

"We can sit in here and watch the film and I can tell you within a half hour whether that guy can play for us or not," Saban told Perles. "Now, you're going to spend the next month on if the kid is motivated and find out everything about him—his strengths and weaknesses, his personality, his work ethic, everything."

Says Perles, "You learned you better damn well know he's our kind of player when he shows up on campus. That's the hard part. It's easy to evaluate the player, but how do you evaluate the person?"

Saban stressed to his staff a few nonnegotiables: the player must love football, must have good character, and must be willing to put in the academic work to get a degree. On the organization's recruiting big board, staffers put colored dots next to players with character issues and academic issues so everyone knew the situation. When those issues became too concerning, Saban took the player off the board even if the talent was there.

At Alabama, everyone played a role in trying to answer those questions. It started with a collection of interns, analysts, and personnel staffers who dig up as much information as possible on all prospective players. They scoured the internet for every little detail they could get, reading through hundreds of stories each week for anything that could be helpful. There was no piece of information too trivial to include in a player's profile if it could help. Hewett remembers including details on how one top recruit liked mustard and another enjoyed eating cereal for dinner.

When Saban called that player, he'd make sure to work in the information. "Hey, man," Saban said, "did you just finish up those Lucky Charms?"

"He made the effort to get that minute, microscopic on an individual prospect in a sea of thousands of prospects," Hewett says. "It shows the level of commitment it takes to be successful on the recruiting trail like that."

Assistant coaches had to work hard to dig up as much information as they could. That meant calling high school coaches, parents, friends, anyone who might give some insight into a player they were interested in signing. Saban wanted to know what made players tick and their internal motivations when considering whether the fit was right. They'd ask about what type of coaching a player seemed to respond best to, both to know whether it would work at Alabama and to have a leg up should that player end up there. Saban purposefully created situations that allowed him and his staff to have one-on-one time with top prospective players so he could assess how they responded to certain things.

Not long after he was hired at Alabama, Saban instructed Alles to put together a big recruiting weekend to host top players and their families on campus. Alles, who previously worked at Ohio State, set it up how he had done so at his previous job—he put them up at the local hotel, set up an appetizer hour for mingling, and then rented buses to take all the players and their parents out to dinner.

That Sunday after everyone left, Saban turned to Alles and said, "What in the hell was that?" Alles was confused.

Saban told him, "We're not herding cattle. You don't just put everybody on the bus and take them some place."

Instead, Saban explained from now on every recruit and his family would be assigned a specific coach for their visit. They'd get a personal vehicle to take them around—Alabama would rent Chevy Tahoes and Ford Explorers for the weekend—and each recruit would have an individualized schedule. The top recruit visiting that weekend was always assigned to Saban, who lavished one-on-one attention that was almost always successful. "If he was laser-focused on getting a kid, nine times out of ten, we're getting him," says Alles.

When he didn't, Saban could take it hard. As a Michigan State assistant under George Perles, Saban was desperate to prove himself as a hardworking coach who could win difficult recruiting battles. It was, at times, an uphill battle competing against more established Big Ten schools like Ohio State and Michigan. He heavily recruited the state of Ohio, where he got to know the Marrow family, who had three sons (Brian, Duane, and Vince) play Division I football.

"When my older brother ended up going to Wisconsin, I watched Coach Saban—he'll kill me telling you this—I watched him cry," says Vince Marrow, who would go on to play for him at Toledo. "That's how much his heart was into recruiting. I was like twelve years old, and I remember watching him, saying, 'Wow.' He was really hurt by my brother going to Wisconsin."

The top target on Alabama's recruiting board would evolve. Saban never let an initial impression of a player preclude him from pursuing or moving on to other options. There was a practical reason for this—remember, we are talking about teenagers, so their bodies can grow in different ways as they age through high school—but it was also an important philosophy that flowed throughout the organization. Saban wanted the best of the best in his organization, and that demanded refusing to go off of old information. Alabama might love a player when he's a high school junior but if he doesn't develop the way the coaches hoped, they are moving on to a different player. It's why Saban instructs his recruiting staff to keep evaluating a recruit's film even after he commits to the program.

In sports, we see organizations fall victim to taking a player for what he was instead of what he would be in the future. Professional sports teams make the mistake of paying a player based on past performance even if there were warning signs if you looked closely. A great example of this is the Los Angeles Angels giving Albert Pujols a ten-year, $240 million contract in 2012 despite evidence that suggested he was already slowing down as a player. After making nine All-Star teams and winning three Most Valuable Player awards with the St. Louis Cardinals, Pujols was an All-Star only once in his Los Angeles tenure. The Angels paid Pujols for what he did for the Cardinals, not what he could do for them.

Alabama tries to avoid this problem in two ways: the recruiting board is constantly changing, and the preference is always to get a recruit on campus for an in-person evaluation. There can be exceptions to that latter strategy—the COVID-19 pandemic in 2020 prevented recruits from attending camps—but Saban strongly believes there are things you can see in person that you can't detail from only watching a player on film. He'd pay attention to the way a lineman walked down a hallway, noting how he carried his weight. When the offensive lineman went through drills, Saban noticed if the player could keep his heel on the ground when blocking. If he couldn't, that meant the player was "ankle-stiff," and Saban would tell staffers like Alles, "You can't fix ankle-stiff," because that player wouldn't generate as much power as the one who could keep his heel planted to the ground.

"He's really sharp in recruiting because he still trusts his eyes," says Rick Trickett, a longtime offensive line coach. "A lot of coaches don't anymore. I think what hurt us at Florida State at the end was we quit trusting our eyes. We cared more about the recruiting magazines telling us we were number three in the nation."

Coaches love to say they don't care publicly about recruiting rankings, but more often than not, they do privately. A top-rated recruiting class can generate considerable buzz for a program that appeases boosters and solidifies job security. There's even money on the line with coaches getting bonuses when their recruiting classes are ranked at a certain level. It can be easy to fall into the trap of wanting a player even more because he's highly ranked and many of your peers also want him. We see this all the time outside of football, too, when demand jacks up the perceived value of something even when it doesn't make sense to you. Do you have the confidence to say, 'I don't care that other people want this'? Or do you follow the crowd?

"From a recruiting standpoint, he's the only head coach who I've met who could care less what a kid's ranked," says Siskey, who also worked at Ole Miss and South Alabama. "I can remember on signing day when the rankings came out, he asked me, 'How did we do?' Coach, we've been No. 1 for a long time. He really has no idea about that."

Getting top recruits on campus allowed Alabama to get accurate measurements like height and weight on the player and provide an up-close look at how he handles the Alabama system. As detailed in chapter one, Saban's conditioning program is no joke, but it serves an essential purpose. At Alabama summer camps, the intensity isn't quite what the players would see once they joined the team, but Alabama coaches would run players through endurance drills and other aspects of the Fourth Quarter Program. How a player reacted to that experience could boost or drop his stock on Alabama's recruiting board.

Hewett, who got his start at Alabama working the summer camps, remembers players coming into the camp highly regarded by the staff and leaving as no longer an option. The summer camp environment combined many of the things that makes Alabama's recruiting approach so successful: the coaches knew what they wanted and had the framework to find it; they adjusted their opinions on players in real time, regardless of a player's reputation heading into it; and they were able to glean valuable information they couldn't get from a scouting report.

"Alabama isn't for everybody," says Hewett. "If you're not that Type A guy who is really intrinsically motivated, it's going to be a difficult road for you. Getting guys in camp and really understanding not only what they physically can and can't do, but more importantly, what is their mental makeup?"

Once Saban built the formula to find the right players, he needed the right strategy to convince them to join the organization. The approach he decided on was tested immediately after he arrived at Alabama and set the stage for all the success that followed.

CHAPTER 3

Only Promise Opportunity

From the moment he landed on Alabama's campus, Nick Saban knew he needed Julio Jones.

After a two-season stint with the Miami Dolphins, Saban furiously worked to get up to speed on who the top recruits were in his first few weeks running the Alabama football program. He was watching as many VHS tapes of top players as he could get his hands on, popping in one video after another. But when Louis LeBlanc, one of Alabama's graduate assistants, told him that Julio Jones' tape was the next one up, Saban stopped him in his tracks.

"Hell, Louis, I may have been with the Dolphins but I know about Julio," Saban said. "He's NFL-ready now. Put somebody else in."

There's no such thing as a sure thing, but Quintorris "Julio" Jones looked as close to one as possible. The 6-foot-4, 220-pound receiver out of Foley, Alabama, was bigger, faster, and stronger than everyone he faced on the football field. He had the kind of elite talent Saban knew he needed to restore Alabama to college football prominence.

Mike Shula, Saban's predecessor, didn't leave a bare cupboard, with several players, such as Javier Arenas, Andre Smith, and Greg McElroy, playing sizable roles under Saban. But in the ultra-competitive SEC, it wasn't considered full, either. Saban knew he needed a talent infusion to build the kind of team that could win it all, and in 2008 that meant owning the Mobile region, which featured future stars like Jones and Mark Barron. That was easier said than done, though, and part of that was Saban's fault. While at LSU, Saban built strong inroads in the Mobile area, and those continued to pay off for new Tigers coach Les Miles even after Saban left for the NFL.

"You had a lot of players leaving to go out of state," says Tim Watts, who has covered Alabama recruiting for more than two decades. "I think he wanted to button up his own state. They had to have Julio Jones. He was the biggest name and everybody watched what he was doing."

Under Shula, Alabama had one assistant coach focus on Mobile, and it wasn't working. Saban immediately doubled up those efforts, including sending down linebackers coach Lance Thompson, who had strong connections in the area, to win over Jones as his primary recruiter. As it got closer to Jones' planned decision timetable, and with rumors swirling he could head to Oklahoma, Saban would bug Thompson as much as five times an hour for the latest on his top target. Whenever Thompson heard coins jingling down the hallway, he knew Saban was coming for an update. Saban did so purposefully, say those who have worked for him. It was a way to let everyone know he was coming—if they were saying anything they shouldn't about him, now was the time to stop. The new Alabama head coach badly wanted Jones and knew if he could get him, it could change the program's trajectory. He wouldn't abandon his principles to get him, though.

When Saban recruited Jones, he delivered what has become a famous pitch: "I would love to win with you, but I will win without you."

There was a confidence in Saban's approach that resonated with Jones. It highlighted an important aspect of Saban's recruiting approach: never offer anything but an opportunity. It's a strategy that Saban sticks to no matter how good or impactful a player might be. While competing schools promised Jones he'd start as a freshman, Saban never budged.

"Saban told him, 'You're gonna come in and you're gonna work hard,'" says Trevor Hewett, a former Alabama recruiting staffer. "If you're the best player, you're going to play. I'd love to have you, but I will be successful without you."

It wasn't just words, either. When Jones was still in high school, he attended one of Saban's first recruiting camps at Alabama. As Saban walked outside to the field, he saw his top target leaning against a wall wearing regular clothes. "Julio, what are you doing?" Saban asked. "We've got practice in three minutes, why aren't you dressed?" Jones went along with Saban's wishes and got put through the full rigors of the summer camp. "We coached the crap out of Julio," LeBlanc remembers. "If he did a drill wrong, we sent him back."

After the camp, as the staff gathered to go over the players, coaches were upset. They were worried running Jones through the wringer would scare him off when other schools were telling him he'd be a starter immediately and didn't have to bother working out at one of their camps. Saban sensed there was consternation among his staff over how he handled the Jones situation, so he used it as a teaching example on building the culture he wanted that first year.

"I know some of you are upset we worked Julio in camp," Saban said. "But if Julio won't work for us in June before his senior year in high school, he won't work for us in August of his freshman year. We need to find out right now."

Jones, of course, signed with Alabama and was one of the best receivers in college football while playing in crimson and white. He was an important part of the undefeated 2009 national championship team, and would later go on to be the sixth overall pick in the 2011 NFL Draft. Landing Jones delivered everything Saban had expected it would, and it only reinforced his beliefs not to sell out for one player. Thompson, Jones' primary recruiter, would later say, "When it wasn't sexy to be at Alabama, Julio came in there and he put the program on his back and said, 'Be like me.' It lifted everybody else."

After Jones, Saban went back to that approach time and time again. He's going to be honest with his expectations and how challenging his system is at Alabama. If a prospective player isn't interested, he's not going to go out of his way to try to sway him into thinking otherwise. As a lifelong fan of the baseball team, Saban likes to say not everyone can play for the New York Yankees. After Saban got his Alabama program rolling, he knew it came with extra pressure for everyone involved, including the players. Some players are better built for it than others. That's why it was so important to make sure a player knew exactly what he was signing up for when he agreed to play for Alabama.

That was especially helpful once the player got on campus and into the program. A growing challenge within college football is the de-recruitment process once players sign with a school and are no longer highly desired recruits. Some coaches will tell them whatever they need to hear to close the deal. They'll give them their preferred jersey number, they'll promise them early playing time, they'll say they'll will build their offense around them. They can be like a new best friend or big brother for some time, alternating between hyping the player up and assuring him his entire life will play out the way he wants if he attends a specific school. It might lead to a short-term win, but it can create long-term cultural issues. If you promise someone the world and then the minute he gets into the organization you flip the switch and start treating him differently, there will be problems. It's bad business, too. Alabama invests hundreds of hours into scouting and recruiting its top targets, a massive time investment that would be for naught if the player quickly left the organization because he felt misled during the process.

"When you start to hear those promises, it starts to become a little bit of a red flag knowing that, hearing a coach promise you this or that when you've heard it might not be like that when you get there," Heisman Trophy winner Bryce Young said. "Coach Saban was always direct with me. He never promised me anything. He only promised me opportunities to compete."

Think about how you'd feel if someone treated you like a rare gem until you signed on the dotted line, and then you were just another piece of coal. If it seems like a flawed strategy, it should. But far too many college coaches make the mistake of telling impressionable seventeen-year-old kids what they want to hear, knowing the minute they get on campus, the man they think is their new best friend will turn into a drill sergeant. They willingly risk unleashing a cancer capable of ravishing the culture to get a momentary win."

Alabama deals with transfers just like any other school but at a lower rate, and rarely does an impact player willingly leave the program. Saban doesn't have to do as much to deprogram these top recruits, because he's up front from the beginning about what it will take to be successful in his system. He'll tell them, "You're not entitled to the outcome. You're entitled to the opportunity to get the outcome." When you set clear expectations from the beginning, it eliminates most potential headaches in the future.

While putting together that first recruiting class that included Jones, Alabama hosted a highly regarded quarterback recruit. The visit went well enough, but at the end, the promising quarterback seemed perturbed when meeting with Saban.

"I haven't heard you tell me I'm the man," the quarterback said.

Saban was confused. "What do you mean?"

"Well," the recruit continued, "you haven't told me I'm the man."

Saban looked the recruit right in his eyes. "I'll give you a chance to prove to me you're the man, but I haven't seen you take a damn snap in an SEC game yet. How do you expect me to tell you you're the man?

Saban wasn't done.

"I'll give you an opportunity to compete for the position, but I'm not going to tell you today you're the man just to commit. If you're afraid to compete, maybe you ought to take other options."

The player opted to go elsewhere.

In a Saban-run organization, it's as close to a meritocracy as possible. Nothing is given to players just because they've been there the longest or are related to a famous former player. No player gets playing time because he was a five-star recruit out of high school whom everyone expected to hit it big in college. It can be easy to promise someone and let the "future you" worry about it, but the bill always comes due. If Saban played someone who wasn't worthy because of an earlier recruiting promise, it would erode the uber-competitive culture he worked so hard to establish. As Saban once explained, "You can't have one guy saying, 'Well, he did this but I'm not allowed to do that' because that creates divisiveness, which is never going to allow you to have the togetherness that you need to be successful in difficult circumstances." The player who gives the team the best chance to win plays, period.

"He's going to play the best eleven, not his favorite eleven," says former LSU offensive lineman Paris Hodges. "You're not the starting quarterback because he really likes you as a kid. You're there because you're the best and he lets you know you worked for that."

Hodges saw the impact of that before he even suited up for the Tigers. A California native, Hodges arrived in Baton Rouge for his recruiting visit knowing what to expect, or so he thought. It was his third official visit, which allowed a player to spend forty-eight all-expenses-paid hours on a college campus, and they followed a similar formula: Players on the team would take recruits out for a night on the town, showcasing the perks of being a football player on their campus, to help convince them that's where they should go. But during the Saban era, LSU players didn't go out on Friday nights during the season. They didn't go out on Thursday nights, either. A big Thursday night out could still impact you on Saturday, so there was a player-enforced mandate not to go out on those days.

"You're going to go out and see the town and instead I'm home at 8:00 p.m. watching the WBRZ news in Baton Rouge with my mom on my recruiting visit," Hodges says. His mom asked him, "You hate this, don't you?" But he didn't. "No," he told his mom, "this is different."

One might think the lack of promises and guarantees would scare off top talent, but it actually seems to do the opposite. Alabama brought in Ken Smithmier, the president of P3 Insights, for his expertise in decision-making and judgments. Smithmier interviewed the entire 2019 freshman class about why they chose Alabama over the myriad of other options at college football's top programs. What he found surprised even him. One-third of the players explicitly said they came to Alabama because Saban didn't make them any promises.

"Saban gets a bunch of guys who absolutely believe they can, and when he says he won't promise anything—in that guy's mind he's [thinking], 'OK, Coach, I'll prove it to your ass. Watch this,'" says Smithmier.

That was part of the appeal for Rashaan Evans. He was a no-doubt five-star prospect ranked as one of the fifteen best high school players in America, according to 247Sports. Everyone in the SEC wanted him, and almost every school that recruited Rashaan told him he'd be a starter his freshman year, his father, Alan, remembers. Except for Alabama. Not only would Alabama not make any promises, his path to early playing time on paper looked onerous. "We knew going to Alabama was going to be a tough road," says Alan Evans. "I let him know that you're putting your head in the lion's mouth going to Alabama."

Add in the fact that Alan played football at in-state rival Auburn and raised his family there, and it felt like a lot of factors were going against the Crimson Tide's favor. The battle for Rashaan Evans became one of the most famous in Alabama history, peaking when an eightieth birthday party for his grandfather the weekend before National Signing Day featured multiple coaches from Alabama and Auburn in attendance dancing and doing everything they could to gain an edge. "It was probably the first time I had ever seen Alabama and Auburn in the same room together having a good time," Evans says. "It was awkward, but it was a very, very exciting atmosphere."

Alabama coaches dancing at a birthday party wasn't what won Rashaan over, though. While other schools focused on the present, Saban pitched the decision as a long-term one and laid out why he'd still be glad he went to Alabama in ten or fifteen years. Knowing that Rashaan's goal was to play in the NFL, he used Alabama's stacked roster, a frequent target of negative recruiting against the school, as a selling point to achieving that dream.

"Coach Saban told us if you want to be the best and want to become the best, then you need to be able to compete against the best," Alan says. "Here at Alabama, you're going to compete against the best and it's only going to make you a better football player moving toward the next level because you'll know how to compete."

There's plenty we can all learn from that strategy. First, Saban takes what could be perceived as a negative and turns it into an opportunity. Yes, he's not going to give you that early security blanket of a promise, but he explains why it'll benefit you in the long run, citing a long track record of former players who succeeded because of that. He sells the competitive culture as a driving force to bringing the best out of you rather than being handed what you want right away. Saban demands relentless competition within his organization, so when an incoming player not only expects it but embraces the idea of competing for everything, his chances of success are high. The established culture has become a beacon to attracting like-minded individuals.

Mac Jones fits the bill. Jones arrived at Alabama in 2017 as a three-star quarterback in the same recruiting class as five-star quarterback Tua Tagovailoa, who at the time was the highest-rated quarterback prospect to ever sign with the Crimson Tide. Oh, and returning starting quarterback Jalen Hurts was coming off an SEC Player of the Year season, one of only two true freshmen ever to win that award, along with iconic Georgia running back Herschel Walker. Jones was initially committed to Kentucky, a school he'd almost assuredly have a chance to play for immediately, but he instead opted for Alabama's crowded quarterback room, a decision that left fans puzzled. He was an afterthought, a lanky kid from Florida who seemed destined to be a career backup at Alabama. But that's not the way Saban's organization operates, even if it's what most fans and media experts predicted.

"There's nobody in there who ever saw Mac as a guy who would just be a career backup," says former Alabama offensive coordinator Mike Locksley. "You could see that Mac Jones had the ability; it was just a matter of getting the opportunity. Coach doesn't recruit backups down there."

In his first season, Jones was relegated to scout-team duty as Hurts started every game that season on the path to Saban's fifth national title at Alabama. After Tua Tagovailoa led a second-half comeback effort in the title game, it became all about Tagovailoa versus Hurts that season. No one cared about Jones. He kept working and working, using practice as his time to better himself and develop as a quarterback. When he first arrived at Alabama, he tended to melt down when things didn't go his way, earning a "John McEnroe" nickname from Saban for his bombastic reactions. Jones' body language was so bad after a mistake, Saban told him he didn't even have to watch the play to know what happened. Saban had one of the program's videographers film Jones' reactions, and the Alabama head coach showed his young quarterback how his actions impacted the whole team. "Do you understand how you're affecting everyone else?" Saban asked him. "This isn't an individual sport." As a quarterback, Jones was held to a higher standard—the rest of the team would look to him on what to do, and if he couldn't control his emotions, everyone would suffer. The lesson proved to be a turning point for Jones, who gained better control over his reactions. He turned practice into a personal game in which he seemed to delight in annoying Saban when he torched his first-team defense with a long touchdown pass. When Saban told him to cut it out one practice, Jones told him, "Tell your defense to stop it." With his confidence and skills growing, Jones waited for his opportunity. It came in 2019 when Tagovailoa went down with a season-ending hip injury, with Jones showing flashes of being a really good quarterback. He built on that all offseason leading to a magical 2020 season that saw Jones break Alabama's passing records, emerge as a Heisman Trophy finalist, and ultimately become a first-round draft pick after winning a national championship. All because he loved the idea of Alabama's competitive culture and how it could make him better.

"Something I appreciated and learned being at Alabama with Coach Saban is [that] most guys would have shied away from coming to Alabama when a guy is coming off [an] SEC Player of the Year award," Locksley says. "But you know kids are competitive and their recruits are competitive and confident in their abilities."

Jones' story is not only a compelling pitch to other self-motivated players, but it's also a strong defense against what Saban knows his opponents will try to use against Alabama.

Think about how much advertising includes a company directly comparing itself to competitors. If you watch any television at all, you've undoubtedly seen a phone company, toothpaste company, or beer company sell you on why it's better than those other guys. It happens in the sales world all the time, too. "Oh, you're with X company; let me tell you why our offerings are a better fit for you," can be a frequent pitch. The wild and chaotic world of college football recruiting is no different.

The 130 programs that compete in the Division I Football Bowl Subdivision level are all competing for the same pool of players. The massive influx of television money has created a vast gulf between the haves and have-nots—a smaller school like Troy isn't going to be competing for the same-caliber recruit as Alabama, for instance—but the competition is intense at every level. In the SEC especially, it can be brutal, with coaches treating certain recruiting battles as the difference between keeping their jobs and being fired. To say those stakes can prompt ugliness among competing schools would be putting it lightly. Former Texas A&M basketball coach Billy Kennedy once said competing schools used his Parkinson's diagnosis against him with recruits.

Saban knows what his competitors will use against him because it largely didn't change after the first few years. Once he got Alabama established as a national power again, opposing schools couldn't criticize his success or coaching prowess. So, instead, they made it about his style of coaching, his age, the unoriginality of playing for Alabama, and, inevitably, the lack of early available playing time. The competitors would tell top recruits that if they wanted to play right away, they shouldn't go to Alabama because there were already too many good players on the team. The pitch could be something like, "Come to our school and you can play right away instead of going to Alabama and getting buried on the depth chart behind all those other guys."

In a video that ended up on the internet, Saban explained his opposing argument when delivering his pitch to highly regarded recruit Enai White.

"First of all, when they tell you that, it's insulting," Saban explained. "I wouldn't be sitting here talking to you if you couldn't play here. Number two, when they say you can play at our place before you can play at Alabama, they're just telling you Alabama is better than them. Number three, if you ask our players on our team, they'll tell you just the opposite. They'll tell you the competition made them better."

If Alabama is the Coke of college football, it doesn't worry about what Pepsi is doing. Saban falls into the line of thinking that even talking about a competitor gives it power. Why draw attention to what someone else is doing when you already have all the tools you need? When Saban or an Alabama assistant talks to a recruit, he'll bring up the national championships, all the players Alabama developed into NFL players, the team's graduation rate, and other relevant discussion points. It's a conversation based on facts, not theory. As former Alabama assistant Billy Napier told me years ago, "We aren't selling hope; we are selling something that's proven."

Hewett remembers the father of one top recruit telling him whenever they visited competing SEC schools, the conversation turned back to

Alabama. There would be direct comparisons and explanations for how that school would knock Alabama off its perch. Eventually, the father and son had a realization: If these rival schools wouldn't shut up about Alabama, why shouldn't the player just go to Alabama? That reaction explains Saban's aversion to making it about anyone but Alabama.

"Negative recruiting is something Coach Saban is adamantly against," Hewett says. "I'm not calling you to talk about what LSU is doing, I'm calling you to talk about Alabama. The advantage Alabama has is we don't have to talk bad about them, all we have to do is talk about our accomplishments."

There are many different ways to recruit people into your organization or to convince a prospective client to go with you. There is no one-size-fits-all approach to guarantee success. When you break Saban's system down, it's pretty simple. He'll never make big promises, he's never going to trash-talk the competition, and he's never going to press to fit a square peg into a round hole if someone is resistant to his style. For Saban, it always comes back to offering just one thing: opportunity.

CHAPTER 4

You Can't Be the Only Leader

Rolando led by fear," says former Alabama running back Ben Howell. "He was a pretty scary guy."

Rolando McClain isn't who you'd consider the prototypical leader. Oft-described as mercurial, McClain could be quiet and distrusting of those around him after a difficult upbringing. At 6-foot-4, 220 pounds, McClain patrolled the locker room in a way that made clear no one should mess with him. In a mostly empty locker room before his first practice as an Alabama player, Howell heard someone yelling "Hey you!" and turned to see McClain trying to get his attention. McClain looked right in the 5-foot-9 walk-on running back's eyes and told him, "I'm going to fuck you up today." On paper, McClain had all the makings of someone to avoid rather than follow, and yet at the end of his junior season his Alabama teammates voted him as a permanent team captain. Beneath that scary exterior was an intelligent football player who knew the defense so well he could tell every player on the field what he was supposed to be doing.

"Everybody was scared of him," says former Alabama linebacker Alex Benson. "You heard rumors of him in high school throwing a kid in a McDonald's deep fryer. I don't know if any of that was true. He was the all-around captain where you were scared of him and whatever he said, you did without question. When he was on the field, there wasn't anyone better."

The McDonald's story was mostly folklore—he got into a fight at one in Decatur that spilled into the parking lot and led to the police being called, according to one report, but nothing about a deep fryer—but it was part of his legend. When he patrolled the middle of the field, he was like a human weapon capable of inflicting damage to opponents. Teammates remember him as a player version of Saban out on the field, with an amazing recall of defensive schemes that benefited every player. He combined his physical demeanor and football prowess to guide his leadership. He used fear to scare his opponents and keep his teammates in line. His teammates, in turn, voted him as the program's "Most Inspiring Player" in 2009.

"Not only did he have a brilliant football mind, but the guy was a freak of an athlete," says former Alabama offensive lineman David Blalock. "He was a big, scary guy to play football against. He had that meanness about him. He's one of the best football players I've ever seen."

Saban is the unquestioned leader of the organization, but he can't lead alone. If Saban was the only leader and the only person trying to hold people accountable, it'd be easy to tune out his voice over time. We see it in sports organizations all the time, where stories come out that the coach lost the locker room and the players were no longer listening to the message. It happens plenty in the business world, too, when a company loses faith in its chief executive officer and the bottom line suffers as a result. Saban needs valued lieutenants like McClain to distill his message and keep the team on board with the organizational vision.

In his book *The Captain Class: The Hidden Force That Creates the World's Greatest Teams*, Sam Walker started with an exhaustive search to determine the greatest sports teams of all time. When he came up with a formula that spit out the sixteen best teams across a host of sports—he excluded college sports teams in the exercise—Walker tried to determine what the commonality was between the success of a 1920s Australian rules football team to the 1960s Boston Celtics to the 1990s Cuba women's volleyball team. What he discovered was each of the most successful sports dynasties followed a typical formula of a coach at the top, talent on the bottom, and a "water-carrying captain in the middle who served as an independent mediator between them."

Walker concluded that those elite captains shared seven primary traits:

1. Extreme doggedness and focus in competition
2. Aggressive play that tests limits of rules
3. Willingness to do thankless jobs in the shadows
4. Low-key, practical, and democratic communicator
5. Motivates others with passionate nonverbal displays
6. Strong convictions and the courage to stand apart
7. Ironclad emotional control

When you review those common traits, you start to look at McClain's leadership qualities differently. He wasn't what the public would tell us makes the best leader, but he possessed many of those elite captain traits. He was a relentless competitor on the field and won the Lambert Award his junior year as the nation's best linebacker. The award was named after former Pittsburgh Steelers linebacker Jack Lambert, one of the sixteen captains on Walker's list. Consider Walker's description of Lambert and see if you see any similarities: "Lambert's most powerful weapon on the field, however, was something intangible. He scared the living shit out of people." You don't have to be a clean-cut perfect citizen to be a good captain; in fact, many of the best ones consistently push boundaries and do things that upset their bosses and the status quo, all in the pursuit of making the team better. McClain fit the mold.

The relationship between Saban and McClain started on rocky terms as McClain didn't always exhibit "ironclad emotional control." During a practice his freshman year, McClain didn't like one of Saban's defensive play calls and decided to change it. When Saban loudly and aggressively questioned what McClain was doing, the freshman linebacker loudly and aggressively gave it right back to his head coach. Saban wasn't pleased, to put it mildly, and punished him through a multi-game benching and other ramifications. However, the incident was significant for two reasons: it established a line McClain knew he couldn't cross again and showed to his teammates he wasn't afraid to challenge authority when he felt it was warranted. Saban and McClain went on to build an incredibly close bond, with McClain becoming one of his favorite players as he stepped up to help lead Alabama to its 2009 national championship.

"A switch flipped with Rolando prior to his last year and he went from being a good leader, a guy some guys looked up to, to if you don't do it the right way I'm literally going to kick your ass," says former Alabama quarterback Greg McElroy. "It was pretty amazing to see how different he became and how the defense and the team as a whole changed because of his presence and willingness to step up and be vocal about his expectations of his teammates."

At a team meeting the week leading up to the national championship game, McClain was sitting next to a couple of teammates when he saw them put pouches of chewing tobacco into their mouths. McClain, who had never done it before, demanded they let him partake despite their objections. As Saban started addressing the team, McClain turned to a teammate and said, "Man, the room is starting to spin." The team meeting broke up as players went to their smaller position group meetings. The buzz of the chewing tobacco overtook McClain, who laid down underneath a table as associate head coach James Willis started leading a defensive film session. For one play, Willis showed a clip and asked his linebackers, "If we are in this defense but the receiver motions across the ball, what do we check to?" Willis looked first at future first-round pick Dont'a Hightower, a player who would go on to make multiple Pro Bowls and win multiple Super Bowls in the NFL. Hightower didn't know the answer. It got quiet as players looked around at each other, unsure of the answer.

Then McClain, lying on his stomach with his head in his hands underneath a table, popped up with an answer. Incredulous, the players turned their gaze to Willis, who affirmed McClain had the right answer. "No one knew the answer, but Rolando did while buzzing his ass off not looking at the screen," Benson says. It was an example of the football brilliance that made players and coaches alike love him.

Saban loved players like McClain because his player leadership philosophy was rooted in trying to make the "alpha dogs" of the team into his best leaders. There can be faults with that strategy, but at his core, Saban believed that if he could turn the alpha from each position group into a good leader, it would dramatically affect the rest of his team. "Who doesn't look up to the best player in each position?" says former Alabama receiver Mac Hereford. "Instead of having them as a toxin on the team, at least try to bring them in."

"What you need is your good players to step up and be leaders," says former Alabama defensive back Will Lowery. "Saban is a master facilitator. He does a great job at getting his leaders to buy in and basically be mini versions of himself as players. He gets them to buy in mentally, and that trickles down to the other players."

Two of the best leaders Lowery witnessed at Alabama were receiver Julio Jones and safety Mark Barron, two of the quieter players on the team. As key members of the 2008 recruiting class that changed the program's trajectory, Jones and Barron didn't scare people as leaders like McClain but instead let their actions on and off the field serve as their leadership blueprint. That meant showing up early to team meetings, staying late after practice to put more work in, and playing hard at every moment. Jones and Barron were not only two of the most talented players but also two of the hardest workers Saban has ever had at Alabama. Former Alabama offensive lineman Antoine Caldwell, a captain on the 2008 Alabama team, can still remember the first time a freshman Jones worked out with the team. As the other offensive linemen were lifting weights, Jones walked over to them, didn't warm up, and did five quick repetitions on the bench of a weight others struggled with before walking off. "I remember all of us looking at each other like, 'What the hell is this?'" Caldwell says. "We always joked Julio should have been blocking for us. He was one of those guys, right away you knew he was a different breed." Jones would use his eyes as his way to tell his coaches and teammates what he thought without saying a word. Both Jones and Barron dispelled the notion that you have to be vocal to be a leader.

"They weren't Hollywood show-timing everybody, skipping workouts and partying all night," Lowery says. "They were really talented and really had a lot of God-given gifts, but they did not take that for granted or rely on that. They put in the work every single day. You didn't have to go looking for the example."

Critically, Saban worked to develop players like Jones and Barron into leaders the moment they arrived on campus. He believes you can't wait until a player is a junior or senior to start preparing him to be a leader. By then, it is too late. The same philosophy can apply to any business trying to groom leaders; you can't wait until after you've promoted someone into a leadership position to start developing those skills. Every day is an opportunity to cultivate leadership qualities from your team, whether they are veterans or brand-new to the organization.

It was important for Saban to establish early what it meant to be a leader, too. It wasn't a status symbol or some source of power over the rest of the team. It was a responsibility, a challenging one in reality, that he was going to hold you to moving forward. The only thing worse than Saban being the only source of leadership is lousy leadership from players more interested in what it means for the individual than the team. It's a challenge that organizations everywhere face when they try to reward talented individuals with leadership opportunities regardless of whether they are worthy. As Walker wrote of the trend in professional sports, "The captaincy had come down to which superstar's ego needed stroking or which player cost the team the most money or which promising teenager they hoped to build around. It had ceased to be a matter of which player was the most fit to lead." Saban tried to avoid that issue with clear communication of what his expectations were for his leaders.

"If you're one of his players who is a captain, those guys not only had to be absolute dogs on the field and in every workout but in everything else they did off the field," says former Michigan State tight end Josh Keur. "Whether it's an interview or having a beer at the bar, Nick expects them to handle it like he was in the room with them. That's not easy to do at that age."

Saban tried to stoke leadership out of everyone but also established a formal peer leadership council. The group was a cross section of the team meant to give a wide variety of different personalities with different opinions and insights. He'd frequently meet with them to discuss what was happening within the organization and whether any changes needed to be made. He'd ask his player leaders if his messages were resonating—and if they weren't, what they'd suggest doing differently. He'd tell them what he wanted to be stressed that week and what each one of them could do to make it happen. Saban would ask how the team was reacting to that week's practices and if he had to tweak anything. "He'd ask them, 'Do you think we need to push them harder?'" Howell says. "Those years we won a championship, I think people were more honest with him. 'Yeah, we need to be pushed harder.'"

They were valuable contributors to the strategy as well as Saban's eyes and ears of the team. The players saw and heard things that Saban wouldn't, and he expected them to pass along any information that warranted his attention. Even more importantly, he expected them to step in and do the right thing when he couldn't be there. "There's some misconception on Nick's side where the casual fan looks at Nick like he's always a tough ass who cusses and fusses, but we saw another side of Nick where he's incredibly passionate," says Caldwell, who was a team captain and member of the peer council. "He wants to know how guys are doing, what he can do to help them succeed or what he can do to be better for certain individuals."

Through the peer council, Saban was building up his players as leaders; he was developing closer relationships with all of them and gaining insight into the team he otherwise wouldn't have gotten. As the program's de facto CEO, Saban had hundreds of people to manage and daily tasks that always kept his schedule packed. By developing leaders in every position group plus his assistant coaches' insights, Saban could get a feel for everything happening on his team. It made a big organization feel more manageable without Saban having to micromanage every aspect of it. He also depended on his leadership council to correct bad behavior and institute punishments as they saw fit to players misbehaving. That included poor academic performances and missed curfews, among other violations.

"If you got to Saban, you really did some bad shit because you had to go through multiple layers to get there," says former LSU center Jimmy Courtenay. "There were a lot of peer checks and balances that were set in place by Coach Saban."

Just as Saban believed he couldn't be the only leader on the team, he felt he couldn't be the sole disciplinarian, either. He had no problems handling punishments or correcting behavior he didn't like—ask any player or coach who has been on the receiving end of one of his "ass chewings"—but he thought it'd carry more weight coming from a peer that behavior needed to change rather than hearing it from him over and over again.

"It's harder to go in and face your teammates versus just a coach behind a closed door," says Taylor Pharr, another member of the peer council. "It was unique, but it makes sense because ultimately if you do the wrong thing, you're letting your teammates down. If one person doesn't pull their weight, it affects everybody."

Even those not on the council were expected to call out bad behavior, whether it was a sloppy play during practice or telling a teammate it wasn't a good idea to go out the night before an important practice. When Saban had his best teams, the player leadership took a no-nonsense approach to anything and everything that could be detrimental to the team's success. The team's leaders would willingly and freely call out behavior to eradicate it before it became rooted in its identity. "If you're not going to practice hard every day, get out," McElroy says. "If you're going to be an anchor to our boat that's trying to set sail, we want nothing to do with you. I think the culture of competition leads to that."

McElroy, a captain on the 2010 team, says the leadership on those early Saban teams could, at times, be a bit "barbaric." The team would call players-only meetings where players would yell at the top of their lungs at each other. They'd get physical with each other during practice if one of the leaders saw a teammate going through the motions. Sometimes it would spill into the locker room, too.

"I can vividly remember Mark Ingram throwing a freshman safety into a locker because the freshman refused to run to the line running sixteen 110s," McElroy says. "As crazy as that may sound, it was effective because guess what? That freshman safety went on to be an All-American. It woke him up because 'the Heisman Trophy winner just beat me up.'

"Once you got called out by the team, the likelihood of you hopping on board was pretty high."

Saban has another subset of the organization capable of fixing the leadership problem: his assistant coaches. Saban's assistant coaches are essentially the middle management of the Alabama organization. They don't have the power to make unilateral decisions, but they are expected to play an important role in shaping their respective units. Saban rightfully gets a lot of credit for his role in Alabama's success, but he must have the right assistant coaches to keep his team, or workforce, engaged and moving in the right direction. Middle managers can be vitally important to an organization's success, as a 2012 Gallup study found out. The study, which analyzed nearly two million employees, estimated that managers account for at least 70 percent of the variance in employee engagement. As it turned out, middle managers had a big impact on how employees viewed their company and whether they enjoyed what they did. In a different study, University of Pennsylvania Wharton School management professor Ethan Mollick studied the impact of middle managers in the computer game industry. He concluded, "The often overlooked and sometimes-maligned middle managers matter. They are not interchangeable parts in an organization."

Alabama's middle managers at times felt interchangeable given the rate they turned over, but there was no question they played an important role. Saban has a reputation for being all business as a leader, sometimes painted as cold when he didn't engage in small talk or niceties. He didn't have time to have a personal relationship with everyone, a source of frustration at times for players and coaches. He tended to be laser-focused on the greater good, a trait they respected him for in the long run, but one that could ruffle some feathers along the way. It would be too simplistic to say Saban needed some good cops to counter his disciplined style, but it was clear he needed different personalities to balance what he brought to the table.

Saban wasn't a big "rah-rah" guy—more on that in chapter seventeen—and wasn't one to freely and easily dole out compliments. It wouldn't have been wise for Saban to surround himself with assistant coaches who did things the same as him. It might have made him feel comfortable, but it was a sure-fire way to alienate portions of the team who needed different tactics. Saban understood that when you are developing leaders in your organization, you don't want them all to look and act like you. At Michigan State, he employed coaches like Pat Shurmur, who would later become an NFL head coach, and

Bobby Williams, who succeeded him at MSU, to bring more encouragement and excitement to their position groups. They were the perfect lieutenants in that they found a different, effective way to deliver Saban's message but they were still all in on the vision.

"He put coaches around us who knew how to build us up," Keur says. "They believed in Nick. You spend so much time with your position coach and when they are blindly following and telling you Coach Saban is the truth, then you start seeing it."

For a long time at Alabama, those two men were running backs coach Burton Burns and strength and conditioning coach Scott Cochran. Burns, a Louisiana native, was a beloved coach who could dish out some tough love, too, but knew how to do it in a way that elicited support. Over his thirteen seasons at Alabama, Burns managed some stacked running backs rooms full of talented players eager to play. He was a master at finding a way to keep all those players happy without losing too many transfers. Burns developed two Heisman Trophy winners (Mark Ingram and Derrick Henry) and had a whopping eight Alabama running backs get drafted in the first three rounds of the NFL Draft. When Burns left Alabama for the New York Giants in 2019, Ingram said he was the best coach he'd ever had. He was a knowledgeable coach who had the right demeanor to handle Saban and still be like another father to the players.

Most former players would tell you Cochran was the second-most-important person in Alabama's organization behind Saban. There was an important practical value to Cochran's job in pushing players through the Fourth Quarter Program, making sure they were getting the necessary work done in the weight room and that they were properly conditioned for the taxing season. All of that was valuable to the organizational strategy, and by all accounts, Cochran was very good at his job. But his real value, the reason he was so much more than just a strength and conditioning coach, was his relationship with the players. NCAA rules grant strength coaches more access to the players during the off-season than the other coaches, meaning no one spent more time with them than Cochran. He developed close personal relationships with the players in a way Saban either didn't have time for or wasn't equipped to do. He was loud and energetic to a point you assumed he did nothing but chug Red Bulls all day, prone to yelling, "Yeah! Yeah! Yeah!" and bouncing up and down, but the players loved him. They found him genuine. He was like a big brother who still held them accountable but with a defter touch.

"If you get in trouble, if you wind up in jail at two thirty in the morning, Coach Cochran is the one you're going to call, and he's going to come bail you out," Blalock says. "He'll run you to death the next day, but he's the one that will bail you out. He's a great guy."

Cochran became Saban's most crucial player conduit. When a player was considering transferring out of the program, Saban dispatched Cochran to talk to him and explain the benefits of staying. Same if a player was considering leaving early for the NFL Draft and Saban's advice to come back for one more season didn't seem to be resonating. Cochran knew how to explain Saban's message in a way that empowered the players and made them fight through the hurdles. He'd fight on their behalf, too, telling Saban when he needed to ease up practices or work in the weight room, accepting any wrath that came with it.

When Cochran left in 2020 to join Saban's protégé Kirby Smart at Georgia, former players were concerned about what it'd do to the culture. They wondered who would replace his role as the person players turned to when they were going through a difficult personal situation or were unhappy with their playing time. "He was the glue," says former Alabama linebacker Keith Holcombe. "He held the team together a lot of the time." I even wrote for AL.com that replacing Cochran would be Saban's most important hire yet.

And then Alabama went a perfect 13-0, won a national championship, and staked a strong claim to being the greatest college football team ever. Alabama winning a national title the year after losing two of its most valued lieutenants doesn't discount their previous contribution to the organization's run of success, but it did spur questions.

When reporting and researching this book, one of my primary goals became finding out the difference between an Alabama national championship team and one that came up short. In his first fifteen years at Alabama,

Saban's program played in nine national championship games, winning six of them. Saban deserved the lion's share of the credit, by all accounts, but he was a constant. He coached winners and losers alike. Was there a common trait on Saban's teams that won it all, though? Or even the ones that didn't?

Every person I talked to who had spent any time within the Alabama organization stressed that, other than Saban's initial 2007 team that went 7–6, talent was never why the Crimson Tide didn't win it all. After recruiting the nation's top class seemingly every year, Alabama always had enough good players to be the best. There's undoubtedly a luck factor in football when it comes to player injuries and actions on the field. Fluky things like the "Kick Six" can happen to doom your title chances.

But then I talked to Hereford, who played at Alabama from 2017–2019. He was part of one of the greatest national championship wins in Alabama history (Tagovailoa to Smith, 2nd-and-26) and the worst loss of the Saban era (2019 title game blowout to Clemson). The core players were primarily the same, and many expected undefeated No. 1 Alabama to repeat as champions in 2019 before the shocking loss to Clemson. What was the difference between those two teams? Hereford believed when you really boiled it down, it was as simple as one or two players swaying the entire team.

"All it comes down to on whether Coach Saban is going to win or not is whether a few of those key chess pieces within the leadership group topple over and invest," Hereford says. When the alpha or two of the team fully invested, he says, it made all the difference. That mentality would spread throughout the team, whether they knew it was happening or not, as players held each other accountable and followed the path of their team leaders. When Alabama had the right player leaders, it won it all. When it didn't, it failed.

"In that leadership system, it's a couple of guys who set the tone," Hereford says. "He uses a smaller group who he could communicate with more closely and pound different things into their heads because if you could get those guys bought in, those guys could impact maybe five or six each, and that's like the whole team."

The simplicity of Hereford's argument surprised me, but it was met with near-universal approval when I presented it to other former players and coaches. When I asked Christion Jones, who played on title-winning teams his first two years at Alabama, what separated his teams that didn't win it all from the ones that did, he fell back on a similar perspective. "The leadership was hidden," he says. "Guys didn't fully buy into their roles."

Holcombe, a member of the 2015 and 2017 title teams, says, "It was really the guys. It just seemed like every guy on the team bought in. Yes, Coach Saban pushed us in the right direction, but it was really the brotherhood of that locker room—all those guys just came together."

Harlon Barnett certainly agrees. As a member of Saban's 2003 title-winning LSU coaching staff, Barnett saw firsthand the tremendous impact possible when the players were fully invested into the mission and willing and able to keep it that way.

"The team leaders, the seniors, must have a good control of the team," Barnett says. "They have to have a pulse of the team; they've got to be able to handle things outside of the football building that the coaches may never hear about or know about. When you have leaders like that, you have an opportunity to be a really good football team."

When Saban talked about the 2020 team that won a national championship after losing two of its key assistants, he referenced the "fantastic leadership" from his veteran players, including team captains Mac Jones, Landon Dickerson, DeVonta Smith, and Alex Leatherwood. "I had the easiest job in America last year," Saban said, "because of the guys we had, the kind of leadership we had, and how they had the respect of the other players and how they impacted and affected what we did on a daily basis."

Saban is the unquestioned man who drives the Alabama organization, but one leader isn't enough. He would have never been able to accomplish what he has without considerable investment from his players and coaches, who were willing to keep each other accountable in the path to success. He needed players like McClain and Jones and coaches like Burns and Cochran to ensure everyone understood the directives. He had to cultivate other leaders and do so as soon as they entered the organization. Leadership is hard, in general, but especially so if you're the only one.

CHAPTER 5

Use Staff Turnover
to Improve

I t's hard to find a more unlikely pairing than Lane Kiffin and Nick Saban. Kiffin was equal parts offensive guru and hellion, a man who seemed to enjoy two things above all else: scoring a lot of points and generally being a pain in the ass. Then there was Saban, the old-school defensive-minded wizard who liked to do things his way and didn't put up with insubordination. It took seventeen years for Saban to get his first head coaching opportunity at Toledo as he put in long hours and jumped from organization to organization to move up the ranks. Kiffin, the son of a longtime NFL coach, was the youngest NFL head coach in the modern era when the Oakland Raiders hired him in 2007 when he was only thirty-one years old. Kiffin loved to troll and poke fun at various targets on Twitter; Saban barely used email, let alone a social media platform. To say the two had lived different lives and possessed different personalities would be a giant understatement.

Kiffin's career came crashing down in 2013 when USC athletic director Pat Haden fired him at 3:17 a.m. in a small meeting room of a private Los Angeles airport following a bad loss to Arizona State. The circumstances behind his firing only a month into the season and the ridicule that accompanied them amplified the precipitous fall from grace for the onetime offensive wunderkind who blew through three premier job opportunities before he turned forty (when you add in his one-year Tennessee stint). Oakland Raiders owner Al Davis hated the Kiffin experience so much he called him a "disgrace" and said he'd conned him in a press conference announcing his firing. Kiffin looked radioactive to prospective employers.

However, Kiffin and Saban shared an important friend: Jimmy Sexton.

The most powerful agent in college sports represented both coaches and brought the two together when Kiffin's career faltered at Southern Cal. "We had actually gone and visited, myself and Jimmy, like a summer or two before just to kind of meet with him for a couple hours and ask him questions and stuff, and get familiar with each other," Kiffin says.

After Alabama lost to Auburn that season, Saban brought Kiffin in as an offensive consultant. The belief around the program was that Saban was upset with how the game was changing, especially the impact of the run-pass option play and its tendency to allow offensive linemen to run downfield, and wanted to do something about it. Kiffin would later say Saban told him, "We're a Mercedes that's getting ready to drive off the edge of the cliff. It looks good, it looks pretty, but it's not working anymore." Even bringing Kiffin in to consult was met with derision. A *Los Angeles Times* story said, "Maybe he wants to hire Kiffin to run his offense? And maybe the whole world has gone crazy?"

Saban did precisely that. He nudged out offensive coordinator Doug Nussmeier, who left for Michigan after the season, and brought in Kiffin as his new offensive coordinator. The Kiffin experience had its share of ups and downs but it served its ultimate purpose of pushing Alabama to revolutionize an offense that was becoming stale.

Kiffin helped Alabama marry pro-style concepts with a faster tempo and more spread option components. Kiffin didn't have much experience with no-huddle up-tempo offenses, but Saban believed in Kiffin's talent and bet on his ability to figure it out. That first year, Kiffin experimented with more tempo to some success, notably helping Blake Sims, a former running back–turned-quarterback, to a single-season school record of 3,487 passing yards. By the end of the season, Saban and Kiffin wanted to move further into faster tempo and no huddle, so they brought in former Washington and Kansas offensive coordinator Eric Kiesau as an offensive analyst. He had previously helped Jeff Tedford, Steve Sarkisian, and Charlie Weis incorporate the no huddle into pro-style concepts.

Saban called Kiesau and told him, "We want to go no huddle, but we just don't know how to do it. Will you help us do it?" Saban flew Kiesau to Tuscaloosa and put him through hours of explaining his philosophies and how they could help Alabama. Saban liked what he heard and offered Kiesau a job the next day.

As Kiesau explained to Saban and Kiffin, it wasn't about changing the play calls necessarily, but about changing how they operate. One early emphasis was changing the play call terminology to be shorter, often one-word play calls, to let the offense move faster. The faster the offense moves, the more plays you can run, which helped a program like Alabama that had a deep and talented depth chart. That paid off in 2015 when Kiffin relied more on the running game and turned Derrick Henry into a Heisman Trophy winner on Alabama's journey to another national championship. There can be a misconception that no-huddle up-tempo teams only pass the ball, but to Kiesau, watching Alabama wear teams down in the second half with its running game was the reason Alabama made the switch.

"When you start going fast, you wear teams down and that's when you get big runs," Kiesau says. "A lot of those big runs you saw with Derrick Henry in the second half were because we were going no huddle, wearing teams down, and then he pops a big run."

In his three seasons at Alabama, Kiffin worked with a different starting quarterback each season but found a way to get the most out of each. He was a savant play-caller who lived for outsmarting and out-scheming his opponents in finding unique ways to get his top players the ball. "He was like Madden," says former Alabama offensive lineman Dominick Jackson. "Before meetings, he'd tell you we're running a play. We get to meetings and the play has been rewritten four different times with four different schemes and four different outlets. He's a mastermind."

Kiffin was what Alabama needed to transform its operation even if he wasn't a seamless cog in the system.

The daily meetings Kiffin was required to attend at 7:30 a.m. frustrated him, as did the regimented approach Saban preferred. Kiffin was more of a freethinker, an artist whose work was beautiful play calls. Ken Smithmier, the president of P3 Insights, identified Kiffin as a people (intrinsic) dominant person while Saban was a vision (systemic) dominant person. In Smithmier's database, only 7 to 8 percent of people are systemic dominant. Smithmier likened it to Israeli psychologist Daniel Kahneman's Fast and Slow theory that as an intrinsic person Kiffin fell under the fast domain and preferred intuitive, fast decision-making while Saban as a slow thinker wanted a more deliberate approach. The differing styles had a way of annoying both sides, with the intrinsic Kiffin wishing to go faster and the systemic Saban wanting his offensive coordinator to slow down and think about it more. Kiffin admitted as much in a *Sports Illustrated* interview, saying, "I was always real fast and I didn't slow down to think things through a lot of times. Coach is so slow when it comes to things like that. And it drove me nuts at first." It took both getting out of their comfort zones to realize that not only would the organization benefit from the balancing of approaches brought on by the arrangement, but so would each individually.

"When you get a great OC like [Steve Sarkisian] or Kiffin, you've got to recognize that that person needs a longer leash," Smithmier says. "And it might make you uncomfortable but the good leaders do it because they think they should. I think Saban is misperceived in his rigidity because he's only rigid about the things he's already determined and have shown over time to really matter."

It wasn't always easy. Saban and Kiffin clashed at times, publicly and privately, in a way that seemed to fascinate outside observers. TV cameras would show the two arguing on the sidelines during games, interactions Saban would describe as "ass chewings." Former Alabama assistant Lance Thompson, who worked under Saban and Kiffin multiple times, told ESPN their personalities were so far apart "it was like Earth and Neptune." Saban indulged Kiffin's antics because he believed it benefited the organization, and he was willing to put his comfort aside because of what Kiffin brought to the table. He was that brilliant an offensive play-caller. There was a sense around the organization that the arrangement wouldn't last forever, though.

"Lane was a ticking time bomb," says former Alabama receiver Christion Jones. "You never knew what he was going to say or do."

That bomb went off in 2016 in the lead-up to the national championship game. Florida Atlantic hired Kiffin after the SEC Championship Game, but he agreed to stay on at Alabama through the season. It was a challenging juggling act that even Saban had struggled with when he took the Michigan State job but was still working with the Cleveland Browns. Kirby Smart successfully navigated the experience the year before on the way to a national championship, but Kiffin wasn't as adept at managing the two jobs. Kiffin interviewed prospective coaches in Atlanta in the lead-up to the playoff semifinal against Washington, with some players even remembering him taking phone calls during practice. Kiffin's behavior that week ahead of a critical game, which included showing up late to meetings, left players deeply frustrated.

"Guys thought he abandoned us," says a former offensive player on that team. "We had been working all season, we were told to buy in, and Coach Kiffin is over here taking interviews. The trust was lost from some of the players because Kiffin wasn't really here."

His media day comments assessing his Alabama experience as, "I don't recall a happy moment. I just recall the ass chewings," was likely said in jest, but it didn't exactly ingratiate him to an already annoyed Saban. The tipping point came when Alabama's offense looked sloppy and ill prepared in its win over the Huskies. When Saban reviewed what went wrong, he found out Kiffin called plays that players hadn't practiced and weren't expecting. Some offensive players voiced concerns to Saban about Kiffin's lack of focus that week. It all added up in a way that pushed Saban to make the bold decision to remove Kiffin as offensive coordinator days before the national championship in a move framed as a "mutual decision." The juice was no longer worth the squeeze.

"Those two guys were never really that happy together," says former Alabama tight end Hunter Bryant. "They weren't having dinner together and hanging out. But they worked well together and respected what each other did. That last year there was some disenfranchisement on Kiffin's part, so when he left I don't think anyone was really surprised."

When Saban addressed the team after the news broke of Kiffin leaving before the title game, he was even-keeled and plainly said it shouldn't change anything, according to players in attendance.

"We still have the plays, we still have the team here, and we are going to go in there and do our job," Saban told them. "If a coach leaves, it doesn't change how we do things at Alabama. We've got to be ready to go regardless."

Alabama had just lost its most prominent assistant coach, a move that became a major national story, and Saban treated it as nothing more than a blip on the radar. The timing was unprecedented, but losing a valued assistant was nothing new for Saban.

Many of us don't like change, especially when it comes to our team. There are actual costs that come with staff turnover, including lost productivity, financial costs, and cultural impact. A 2012 Center for American Progress study determined that replacing a senior executive type like Kiffin could cost up to 213 percent of that person's salary, meaning for an organization like Alabama the loss of Kiffin could cost millions. There was also the mental cost of losing a trusted and valuable employee. Former Minnesota head coach Glen Mason told me it would ruin his summer when he lost a quality coach because he knew all the hard work that would go into having to replace the person. Too much staff turnover threatens to disrupt continuity and, ultimately, progress and growth.

During Alabama's successful run, Saban has dealt with extreme turnover. He had a few long-tenured lieutenants like Scott Cochran and Burton Burns, who each stayed with him for more than a decade, but the average assistant coach spent a few seasons before moving on. There are several reasons for that, but the biggest is the copycat effect within college sports. Competing organizations see Alabama having considerable and consistent success, so they try to copy it by hiring away one of Saban's top assistants. Since 2007, nine schools have directly hired Alabama assistants or staffers away to be their head coaches. They've left for everything from smaller FBS schools like Florida Atlantic and Marshall to the most prestigious in the country like Texas and Georgia. That list doesn't even include Miami hiring Mario Cristobal, Florida hiring Billy Napier, or Michigan State hiring Mel Tucker—all Saban disciples who worked for him in Tuscaloosa. Not surprisingly, the years with the most extensive turnover came after Alabama won a national championship. Saban's 2015 championship-winning staff featured six future

FBS head coaches, including graduate assistant Dan Lanning, who would go on to become Oregon's head coach.

Consider the turnover after Alabama's championships in 2015, 2017, and 2020.

2015

Defensive coordinator Kirby Smart (Georgia head coach)
Defensive line coach Bo Davis
Defensive backs coach Mel Tucker (Georgia defensive coordinator)

2017

Offensive coordinator Brian Daboll (Buffalo Bills offensive coordinator)
Running backs coach Burton Burns (Off-field role)
Defensive coordinator Jeremy Pruitt (Tennessee head coach)
Defensive line coach Karl Dunbar (Pittsburgh Steelers DL coach)
Defensive backs coach Derrick Ansley (Oakland Raiders DB coach)

2020

Offensive coordinator Steve Sarkisian (Texas head coach)
Offensive line coach Kyle Flood (Texas offensive coordinator)
Associate head coach/running backs coach Charles Huff (Marshall
    head coach)
Defensive backs coach Karl Scott (Minnesota Vikings DB coach)
Special teams coordinator Jeff Banks (Texas assistant HC/special teams)

Replacing one key assistant could be challenging enough. Now imagine having to replace five of your top ten employees in a month. Saban not only had to find quality replacements, but he also often had to do so under a time crunch due to recruiting pressure. It had the potential to wreak havoc on the organization, yet somehow Saban found a way to keep the organization chugging along despite the consistent turnover.

"His ability to be able to do that is unparalleled," says former Alabama receivers coach Mike Groh. "One of the least things that's ever factored into winning is continuity. And there's been an extreme lack of continuity over the years, particularly in terms of losing coaches."

How does Saban succeed in the face of the turnover? First, he prepares everyone in the organization for the inevitability of it. During the recruiting process, Saban is candid with prospective players that they might lose their position coach or coordinator during their time at Alabama. It sets clear expectations so there are no surprises when a coach leaves that might prompt unrest or possible departure. All Saban had to say was he would be there, the "Process" would be there, and then point to his strong track record of hiring assistant coaches.

To hire the right replacements, he relies on trusted friends and advisors. To be considered for an on-field coaching position you had to be a good recruiter and a good teacher, but more than anything, you had to be committed to doing things the "Alabama way." Finding the right people requires lots of research and phone calls. Throughout his career, Saban built up a network of people he can trust and go to when he needs to make hires.

Other than his wife, Terry, Jimmy Sexton has long been Saban's most trusted advisor. The co-head of Creative Artists Agency's football division, Sexton represents many of the biggest names in college football, including Smart, Jimbo Fisher, and Dan Mullen. Still, Saban has been his most important client for years. The two connected while Saban was at Michigan State and dissatisfied with how his previous agent handled his NFL interest. Sexton was a shrewd yet affable man whose clients always seemed to come out on top in deals but he still found a way to make everyone involved feel good about the process. It's why he got so much repeat business and elicited such trust from coaches, athletic directors, and other industry folks. Once the two linked up, Sexton played a significant role in every major career decision Saban made.

He facilitated a conversation with LSU, he advised Saban to weigh what he really wanted to be known for when considering the Miami Dolphins job, and he has been the consigliere to Saban's Godfather status at Alabama.

"Jimmy is so good at his job, and Nick trusts him," says former LSU trustee Charlie Weems, who dealt with Sexton frequently while Saban was in Baton Rouge. "I think that trust extends beyond the principal-agent relationship. They're friends, and Jimmy's always had Nick's best interests at heart. When something wasn't in Nick's best interests, he'd tell him. He's been such a good thing for Nick."

Says a former Alabama staffer, "I think Jimmy had a lot more to do with what came out of [Saban's] mouth when there was a real problem than probably anybody else."

Sexton connecting Saban with Kiffin was one of the little-discussed ways he demonstrated his value to the Alabama head coach. Sexton is best known for getting big contracts for his clients, a service he delivered numerous times for Saban as he was regularly the sport's highest-paid coach once Sexton started representing him. As Saban lost more and more assistants, though, the CAA agent's biggest value may have come from advising him on prospective hires. Sexton had a deep client list and built a team of people expected to identify the top up-and-coming coaches Sexton would want to add to his roster. That came in handy when schools regularly pillaged Saban's staff looking for new head coaches and coordinators. Sexton had the valuable knowledge of the type of person Saban wanted and the coaches best suited to work well under him. After Jeremy Pruitt, a Sexton client, left to become Tennessee's head coach, Sexton's team played a direct role in Saban hiring Pete Golding, also a Sexton client, away from the University of Texas at San Antonio. Saban knew little about Golding and had never met him before Sexton put him on his radar. Saban also called his former defensive line coach Bo Davis for his honest opinion on Golding after the two worked together at UTSA. Former Ole Miss head coach Hugh Freeze, another Sexton client, was expected to join Saban's staff that same offseason before the SEC intervened and discouraged the hire.

Sexton's staffing help began long before Kiffin, too. In his first week at Alabama, Saban faced a whirlwind of activity trying to put together a recruiting class and his first staff at the same time. As Saban was flying around the country to meet with prospective players, Sexton and two of his subordinates parked themselves in Tuscaloosa for days to help Saban get the right people in place. On opposite ends of a long table were Saban calling recruits and Sexton calling coaches nonstop.

When it was time for Sexton to leave, graduate assistant Louis LeBlanc drove him to the airport. Seeing the tension on LeBlanc's face as he drove, Sexton asked him if everyone in the organization was on edge as a new regime took over. When LeBlanc said yes, Sexton offered his advice.

"Coach Saban is more about trying to change people than change out people," Sexton told him. "Just buy in, do what he asks, and he'll be incredibly loyal. If you go in and try to do your own thing, you're probably going to get rooted out. He doesn't want to fire people; he loves it when they buy into his vision."

Sexton's advice is a refrain shared by many former Saban assistants. There was a system in place and while Saban was willing to adjust it as he did with Kiffin, he wanted it done only if it best served the players. A good example: In football, every coach has different terminology they use for their play calls. Even if the plays are similar, the verbiage can be very different. It's common when a new coach comes in to bring the plays they are accustomed to calling and everyone has to learn the new terms. But Saban didn't believe in that. Why should fifty or sixty players have to learn entirely new descriptors as opposed to one coach having to do it? So when Saban hired Bill O'Brien, fresh off a seven-year run as an NFL head coach that included four playoff trips, O'Brien was expected to adjust his playbook to fit what Alabama players knew. It didn't matter that he had a reputation as a quarterback whisperer after working with Tom Brady in the NFL—the same standards applied to everyone. "He has the program in place, you learn," says longtime offensive line coach Rick Trickett, who worked with Saban at two schools. "If you have good ideas, that's fine—let's put it in our language."

O'Brien admitted that was "very challenging" early on in his transition to working at Alabama. He had spent five years working for Bill Belichick's New England Patriots so he knew what to expect working for Saban, but it still took hard work to train himself to take his knowledge and use it within

Alabama's parameters and not simply how he had done it elsewhere. Long-time defensive line coach Pete Jenkins, who worked with Saban at LSU and now consults at Alabama, watched O'Brien's transformation unfold over the 2021 season. Jenkins visited Alabama that spring and saw O'Brien trying to figure out how to operate under Saban. "When I went back for training camp [in August], I could see where he had made the adjustment to Coach Saban," Jenkins says. "And then I was there the week before the semifinal game, and I thought Bill O'Brien had made a tremendous adjustment."

As Jenkins explained it, "It don't make a damn [difference] where you've been." The secret—and challenge—to working for Saban is that it doesn't matter what you've been or done before you arrive in his organization. Whether you are a first-time assistant coach or a former Super Bowl–winning coach, you get treated the same way. Not long after Saban hired Jenkins to his first LSU staff, the two were discussing technique when the veteran defensive line coach mentioned his previous success in getting at least one of his nose guards to make first-team SEC for ten years. Saban said that was impressive but they were still going to play his preferred way.

"Whatever you might think, it's his offense, his defense, his special teams, his recruiting operation, his offseason program, and he plugs people into it," Jenkins says. "Some guys can't adjust to it."

That mentality flowed throughout the organization and is something Saban would directly address during the hiring process. When Tyler Siskey interviewed for a job at Alabama after having success at Ole Miss, Saban told him, "I'm not hiring you to do what you did at Ole Miss. I'm hiring you to do what we do here at Alabama and to run it." The Alabama coach would explain what the role entailed and make sure the prospective hire was comfortable with what he expected. Saban believed in his approach wholeheartedly and wanted people who generally felt the same. He knew other organizations might offer more freedom to their assistant coaches, so he wanted to know they were on board with the primary tasks of coaching up the players and getting them to best understand the system already in place. Transparency and clear expectations are critical when bringing someone new into your organization.

"He's going to put pressure on everybody in the organization every single day," Groh says. "Every day. Without fail. He had a clear definition of the standards and really the job description of each position within the organization, from the very top all the way down to the very bottom person. You were expected to uphold the standards of whatever that job description might be."

When a hire went poorly, more often than not, a coach hadn't liked that approach or had used the organization as a temporary stepping-stone to get a bigger job elsewhere. After the 2017 national championship when Saban lost both coordinators along with other valued coaches, he skewed too far in one direction when picking their replacements. He thought recruiting was slipping and wanted younger, hungrier coaches who could boost Alabama's efforts in that area. His departing protégés raided his stash of talented young coaches on the way out, a move that greatly frustrated Saban, so there weren't as many obvious in-house replacements. Kiffin explained it as Saban "went out of his loop" that hiring cycle and opted for coaches with few to zero previous ties to his system. "He didn't know these guys, they came in, and it was different for them," Kiffin told me. "Their goal was probably to get to the next place."

That reared its head in the Tide's ugly title game loss to Clemson in January 2019. The staff never gelled the way Saban wanted, and he attributed it to distractions that included coaches looking for the exit before the season was over. It prompted a mass exodus of six assistants out of Tuscaloosa: offensive coordinator Mike Locksley (Maryland head coach), co-offensive coordinator Josh Gattis (Michigan offensive coordinator), defensive coordinator Tosh Lupoi (Cleveland Browns defensive line coach), quarterbacks coach Dan Enos (Miami offensive coordinator), offensive line coach Brent Key (Georgia Tech offensive line coach), and defensive line coach Craig Kuligowski. With all the exits came stories questioning whether Saban's management style was running coaches out of the organization who didn't want to deal with such a demanding boss. It's a reputation Saban has had to fight back against for years.

A famous story that seemingly showed how hard a boss Saban could be popped up after he left Michigan State for LSU. The story, which has been retold in books and newspapers, is that after accepting the LSU job, Saban sent a plane up to East Lansing to bring his MSU assistants down to Baton Rouge with him. He wanted the majority of his assistants to follow him, according to the accounts, to bring their knowledge of his system and serve as his loyal disciples in the SEC. But the plane landed in Louisiana empty. "It was an embarrassing thing for Nick," Michigan State offensive line coach Pat Ruel said in one interview. The many retellings of the story of a coach no one wanted to follow only furthered the embarrassment.

The truth, though, was very different.

"There was never a plane that dropped down to East Lansing and no one showed up," says former Michigan State assistant Bill Sheridan. "There was never a plane that was ever sent. That whole story is all bullshit."

According to Sheridan's telling, Saban talked to all his assistant coaches before he left to take the LSU job. He told them that as he was putting together his first LSU staff, the top priority was getting coaches who had experience either in the SEC or the South in general. Saban had spent the vast majority of his career in the Midwest and knew he needed coaches with already-established relationships down south if he was going to be success-ful in recruiting. During his job interview, he even told LSU officials that he wanted to bring in Jimbo Fisher as his offensive coordinator and John Thompson as his defensive coordinator because of their SEC ties. Saban was interested in taking three of his MSU assistants with him in Ruel, defen-sive line coach Brad Lawing, who previously worked at South Carolina, and defensive coordinator Bill Miller, who had recruited in Florida when he was at Miami. Sheridan was interested in following Saban to LSU if he would take him, but he didn't have any preexisting SEC recruiting ties. When the two met, Saban thanked him for his loyalty and all the hard work he had done but said he couldn't commit yet to taking him with him. "That's kind of how it was for everybody," Sheridan says.

As Saban started putting together his LSU staff, a movement was afoot to have Bobby Williams succeed him at Michigan State. Williams, a popular coach on the staff, was named the interim head coach and guided the Spar-tans to a Citrus Bowl win over Florida. It was strongly implied to the staff that if they all banded together to stay at MSU, Williams would get the permanent job and they'd all keep their jobs. That meant stability and no need to move their families to Louisiana, a welcome reprieve for the nomadic lifestyle most were accustomed to as college coaches.

"Our entire coaching staff all went over to the athletic director's house and said, 'We are coming off one of the best years in the history of Michigan State, we've got good players coming back, and Bobby could and should be the head coach,'" Sheridan says. "And if he does, we'll all stay—none of us will be going to LSU. That was the pitch and that's what happened.

"The story of a plane being sent to East Lansing to bring three or four assistants that he had offered jobs to and guys not showing up at the airport to get on to them, that's completely fabricated. There's not one ounce of truth to that."

Michigan State leaders didn't hide the fact that they liked the idea of running it back and keeping the band together. After Saban accepted the LSU job, MSU initially offered the job to his old friend Glen Mason. However, there was a stipulation. "They wanted me to keep his staff," Mason says. "You have to have the right to hire your own staff. The president wanted me to keep his staff, and I said I'm not going to do that. I might keep some of them, but it can't be a prerequisite."

The Michigan State plane story fits a perception Saban has struggled to shake. Following years that had more coaching turnover than usual at Alabama, another crop of stories about Saban as an impossible-to-please boss sprang up. They weren't altogether inaccurate; there is no question Saban is a demanding boss who asks a lot of everyone in his program. He holds them to a high standard and expects them to put the organization before themselves. That style isn't for everyone, and it certainly led to coaches over the years deciding to continue their careers elsewhere. More often than not, though, it was because a better opportunity awaited them.

"People say, 'All the turnover, people must hate it there,'" Siskey says. "No, they don't hate it there. It's just that they've created so much value in the short time they are there, they're going to capitalize on their value."

The truth was, Saban saw the value in the turnover, too, even if its frequency could frustrate him. It helped limit complacency to bring in new

blood with new energy and ideas. Continuity may have made his life easier, and he would never say otherwise, but it was almost like deep down the
ultra-competitive Saban liked the challenge of having to replace talented
people after a success. It was another hurdle for him to overcome, a way for
him to test himself against an industry desperate to knock him off the throne.
The turnover also led him to innovation: he had to find a way to better prepare for the inevitable departures and have more talented in-house talent
available to be promoted. While other leaders might bemoan the loss of a
talented staffer, Saban views it as an opportunity to improve.

CHAPTER 6

Give Distressed Assets Another Chance

Butch Jones' fall from rising star to butt of jokes was steep and abrupt. Before becoming Tennessee's head coach, Jones had considerable career success, emerging as one of the hottest names in the business after building winning programs at Central Michigan and Cincinnati. Tennessee had spun through head coaches in a dizzying fashion, from Phil Fulmer to Kiffin to Derek Dooley in a four-year span. Tennessee hired Jones to bring stability to a drama-filled program and get the Volunteers back to competing with Alabama again after a long losing drought.

Jones recruited very well at Tennessee, signing the nation's seventh-best class in 2014 and fourth-best in 2015, according to 247Sports. Those classes included future NFL pros Alvin Kamara, Jalen Hurd, and Derek Barnett. He achieved back-to-back 9–4 seasons, better than anything his two most recent predecessors in Knoxville had accomplished. But when the fan base and media turned on Jones, they did so viciously. He got crushed on social media for cheesy motivational slogans like "champions of life" and "five-star hearts." He had his issues as a coach, and fans had every right to demand more than four-loss seasons, but he was labeled a laughingstock even if the results really didn't indicate that.

After Tennessee fired Jones in 2017 amid a 4–6 season, he weighed what his next step should be. With a big buyout supplying a salary for years to come, he benefited from not having to jump at the first opportunity. Typically, a coach in his situation would work in television for a year or two or try to land a position coach job at a lesser school.

Jones opted for door number three: to become an analyst at Alabama. "Quite frankly, when I was probably at the lowest point of my career, [Saban] welcomed me into that football program," Jones says. "And I'll forever be grateful."

At Alabama, Jones would get a chance to learn under Saban and rehabilitate his battered reputation, while Alabama got a veteran coach in a position that fifteen years earlier would have been occupied by a young coach with a fraction of Jones' experience. It was a mutually beneficial arrangement and gave Saban's program yet another advantage over its competition.

It required foresight and openness from Saban to see the value in hiring coaches deemed failures elsewhere. He established it was about what those coaches could do for Alabama, not what they had done elsewhere. A coach like Jones may have failed as a head coach somewhere else but, typically, he had to have done something right to have gotten that opportunity in the first place. Rather than focus on the failure, Saban sees a distressed asset that can be acquired cheaply, will be motivated to prove his doubters wrong, and has significant experience that can be valuable to the organization. Saban destroyed his competition, hired away their top people in lesser roles, and established Alabama as the place to go after you've failed elsewhere, which attracted high-quality job candidates.

"He's a coaching whisperer," says former LSU offensive lineman Paris Hodges, a member of the 2003 national title team. "He knows what he wants, he knows what he sees, and he knows how to utilize their strengths. Whatever their weaknesses are, he helps make them stronger."

NCAA rules prohibited analysts like Jones from actively coaching, but they could still interact with players, help assistant coaches with game planning, and break down film to allow coaches to focus on other tasks. They brought valuable insights as former head coaches on knowing how and how not to run a program. They were overqualified for their positions but eager to take them to better their future career prospects after working for Saban.

"It's an opportunity to be around and learn from arguably the greatest of all time," Jones says. "You're always going to be challenged; you're always going to be around experts and great people who are like-minded in competitiveness and inner drive to be the best. Not only being around Coach Saban every single day, which was the biggest factor for me, but also being around other great football coaches."

Saban was capitalizing on a growing market inefficiency. Tennessee owed Jones $8.26 million, due in monthly payments, when it fired him in 2017. Those payments were mitigated by whatever salary Jones made until Tennessee fully paid the buyout, but knowing he had a $200,000 check coming in every month made it easier for someone like Jones to accept an analyst role at Alabama for a $35,000 annual salary. As television money poured into college football, so did the willingness for schools to pay large buyout sums, otherwise known as liquidated damages, to make their coaches go away. The numbers could be obscene, like when Auburn ate a $21.5 million buyout to fire Gus Malzahn in 2020 or Notre Dame paid Charlie Weis nearly $19 million to leave in 2009. When South Florida fired Charlie Strong in 2019 and owed him a $2.5 million buyout, Saban and Alabama were more than happy to take advantage of the situation to add the former Texas head coach as a defensive analyst. It was a similar story adding former Houston head coach Major Applewhite, whose old employer owed him a $2 million buyout. Schools were so desperate to dethrone Alabama, especially those residing in the SEC, they threw gobs of money to replace their coaches only for those actions to inadvertently make Saban's program even stronger. "We pay them to beat us again," says an administrator at a rival organization.

It all started in 2009 with Mike Groh, who says he invented the analyst position. The son of former New York Jets coach Al Groh, Mike saw his career was on the rise in the mid-2000s. He moved up the ranks on his father's Virginia coaching staff to become the offensive coordinator in 2006 when he was in his early thirties. However, a power struggle in 2008 between his father and the school's athletic director forced the younger Groh out.

While it wasn't his father's decision, on paper Mike Groh got fired by his dad and now needed a job.

He considered different options and decided on one that caught people by surprise; he was joining Saban's nascent Alabama program as a graduate assistant. With one decision, Groh went from being an offensive coordinator in the Atlantic Coast Conference to a low man on the totem pole at Alabama. He was taking over a job typically reserved for a recent college graduate thirteen years after graduating from Virginia. It might not have been where a thirty-seven-year-old Groh expected to be at that point in his career, but it gave him a front-row seat to Saban guiding Alabama to its first national championship since 1992. "It says a lot about his vision and how the game can grow in any way he can get an advantage," Groh says.

Groh spent one season as a graduate assistant before jumping at a quarterbacks coach job at Louisville. A year later, Saban brought him back as his wide receivers coach and recruiting coordinator after being impressed with what he saw from Groh in 2009. That was the start of a pattern of established coaches joining the organization in lesser roles and being rewarded. That same year, Billy Napier, fresh off being fired as Clemson's offensive coordinator, joined the program as an analyst. Like Groh, Napier went from being a hotshot young offensive coordinator on the rise to seeing his career crumble before his eyes when Dabo Swinney dumped him for another coach.

"That was probably the best year of my coaching career," Napier told me years ago. "I coached for ten years, came to Alabama, and the eleventh year I learned more in that one year than I did in the prior ten. It's a great environment to learn and grow as a coach."

Not only did it help Napier grow as a coach, it rejuvenated his career. He worked closely with Alabama offensive coordinator Jim McElwain, who took him to Colorado State as his assistant head coach in 2012. After Groh left for the Chicago Bears a year later, Saban called and brought Napier back in Groh's old spot. He flourished as one of Saban's nine on-field assistant coaches for three seasons, and it helped him get a promotion at Arizona State and later the head coaching job at Louisiana. His time at Alabama gave him the blueprint for running a college football program, which he established to great success at Louisiana, emerging again as one of the nation's top young coaches a decade after being fired at Clemson. After four successful seasons at Louisiana, Napier left to take over one of the premier college football programs in the country as Florida's new head coach.

Following Napier's success, a who's who of failed coaches lined up to get some of that Alabama winning cologne sprayed on them. That trend didn't make everyone in college football happy, with some rival organizations pushing for a cap on the number of analysts an organization could employ. It was another reminder that as you push the boundaries to find new, innovative ways to be successful, it will upset people happy with the status quo. Saban pointed out to the media that everyone had the same opportunity to do what his organization was doing and continued bolstering it through cheap, experienced coaches eager for a second chance.

Known as one of the nation's top recruiters at Washington, Tosh Lupoi signed up to be an "intern." Like Napier, Lupoi told me years ago, "It's probably the best decision I've ever made in my life." Lupoi, a well-known recruiter, would eventually be promoted to outside linebackers coach and later to defensive coordinator. It set up a familiar path: a well-known coach joins the organization in a lesser role, and after a year or two when there's an assistant coach opening, he slides into the job. The setup gives that coach a chance to get familiar with Saban's system to see if it's a good fit, while allowing Saban to maintain some continuity amid all the turnover.

"He has a system that really changed college football," says former Georgia head coach Mark Richt. "He's got people in-house learning the system, being groomed for on-the-field positions, coordinator positions. He's got people in the building who are highly qualified guys that are learning the system, learning the way he does things."

That was the case for Mike Locksley. After a stint as Maryland's interim head coach, Locksley chose an Alabama analyst position over multiple on-field assistant jobs at Power Five programs. Saban rewarded him with two promotions, first from analyst to co-offensive coordinator, and then to offensive coordinator. In his final season at Alabama, Locksley won the Broyles Award as the nation's top assistant coach. In three seasons in Tuscaloosa,

Locksley completely transformed his reputation after a disastrous stint as New Mexico's head coach that was full of losing (2–26 record) and drama. Three years after not getting the job he badly wanted, Locksley returned to Maryland as the program's new head coach armed with notebooks full of knowledge he gained working alongside Saban. "Took the chocolate chip cookie recipe from down there," Locksley says, "and trying to make it work the same way." Locksley was so thankful for what Saban did for him, he kept recruiting for Alabama in the final month before signing day even after he had already accepted the Maryland job.

After Locksley left, Saban tried to complete his greatest reclamation project yet: Steve Sarkisian.

Sarkisian was a very talented offensive coach who quickly rose through the ranks to become the head coach at Washington and later Southern Cal, one of the country's premier programs. It all came crashing down in 2015 when Sarkisian reportedly showed up to USC football practices drunk and had an embarrassing encounter at a booster event. USC fired him with cause, and he was all but radioactive in the college football world. He initially planned to work at Fox Sports, but Lane Kiffin, a former colleague at USC, connected him to Saban and brought him to Alabama in 2016 as an analyst.

It was a significant risk for Saban, who seemingly should never have to take one. Why would he even bother taking on an embarrassed head coach with an alcohol problem and all the possible negative publicity that would come if the situation went poorly? Yet Saban didn't see it that way. He saw a talented coach who could bring value to his organization that Alabama didn't have to make a big investment to hire. Saban strongly believed in the culture he had already established and that it would provide the necessary structure for Sarkisian to get back on his feet. That isn't to say he made the decision lightly, because he didn't. Anyone who interviews for a job at Alabama, let alone gets an offer, is run through the gauntlet of talking to multiple people within the organization to make sure it was a good fit. Saban made the final call but he wanted input from the academic support staff, the strength and conditioning coaches, and other assistant coaches on the staff, among others, to ensure the prospective hire not only had the necessary skills to do the job well, but also would fit in personalitywise with the rest of the organization. Saban realized he asked a lot of his staff, including long hours at the office, so he didn't want to bring in anyone who would disrupt the operation and create internal strife.

That process wasn't perfect. Saban made unsuccessful hires like any hiring manager could, but overall he had a very successful hit rate. After taking in all the information, Saban was adroit at reading people and sussing out who was real and who was just saying what they thought he wanted to hear. A former assistant coach once praised Saban for how quickly he could identify people for who they truly are. Saban told him it was a skill he learned early in life. "When I was a kid growing up in West Virginia, there were a pack of dogs that ran in our neighborhood," Saban told the coach. "Some you could pet, and some would bite the hell out of you. You had to identify one from the other real quick."

With Sarkisian, Saban did his due diligence and came away believing it could be a win-win for everyone involved. "Saban is like, 'I'm giving you your second chance,' and helped him through all that stuff and that created more passion from Sark's point of view," says former Alabama receiver Mac Hereford. "He then has the mentality of 'I really want to be a part of this program for someone who's giving me a chance and wants me to succeed.'"

The move to Alabama proved to be precisely what Sarkisian needed. He could disappear into the work, not having to worry about media obligations or TMZ tracking him down at the airport. That first year, Sarkisian just had to worry about football, specializing in helping Kiffin with red-zone strategies. When Kiffin left to be Florida Atlantic's head coach, Saban promoted Sarkisian to offensive coordinator, though he stayed in that job for only a month before leaving to become the Atlanta Falcons offensive coordinator. When the Falcons fired him two years later in 2018, Saban again turned to Sarkisian to be his offensive coordinator. This time, Sarkisian couldn't say no.

"I didn't know enough of the 'whys,'" Sarkisian told CBS Sports. "I knew what Coach Saban was doing. I knew how he did it. I didn't know why he did what he did. I just said, 'I have a chance to go back to Alabama to get the finishing touches on my career, which is to be a head coach again.'"

Sarkisian did such a good job at Alabama that Saban turned to him to coach the 2020 Iron Bowl when he could not do so because of a positive coronavirus diagnosis. That gesture was "almost like the last piece of the puzzle for me," Sarkisian said, and further empowered his growth as a coach when he guided Alabama to a 42–13 win. After his second season as Alabama's offensive coordinator, Sarkisian went from being once considered unhirable to getting one of the top five jobs in college football as Texas' head coach. Sarkisian's total rehabilitation made it that much more desirable for down-on-their-luck coaches to put their egos aside and come to Alabama. "They've seen other people go before them and what it's done for their careers," Groh says. "When you get that call, you have to listen."

"Butch Jones was dead in the water," says former LSU defensive line coach Pete Jenkins. "Lane Kiffin, dead in the water. Sarkisian, dead in the water. That man's helped so many people, he just doesn't toot his horn. He does them for the right reason, and he doesn't spend a lot of time patting himself on the back about it."

The way Saban helps fired coaches like Sarkisian get back on their feet through association with his successful operation prompts real gratitude and loyalty. Any time Saban picks up the phone and says he needs Jenkins' help, the octogenarian defensive line coach packs his bags and heads to Tuscaloosa. *Sports Illustrated* compared Jenkins to Harvey Keitel's Winston Wolfe character in *Pulp Fiction* in a story on the pair's long-standing working relationship entitled "Alabama Coach Nick Saban's Secret Weapon? Meet Defensive Guru Pete Jenkins." Saban earned Jenkins' undying loyalty when he hired him back at LSU on his first staff, a move Jenkins to this day says is one of the keys to his happiness and was possible only under Saban. Jenkins had spent ten seasons working at LSU before being fired in 1990, ending a lifetime dream of coaching at the school. He was so desperate to get back to LSU that Jimbo Fisher told Saban, "If you offer Pete a job here at LSU, he'll run down I-10 naked to get here." After Saban hired him, Jenkins joked with Fisher that the only reason he didn't was because Saban didn't ask him to.

"I had a hole in my heart, and I think it would have been there for the rest of my days if he hadn't given me a chance to come back," Jenkins says. "I've always told Coach Saban I will be indebted for the rest of my days for giving me that chance to come back to LSU."

When Sarkisian left for Texas and took offensive line coach Kyle Flood with him, Saban replaced the outgoing assistants with Bill O'Brien and Doug Marrone, two NFL head coaches the previous season. Only Saban could lose the nation's top assistant coach and replace him with a man who had held one of thirty-two coveted NFL positions just months prior. Convincing Marrone, who guided the Jacksonville Jaguars to the AFC Championship game in 2017, to be a college position coach might have been even more noteworthy. Even established coaches like O'Brien and Marrone knew time inside the Alabama machine would be good for their careers. "It was the only phone call I got last year," O'Brien said. "And so he had a job opportunity for me, and I couldn't ask for a better opportunity."

Adding former NFL head coaches took both confidence and humbleness to make it work. Here's what that means: Saban isn't threatened by bringing experienced former head coaches into his organization. There are plenty of organizational leaders, including in sports, who don't want to surround themselves with talented, experienced lieutenants. They don't want to inadvertently groom their successor, so they'd rather have less threatening, less talented people below them, so they don't lose power. Conversely, before Sarkisian left for Texas, Saban did everything he could to try to keep him, including intimating to him that Sarkisian would have a chance to replace him one day at Alabama. While it helps that Saban is entrenched enough in his position that he doesn't have to worry about being ousted, it still takes a certain mindset to want to be surrounded by high-profile veteran coaches who might have a different perspective. O'Brien and Marrone are two strong-willed men used to running their own organizations, but Saban so emphatically believes in the culture he's established that he's not worried about their presence creating problems. It always goes back to this: if he thinks a person or thing can benefit his organization, particularly his players, he's going to do it.

"One of the biggest things at Alabama that you can sell is of course you have nice facilities, and of course the record shows for itself, but I think it's the people that make that program go," says Andy Kwon, who spent three seasons as an Alabama offensive graduate assistant. "There's a reason they are successful every year, because Coach Saban obviously is the CEO of the program, but he's always going to hire the best people in the country to support his players."

For the coaches, it takes humbleness to accept a lesser role. It can be an ego hit to go from being a high-powered head coach who makes millions a year to holding an ambiguous "analyst" title and making $35,000. It means going from a spacious office with a great view of the practice fields to a cramped Alabama auxiliary meeting room where the only accommodations are two folding tables and some chairs. Those coaches have to come in with the right attitude or it isn't going to work, and that requires some level of sacrifice from the coaches. There's less pressure in these roles, a nice perk, but there's also far less adulation.

"You're like, man, just months ago these guys were at the pinnacle of what they thought their career would be," says Hunter Bryant, who witnessed the peak of the offensive analysts at Alabama from 2014–2017. "Those guys had to come to the agreement, 'You're not going to be given any glamor, there's not going to be a lot of hoopla around you, you're not going to be treated any differently.' The feeling in meetings was what those guys said carried a lot of weight, but outside of those meetings, you didn't know they were there."

Bryant says there would never be any real announcement that a high-profile coach was joining the growing legion of analysts. He can still remember being in an offensive meeting one day, noticing a familiar face sitting in the back, and saying to himself, "I think that's Steve Sarkisian." But Lane Kiffin, the offensive coordinator at the time, never addressed it and neither did Saban. There was a point behind the strategy: those coaches, no matter how famous they were outside the football building, would be treated just the same as everyone else.

Jones went from trying to figure out ways to beat Alabama in the annual "Third Saturday in October" game as the face of Tennessee's program to being just another face in the Alabama army of analysts and coaches on the opposing sideline. CBS Sports analyst Gary Danielson told me it seemed like

Jones' primary job at Alabama during games was to "keep Najee [Harris] from blowing his top." "When you're used to being the one in the front of the room and you're used to setting the tone and you're used to setting the vision, it's very humbling," Jones admits.

A friend told Jones he had a "competitive advantage over everyone else in the country" once he accepted the analyst job at Alabama. Jones, fresh off a firing and now in a low-level position, asked him what he meant, and the friend said that at the halftime of his career Jones was getting a chance to spend it in college football's best program with college football's best coach. Jones, the friend believed, was setting up the second half of his career perfectly. The message hit home for the former Tennessee head coach, who got another head coaching opportunity at Arkansas State following three years at Alabama. He took Kwon with him as his new tight ends coach after working closely with him.

"I tried to take everything in, I tried to ask a lot of questions, I tried to evaluate a lot of things," he says. "Even though, yeah, it's hard when you're used to running your own program, it was very refreshing. I think it was needed for me from a professional and personal standpoint. I needed that time to self-evaluate, watch and learn, and try to bring value to Alabama in every facet."

The best leaders find ways to improve their organizations in big and small ways. Saban pioneering the analyst position isn't exactly Johannes Gutenberg inventing the printing press, but it offered a new way for Alabama to populate its organization with talented people at a discounted price. It capitalized on a market inefficiency and challenged the status quo, eliciting a fair share of detractors along the way. And as is the case with most innovations, it produced plenty of copycat efforts.

Competing programs realized Saban was on to something impactful and built their own mini-analyst armies. Saban protégé Jimbo Fisher became one of the most devoted followers, stocking his staff with analysts and well-known GAs like former Florida State co-offensive coordinator Lawrence Dawsey and former NFL cornerback Antonio Cromartie. When South Carolina fired Will Muschamp, another Saban protégé, and owed him a $12.9 million buyout, it wasn't much of a surprise to see him end up on friend Kirby Smart's Georgia staff as an analyst. Muschamp even reportedly turned down a chance to be Sarkisian's defensive coordinator at Texas to team up with Smart in a lesser role.

All around the country, organizations started adding experienced coaches in off-the-field analyst jobs. Former St. Louis Rams head coach Scott Linehan popped up as a Missouri analyst. Florida hired former NFL kicker Shayne Graham and former Georgia Southern head coach Tyson Summers. Other prominent analyst hires included former Miami head coach Randy Shannon (Florida State), former Iowa State head coach Paul Rhoads (Ohio State), and former North Carolina head coach Larry Fedora (Texas).

"They're building bigger buildings to do it and they are paying guys salaries that wouldn't have existed a few years ago," Richt says. "But the proof is in the pudding."

They have the recipe because Saban was willing to think outside the box and hire the most veteran graduate assistant he'd ever had in Groh. That one hire forever changed how organizations looked at their off-field hires and highlighted what was possible when you strived to be better rather than be comfortable.

CHAPTER 7

"The Process"

T he co-creator of Alabama's most famous product is a slender man who wears a long gray beard and thick glasses and is nicknamed "Gandalf" and "Lonny Graybeard" by players. "The guy looks like they dragged him off the streets of Seattle from a homeless shelter," says former Alabama staffer Todd Alles. "But he was absolutely brilliant."

Dr. Lionel "Lonny" Rosen's day job is as a Michigan State University psychiatry professor, but he's most famous for his role in creating "The Process" alongside Saban. Not that the media-shy Rosen wants any credit for that.

The Process is the engine that powers the Alabama organization, the system and mindset that everyone must follow. Competing organizations have tried to copy it, though no one has perfected its execution like Saban and Alabama. The Process is many things; most importantly, though, it is a daily way of living. It focuses on completing the task ahead of you at that moment and not worrying about what happened in the past or what might be around the corner in the future. You can't worry about what anyone else around you is doing. As New England Patriots coach Bill Belichick would say, you just do your job.

"It's broken down to such a granular level that you're not worried about the big picture," says Trevor Hewett, who spent six years working at Alabama. "I'm worried about this one specific task. It makes things so much simpler and clearer, not just at the top but all the way down to the bottom. We are here to accomplish this mission, and that's what we are going to do."

The Process is Saban's life work, the culmination of his upbringing, personality, and what he has determined is the best path for success. Many of the trademarks of what we've come to understand about The Process are things Saban has been preaching for most of his coaching career, dating back to when he was a young assistant coach. It's why it would be mostly inaccurate to say The Process was born on any one day. However, the most popular theory is that it crystallized for Saban in 1998 with Michigan State struggling with consistency and achieving the desired level of success.

In his first three seasons at MSU, Saban managed only a 19–16–1 record, a far cry from the success he'd later achieve at LSU and Alabama. Saban inherited a program that was hit with a scholarship reduction and put on probation in 1996 that slowed his expected progress. MSU players could see themselves getting better and the program was getting closer to being competitive on the field, but the results didn't always match up with that feeling. As Saban struggled to get the Spartans winning more, an unlikely friendship blossomed with Rosen. Saban had long been interested in human psychology, and Rosen introduced him to process thinking that emphasized breaking down big things into more easily completed tasks. Ahead of a game against No. 1 undefeated Ohio State, Saban asked Rosen an important question: What do you tell a team that thinks it has no chance to win?

Rather than identifying winning the game as the goal, Rosen encouraged Saban to stress winning each play instead. If players could zero in on what they needed to do a few seconds at a time to win the play—and could repeat that behavior throughout a game—they'd tend to get the desired big result without making it the focus. It took a sixty-minute game and broke it down into hundreds of seven-second plays. The idea deeply resonated with Saban, who told his team that week to focus on the process rather than the results.

It was put to the test early in that game when Ohio State raced out to a 17–3 first-quarter lead. To outsiders, it looked like more of the same for the 4–4 Spartans. The MSU players, though, focused on what they could control—trying to win every play and not worrying about what the scoreboard said. They battled back and won, 28–24, when Renaldo Hill intercepted a pass to end the game. It was Saban's biggest win as a coach to date and a sign that he was on to something emphasizing process thinking. It was further solidified the following year when Saban put together his best season as a head coach. He finally had the right mix of experienced staff and talented veteran players like receiver Plaxico Burress and linebacker Julian Peterson, who became first-round NFL draft picks, all in on the vision. The Spartans went 10–2 in 1999, which included another win over OSU, and Saban became a hot coaching commodity.

Rosen stuck with Saban as he jumped first to LSU and later to Alabama. Saban had complete trust in Rosen, especially his evaluation of people, and would send players to him to get his thoughts. It started at Michigan State as Saban looked for possible solutions for players going through a tough time, but it evolved to most players by the time he got to Alabama. Rosen helped Saban develop an individualized approach to each player, focusing on what made the person tick. Rosen could be blunt and would tell Saban if he thought a certain coach or player wasn't a good fit in his system. "He'd say, 'This kid isn't worth fighting for,'" Alles says. "'He wants to leave; let him go.'"

Seeing the success of his partnership with Rosen, Saban dove even deeper into the world of sports psychology. He connected with sports psychologist Dr. Kevin Elko while at LSU after hearing him talk about hockey star Jaromir Jagr wearing the number 68 as a way of remembering his grandfather. Jagr wore the jersey to remind him of what he was playing for—his why—so Elko would instruct his audience to find their 68. He brought in IMG mental conditioning coach Trevor Moawad, who helped Alabama players work on their communications skills, how to eliminate negative thoughts and how to sustain the right attitude amid challenging situations. Rosen and Moawad, who developed a close partnership with NFL star quarterback Russell Wilson, made an unusual pair but were very effective at engaging with the players in different ways.

"Sometimes you would do it and feel like you were hypnotized when you left, but it was really good stuff," says former Alabama captain Antoine Caldwell. "It's stuff that we had never been turned on to and never even thought about. I think it really helped guys like myself who were leaders and did things the right way just as much as the guys who were slacking and had things going on."

After a roller coaster 2007 season that ended with a 7–6 record, Saban hired The Pacific Institute, a Seattle-based company focused on how the mind works and how to "actually hack your mind," according to CEO Mark Panciera. Then-USC head coach Pete Carroll recommended the company to Saban after the success he saw it had with his program, which won national championships in 2003 and 2004.

The Pacific Institute came armed with a recently developed interactive program called PX2 specifically designed for young adults that featured founder Lou Tice on video and in-person facilitators like former NFL player Antowaine Richardson to guide the team through the lessons. The program, which Alabama primarily used with its underclassmen, focused on the metaphor of writing your own movie and then creating the script for said movie. The Pacific Institute emphasized the importance of self-talk, that inner voice we all have that can impact how a person views himself.

In basic terms, negative self-talk could be self-defeating and had a way of becoming a self-fulfilling prophecy. If a player walked into a big game thinking, "I always seem to play my worst in big games," it made it that much more likely to happen. It could turn a small mistake into a catastrophe if a player spiraled during a game because of it and couldn't regain control of his thoughts. To counteract it, The Pacific Institute taught them a technique called "the next time," so when a mistake happened, they focused on what they'd do the next time they were in a similar situation rather than defaulting to negative thoughts. When Carroll worked with The Pacific Institute at USC, he taught himself that anytime something bad happened his default saying would be "something great is about to occur." They were teaching the players that they had to be disciplined in the thoughts and mental pictures they allowed into their minds to be successful. "We aren't teaching people things they haven't done," says John McNeil, who helped write the PX2 program and worked closely with Carroll. "We are teaching them what they did when they were at their absolute best. And they know it; they connect with it."

"When those guys got brought in, this was the kind of stuff that really resonated with me because I knew I was going to be able to apply it," says former Alabama linebacker Alex Benson. "These Pacific Institute guys were legit. You knew you were going to be able to use that stuff for the rest of your life."

Every organization, even the most successful ones, inevitably faces challenges that could have a dramatic impact if not appropriately addressed. It is crucial to gauge the temperature of the people within the organization, from the high-level executives to the most junior employees, on what they believe to be the problems currently plaguing the company. Simply put: you can't fix a culture problem until you identify it first. One tactic The Pacific Institute used that could be applied to any organization was gathering employees and breaking them into small groups. The facilitators would ask them to identify what each employee believed was the biggest limiting belief occurring within the organization. It could be an "us versus them" mentality, a lack of resources needed to win, little faith in management, or many different concerns. Once you identify the primary limiting belief, you evaluate how it impacts the organization and what can be done to fix it. If the top issue was an "us versus them" mentality, that meant identifying the consequences of that belief like employees refusing to share good ideas. Ultimately, the goal was to use that limiting belief and turn it into a positive organizational affirmation like an "us environment" that everyone was expected to buy into.

Through that process at Alabama, the team came up with positive affirmations like "We fly to the ball seeking to cause big plays on every down" and "Our team is a family. We will look out for each other. We love one another. Anything that attempts to tear us apart only makes us stronger." There was real power in visualizing through affirmation, according to Panciera, who says, "When you affirm with the emotion and the picture vivid in your mind, you start moving toward having that mindset."

When former NFL defensive back Ron Medved, the Alabama project director and a vice president of sales for The Pacific Institute, returned after the season, he was stunned when he saw Alabama's team affirmations on a poster in the weight room. "I swear I'm not exaggerating that I gasped when I saw those team affirmations because they were freaking scary," Medved says. "The attitude and the experience that those affirmations said they wanted to create on the field for their opponents."

When he watched Alabama defeat Texas in the national championship that season, he saw the affirmations come to life. It served as a reminder to him that to establish a winning mindset, "you've got to work on it, you've got to build it, you've got to train it. You have to practice that mindset before you do that mindset." Seeing the impact The Pacific Institute had that year on Alabama, then-Oklahoma head coach Bob Stoops called up Richardson and said, "I want exactly what Alabama got."

Alabama builds its winning mindset without actually discussing winning. At the very heart of The Process is Saban's deep aversion to a results-oriented strategy. If Saban ran a car dealership, as he has often said was his initial career plan, he'd suspend all monthly sales quotas. He didn't believe such a specific outcome-driven strategy was effective or sustainable in the long term. Not long after he arrived at Alabama, he told one staffer how disturbing he found the mentality of a season boiling down to a national championship or bust.

"People think you've got to win a national championship every year, and if you don't, the season is a waste," Saban told him. "We can't teach that to these kids. Our goal is to be better today than we were yesterday."

Nowhere in Alabama's facilities will you see stated goals of winning the SEC or winning a national championship. You'll never see Saban circle a big rivalry game weeks in advance as a motivational technique. The expectation is to put in the required level of work to be successful regardless of the circumstances. He wanted everyone in his organization working just as hard preparing for Mercer as they did for rivals LSU and Auburn. Former Cleveland Browns general manager Phil Savage accurately captured that mindset when he titled his Alabama football book *4th and Goal Every Day*. That was the mentality Saban wanted everyone in the organization to come to work with every day, to treat each task as if it was as important as deciding what to do when it was 4th and 1 with the game on the line, whether it was the day of the national championship or a random Thursday in April. Every day mattered, and every day required the same level of dedication and effort. While difficult to maintain at times, that mentality is one reason Alabama has largely been upset-proof in the Saban era. After the 2020 season, Saban had an FBS-best ninety-eight consecutive wins against unranked opponents, the result of actually practicing what Saban preached about treating every opponent the same.

"You can't ever be that guy who is happy with a win or feels good about that and is up and down," says Rick Venturi, who worked with Saban with the Cleveland Browns. "By the end of Monday, you don't know if you won that game on Saturday or not. He's going to keep the heat on you; he's going to strive for perfection at all times."

For Saban, The Process really came down to discipline. His system was predicated on everyone in the organization having the discipline to avoid the things they knew they shouldn't do and do what they knew they should even if they didn't want to. That could be anything from getting to bed early rather than going out with friends to giving it your all on every single repetition during a grueling fall camp practice in August with the Alabama heat beating down on you. If you could master those simple concepts, you flourished in Saban's system. He'd tell his team that everyone has the ability to invest in The Process—it just comes down to whether they have the desire and discipline to do so. He framed it as a decision everyone had to make: "Do you want to live with the pain of discipline or the pain of disappointment?" He told them he'd always choose the pain of discipline because it meant he'd never deal with the pain of disappointment.

When Saban woke up each morning, he believed there were only two options available: you either got better or you got worse. There was no such thing as maintaining the status quo in Saban's mind. You either did something that made you better and brought you closer to being a champion, or you didn't. Being a champion, Saban would say, was about focusing on what it took to get there and not on simply getting there. It was about investing your time rather than simply spending it, a metaphor he'd repeat frequently to his organization.

"We're focused on what it takes to win and doing what it takes to win, not talking about winning," says former Alabama offensive lineman Taylor Pharr. "He's always talking about what we are doing and what we are not doing. And if we're not doing it, how do we fix it to get back to what we do?"

With considerable player and coach turnover after every season, Saban annually had to train an influx of new people to ditch their results-driven outlook for his Process. That meant avoiding individual goals like how many touchdowns a player would have that season. It was always about the team—a point Saban would often remind his players, sometimes in colorful fashion—and about getting better. He detested focusing only on the results, because he felt it could obscure the actual process of getting better. Alabama players were going to win the vast majority of their games, but that didn't mean they were improving individually or as an organization. And if that's all anyone cared about, how would he keep them motivated once they won it all, as every Saban recruiting class at Alabama eventually would? It had to be about more than just the results, or it'd be almost impossible to avoid complacency setting in once players achieved them. Saban created a Sisyphean-like task to ensure long-term success.

"The opponent doesn't matter, the standard is perfection," Hewett says. "Our opponent is perfection. Whoever is on the other side of the field is totally inconsequential to what we're trying to accomplish today."

Saban practiced what he preached. When you've spent time around one of Saban's programs or even just watched enough of his team's games on television, you learn to expect a strong reaction or two when his team gets up big against an opponent. He demands his team play hard no matter what the scoreboard reads, but that can be easier said than done. It's human nature to ease up when a positive result is guaranteed, and even the well-trained Alabama players can fall victim to that mentality. Saban refused to accept that behavior and could always convince himself of the long-term impact of a lapse in attention late in a game. When he saw what he felt was a careless mistake because of it, he quickly made an example. It could look like borderline crazy behavior to an outside observer to watch Saban seemingly lose his mind on a player who made a mental error late in a blowout win. Even if you could predict it, it wasn't an act.

Michigan State secondary coach Harlon Barnett saw it countless times as he orbited the Saban universe. Barnett saw it when Saban was his position coach at Michigan State, he saw it when Saban was his defensive coordinator in the NFL, and finally he saw it when Saban was his boss at LSU. "He's dead serious when he tells guys, 'Don't look at the scoreboard,'" Barnett says. "He's coaching every play. They are up 45–3, they've got the backups in, and he goes off for a blown coverage; he's dead serious. He's playing each play, one play at a time."

The message was simple: just because the likely outcome is good doesn't mean we abandon our principles. Corey Miller, who played nine NFL seasons with the New York Giants and Minnesota Vikings, watched Saban do it to his son Christian late in a blowout win against Louisville. While up 34–0, Miller committed an unsportsmanlike penalty that kept a Louisville offensive drive alive that eventually resulted in a touchdown. The late touchdown wasn't going to change the game's result of an easy Alabama win, but Saban let Miller have it as he came off the field.

"What he said was, 'Son, I know this game is over, but if you make that mistake in a close game, it could cost you and it could cost the team,'" Miller says. "He wasn't coaching about that moment, that particular play, he was coaching for the future. He wanted to get them to the mindset that even if we're up thirty, we have to be disciplined."

Saban liked to reference Martin Luther King Jr., with one story serving as a perfect metaphor for his Process. In King's sermon "The Three Dimensions of a Complete Life," he told the story of a man who shined his shoes in Montgomery, Alabama, who was above and beyond the best he had ever seen at shining shoes. He said it was like the man had a "PhD in shoe shining." What it taught King was if you have to be a street sweeper, to sweep streets "like Michelangelo painted pictures." It was to take pride in your work and do the best you could no matter what it was.

"There's no better feeling than knowing you did the best you could be," Saban said, referencing King's sermon. "I don't care if it's what you do, what I do, what the street sweeper does. It really doesn't matter. It's not all about results."

Telling someone just to do their best is about as cliché as it gets. Actually living every day striving to do your best isn't. Saban isn't a profound philosopher who came up with phrases we'll be quoting for a century. He is a football coach who relied on some of the inspirational quotes the rest of us have read. The difference was how he molded them to fit his approach and how he could explain them to his organization in a way that felt new and unique. One of his favorite quotes is, "Your actions speak so loudly I can't hear what you're saying." It was a Ralph Waldo Emerson quote, but Saban said it so frequently and authentically, one former coach admitted it took him years to stop attributing it to Saban in emails to players and parents.

As Alabama likes to point out, The Process has been "often imitated, never duplicated." Focusing on the process to success rather than results is something that any organization can do. The challenging part is following through with it every day, not letting negative self-talk overtake you, not worrying about your monthly sales goal or what one of your coworkers is doing. The Process requires supreme focus and commitment, which Saban has proven to his organization gives it the best chance of being successful.

The Process is simple, really. It might leave the destination off, but it's a road map to success. It's up to the individual whether to be committed enough to follow it.

CHAPTER 8

Don't Let Outside Factors Impact Your Goals

T he stories feel apocryphal, too unbelievable to actually be true. Former coaches swear they've never seen him yawn before. Players tell you they've never seen him cough or sneeze, let alone actually get sick.

It all sounds ridiculous, but they tell you these stories with such earnest appreciation you can't help but start believing them yourself. If Saban can get sick, they tell you, they've never seen it happen before.

"'Death, taxes, and Saban showing up,' is what we said," says former Michigan State tight end Josh Keur. "I never saw the guy sick. If he was, he hid it well. I don't ever recall him taking a day off."

"I never, ever remember 'Coach isn't at work today, he has the flu,'" says Trevor Hewett, who spent six years working for the program. "I have no recollection of him ever being sick. I never remember him missing a day of work or taking off early because he wasn't feeling great."

After hearing story after story from former players and coaches that Saban never gets sick, I investigated the seemingly ridiculous premise for a 2019 story I wrote for AL.com. Former offensive lineman Josh Casher told me he thought it was "probably vitamins" that allowed Saban never to get sick. A former staffer said he thought the Alabama coach's regimented eating schedule and doing the same thing every day prevented illness. Lane Kiffin, who said in three seasons with Saban he never saw him sick, attributed it to "how powerful your mind is that you're not allowed to get sick so you don't get sick."

Despite all the devoted testimonies, I learned Saban is, of course, capable of getting sick. He's not some robot impervious to all human illnesses. The difference with Saban is he never lets it slow him down. Former Alabama player Keaton Anderson may have summed it up best.

"He's never taken a day off, never missed a second of a meeting, never missed a second of practice," Anderson said. "You'll never know if he's having a bad day, good day, sick. It's the same mentality—put in the work."

Saban is a big believer in practicing what you preach, and one of the biggest components of that is not allowing outside factors to impact your goals. He wants everyone within his organization locked into completing their assigned tasks and not letting outside factors—he calls it "clutter"—derail those tasks. In simple terms, it is, "Control what you can control." Not letting sickness slow him down is the physical manifestation of doing what needs to be done regardless of the circumstances. He knows that whether you're a player or a coach in his system, there will be days you face obstacles, days you aren't sure of whether you have the ability or resolve to push through. He presents himself as an example to follow so that everyone knows what can be accomplished when your mind and body are locked in. He'll never complain about being sick because he'd never accept the same behavior from one of his players.

"Whether we feel a little sick or we feel a little hurt, you're going to go through it," says former Alabama receiver Mac Hereford. "That was one of the best things ever because now in life when I'm not feeling great, I have to get up and perform. Not a lot of people get to experience that or be in that environment. It makes it so you're unstoppable. It gives you the mindset that anything that comes my way, it's not going to prevent me from doing my job."

When I first asked Scott Cochran, Saban's long-time strength and conditioning coach at Alabama, whether Saban ever got sick, he reacted as if I had just asked him to reveal a deeply guarded secret. The normally boisterous and confident Cochran became nervous, his eyes darting around, as he considered what to say. "This is a really tough question to answer," Cochran started before admitting that, yes, Saban was capable of feeling under the weather. "I would say, uhh, yeah, I've seen him down and out, but it never affects him."

Cochran explained that how Saban handled external factors like a cold always came back to putting the team over himself. "What he wants for the players is way more important than how he feels," Cochran says. "If you ever really got to know the man, you'll understand why he has so much success, because he doesn't care about the rings, he doesn't care about the championships, he cares about the kids. And that's the difference between him and everyone else."

Cochran, who spent thirteen seasons at Alabama, said Saban had a bulging disc in his neck his first three seasons at Alabama. It was only after winning a national championship in 2009 that he agreed to deal with it. There was simply too much work establishing the Alabama culture beforehand. When he finally got the surgery done, Cochran said he was back to work that day.

Nearly a decade later, it was more of the same for Saban. After struggling with a balky right hip, Saban agreed to undergo hip replacement surgery after wrapping up 2019 spring practice. Knowing that his advancing age amplified by getting a new hip could be used against him in recruiting, Saban returned to work less than forty-eight hours after the surgery. He was forced to use a walker for a day before he ditched it, a signal to the world that even hip surgery wasn't going to slow him down. It didn't stop there, though.

When Saban returned to work that Wednesday morning after his Monday surgery, he walked into his bathroom and saw two handicap grab bars around his toilet. They were installed in case Saban had trouble getting off the toilet after his hip surgery. The sight of them left Saban furious. What if a recruit walked into the bathroom and saw the handicap rails, Saban asked. His office is in many ways the epicenter of Alabama's recruiting efforts, where he invites in the program's top targets and sells them on his future. Beyond practical purposes, the office is one big stage to attract recruits, with all of Saban's national championship rings prominently displayed as soon as you walk in. Handicap rails in the bathroom would make Saban look ancient, vincible even, and would almost certainly be used against him on the recruiting trail if anyone found out. That was unacceptable to a man who over the years dyed his hair, among other age-defying tactics, not out of vanity but for recruiting purposes. He demanded that a facilities handyman come down and unscrew the rails immediately as he inspected the work.

The message was clear: Saban always wanted to present himself a certain way, even if it inconvenienced him.

In 2020, it became even more evident Saban is mortal just like the rest of us when he tested positive for the coronavirus just days ahead of the Iron Bowl against Auburn. Saban fortunately experienced only minor symptoms from a virus that tragically killed hundreds of thousands of Americans. The rules were clear, though, that Saban wouldn't be able to coach in the game inside Bryant-Denny Stadium even if he was dealing with symptoms equivalent to a head cold. Not being at the game was difficult for Saban to accept, as he hadn't missed a game since his father died in 1973 when Nick was a Kent State graduate assistant. As hard as it was for Saban to not physically be there, he did everything he could to stick as close to the regular routine as possible. He handled team meetings at the same time as usual—he just had to do them from home over Zoom. That's a sentence that would have made Saban's head spin a year earlier but had already become pretty normal in 2020. For practices that week, he watched at home via a live feed and barked out orders over the phone to former Texas head coach Charlie Strong, who served as a defensive analyst at Alabama. It was unquestionably weird, and if Saban had missed any other Iron Bowl it would have sent the state of Alabama into shock, but it was the culmination of the most bizarre and challenging season in college football history.

That 2020 season represented a massive challenge for everyone involved with the sport. Coaches like Saban had to quickly become accustomed to quarantines and isolation, frequent, if not daily, COVID-19 tests, and other tasks that they would never have thought about previously. There was no such thing as playing while sick so coaches had to deal with depleted rosters and plugging players into playing time before they were ready. There were last-minute game cancellations and postponements, with coaches having to pivot from planning for one opponent to a new one with only a few days' notice. The desire to keep players safe and healthy demanded creating as close to a "bubble" as possible, depriving players of normal social activities. Some programs struggled with virus outbreaks after team members went out to bars and house parties. Top players opted out of the season for health reasons, and as the season progressed, it got increasingly difficult for programs to sell that it was all worth it as a rash of players opted out during the year. It was a lot for anyone to deal with, and it became evident quickly that some competing programs weren't up for the unique challenge and crumbled under pressure.

Outsiders openly wondered whether all the moving parts and new hurdles would derail the famously regimented Saban. The assumption was he wouldn't be able to handle the last-minute changes and inability to plan far in advance. But it ignored his gift of not letting outside factors disrupt his pursuit of the ultimate goal. March 13, 2020, was supposed to be the first day of Alabama's spring practice. Instead, the world was changing. The NCAA men's basketball tournament was canceled the day before, and later that day Alabama would be forced to shelve its spring practice slate. With all that coming to the forefront, Saban walked into the staff meeting that Friday morning and asked his staff, "Did anybody see a dinosaur on their drive in to work this morning?"

Everyone in the room, which included his former LSU assistants Pete Jenkins and Rick Trickett in for a visit, looked around at each other, confused. No, they said, there were no dinosaurs roaming around Tuscaloosa.

"I didn't either," Saban told his staff. "The reason there were no dinosaurs on the way in this morning was they couldn't adapt, they couldn't adjust. They couldn't adapt and adjust so they are gone now, and that's what will happen to us when we get to where we can't adapt and adjust."

Saban then launched into laying out exactly how Alabama was going to tackle the burgeoning COVID-19 pandemic, from team protocols to communication and everything in between. "It was one of the most impressive meetings that I've ever been in my whole career," says Pete Jenkins, who has coached for nearly sixty years at places like LSU, Florida, and Auburn. "But that's not uncommon for him."

And, true to tradition, Saban still went over the five recruiting prospects he watched the previous night and offered his assessments in the meeting. Even at the start of a worldwide pandemic, ignoring recruiting was a non-negotiable for Saban.

Saban told his team that the program that could manage all the unexpected issues best would be the one standing victorious at the end of the season. He was perfectly suited to guide his team through a pandemic because he had always preached, "Focus on what you can control, adapt to what you can't, and do your job." He willingly served as the example of that for everyone.

"The job Coach Saban did of managing and staying in control of very, very tough circumstances is really a tribute to him," says Butch Jones, Saban's special assistant in 2020. "Obviously, you're known for what you do on the field, and obviously, he's known for all the national championships, but I really think the management behind the scenes of this year really defines what he is as a leader."

Saban himself called it the best team he had coached at Alabama for the way it navigated such a challenging season. "This was the best team that was committed to a standard of excellence and to each other to accomplish something of significance, and winning the national championship is something that will stay with every one of these players for the rest of their life."

Will Lowery, a member of the 2009 and 2011 national championship Alabama teams, agrees with Saban's assessment. "His whole system is built around blocking out the noise, and this year was the best example of it. This is the kind of environment where Coach Saban's Process shines the most."

If there's a secret to Saban's approach to avoiding "clutter," it is his focus on the tasks at hand. He's almost like a thoroughbred horse with blinders on, fully immersed and dedicated to completing the specific job. It can help explain away some of his awkwardness when players or staffers would walk past him in a hallway and not even get a courtesy hello. It can be a blessing and a curse for Saban, who has rubbed some people the wrong way over the years with his absence of polite niceties. Rick Venturi, who worked with Saban in Cleveland, said he has the unique ability to be all in on one topic with zero distractions and then shift to whatever is next on the schedule. He isn't worried about his mortgage or what he will have for dinner that night or even what he needs to do for his next appointment. He's fully present in the moment, and when it's over, he's fully on to the next thing.

"He'd be with you in a defensive meeting for an hour and he might not even know you the next hour because his focus is now the drapes in that [recruit's] living room and what they need to do to go get him," says Venturi.

Alan Evans, whose son Rashaan was a starter and team captain at Alabama, enjoyed getting to know Saban over the years. His wife, Chenavis, worked closely with the Alabama football program through a workshop called ILEAD. He had authentic conversations with the Alabama head coach, both during his son's recruiting process and once he got to Tuscaloosa, and grew to really like him. But the charismatic man who had sat across the table from him while recruiting his five-star son was gone on Saturdays. Evans says Saban is so locked in on game days, so focused exclusively on football and what he needs to do to guide his team to a victory, it's like he's turned off every other part of his mind. "When you see him on game day, that football light is turned on," Evans says. "You can't penetrate it. He's a different animal on game day." That level of focus isn't easily achieved, especially for eighteen- and nineteen-year-old kids.

That didn't stop Saban from trying to rid the "clutter" out of their heads so they could focus on the tasks at hand. When he talked of clutter, he meant it both physically and mentally. He'd instruct the players to pick up any pieces of trash they found lying on the floor of the football facility. More than anything, though, he focused on the mental clutter, the distractions that come with being a football player on a college campus. When you oversee more than one hundred college football players, you're going to run into problems inevitably. Girlfriend problems, legal problems, drug problems, you name it. Saban's strategy was to try to limit those as much as possible by trying to keep the players' focus on getting better. He didn't tell them they couldn't go out and have fun, but he preached responsibility. He had little sayings for the players, like "Nothing good happens after midnight." He could be funny in how he broached the subject with his team, cracking players up with his old-school West Virginia sensibilities. In one meeting before a practice, Saban said he heard a bunch of players were going to fraternity parties and considering joining social fraternities. Saban brought up the risks in doing that, but more than anything, he said he didn't understand why. "Anyone who has to pay to have people to hang out with is a loser," Saban deadpanned as the team broke out in laughter.

If someone got in trouble, Saban would address the team and say the player created clutter not only for himself but also for the whole team, because it impacted everyone. It was all about accountability. Saban's philosophy of ignoring clutter was put to the test in 2003 when his LSU team arrived in New Orleans for the national championship game. New Orleans could be a dangerously fun city, one that many of the Louisiana-born Tigers knew well. Rather than trying to control his team too much and risk a rebellion, Saban eased up on the curfew and showed them that he trusted them. LSU players caroused as kings of New Orleans early that week, frequenting the Daiquiri Deli in the French Quarter, which named daiquiris after players. "The first couple of days, we had a lot of fun," says former LSU offensive lineman Jimmy Courtenay, a ringleader of the late-night activities that week. "I mean a lot of fun."

Players were allowed to stay out late—some remember being out all night—but everyone was expected to be at practice the next morning at 8:00. It was Saban's way of showing that no outside influence was going to derail his program's pursuit of a national championship.

"Those practices were hell," says Paris Hodges. "It was all gas, no brakes. It had nothing to do with what we consumed and everything to do with him saying, 'OK, you want to party hard and play hard, you're going to work hard.' He knew what he was doing."

As the week progressed, fewer and fewer guys went out on the town knowing what was coming for them the next morning. It paid off when an underdog LSU beat Oklahoma a few nights later to win a national championship, setting off a legendary night of celebration in New Orleans for all those who rooted for the purple and gold.

Saban once explained that the best teams, deep down, are resilient. "No matter what is thrown at them, no matter how deep the hole," Saban said, "they find a way to bounce back and overcome adversity." That's what eliminating clutter and not letting outside factors impact the greater goal is all about. The best leaders have the emotional resilience to persevere through challenging situations and not get sidetracked on the journey to success. Saban not calling out sick isn't a display of masochism, it's living up to the standard he's set. As Anderson put it to me, it is standard over feeling.

CHAPTER 9

Pick Where You Can Win

M ichigan State had just wrapped up a 9–2 regular season in 1999 featuring wins over Michigan, Notre Dame, Ohio State, and Penn State. The Spartans had finally broken through under Saban with the help of Lonny Rosen and had the feel of an ascendant Big Ten program ready to challenge the status quo hierarchy.

"With the recruits you have coming in and the personnel and all those kinds of things, things are really about to take off," remembers Mike Vollmar, then Michigan State's director of football operations.

With everything seemingly on the upswing for Michigan State, Saban called his old Kent State teammate Gary Pinkel, who had replaced him as Toledo's head coach, and told him he was leaving for Louisiana State.

"Why would you go to LSU?" Pinkel asked him. "You just started to build this program."

Saban responded, "I'll never be Michigan."

"He knew you had to go to a place that has all the resources to be great," Pinkel says. "LSU is one of them. Alabama is on that same list. There's about ten of them in the country."

In college football, every school is not created equal. Some have inherent advantages, from a fertile recruiting area to a large fan base to wealthy boosters willing to pay for the latest and greatest facilities. There are certain programs better equipped to achieve greatness than others, and Saban realized that in Michigan. No matter what he did in East Lansing, Michigan State would never have the large fan base and dominate the conversation the way the school in Ann Arbor did. He told another coaching friend he knew he'd "always be second fiddle to Michigan." That was made clear to him when the Orange Bowl picked Michigan over Michigan State that year despite the Spartans beating the Wolverines. Saban could have banged his head against the wall for years trying in vain to change that, or he could find a place that had the necessary ingredients to compete for national championships.

Saban was painted as overly ambitious early in his career, jumping from place to place to move up in the business rather than appreciate where he was. That can be cast as wanderlust or disloyalty, but there's something to be said about working hard to find a job and organization that can help you achieve your goals. Saban garners buy-in from his players because while they know his system is difficult, they also know that it'll be mutually beneficial if they put in the work. Everything within the Alabama organization is geared toward making the players as successful as possible so that both parties derive value from the relationship. There's nothing wrong with seeking out the same for yourself.

Two of the most impactful relationships of Saban's career came from being proactive. As a young coach, Saban went out of his way to forge relationships with George Perles and Bill Belichick that would completely change the direction of his career. As just a twenty-six-year-old West Virginia assistant, Saban would make frequent trips to Pittsburgh to visit with Perles, the Steelers defensive coordinator, to pick his brain and learn more about the famous "Steel Curtain" defense. When he later moved on to Navy, he worked with Steve Belichick, Bill's father, and started an annual tradition of visiting Bill to talk football for hours. His friendship with Belichick would become one of the most defining of his career and even the source of a documentary, *Belichick & Saban: The Art of Coaching.* When Perles got the Michigan State job in 1983, he quickly plucked Saban away from Navy. "I hired him because I got to know him from coming around," Perles told AL.com. "He was so interested and so dedicated." The story was similar when Belichick became the Cleveland Browns' head coach in 1991 and convinced Saban to leave Toledo to be his defensive coordinator. Saban didn't wait for those opportunities to come around; he actively sought them out through building relationships and showing an active desire to get better.

"My dad had seen a lot of coaches come through the Naval Academy," Belichick told *Sports Illustrated*. "So when he would say to me, 'This is one of the best coaches I've worked with,' I always kept that in the back of my mind."

That mentality didn't stop when he started moving up the ranks, either. When Saban was at Michigan State, Perles would annually bring in top coaches like San Francisco 49ers coach Bill Walsh to speak at his clinics. Even as a rising star, Saban sought out the other speakers to not only develop relationships but also to pick their brains for any little piece of information that could help him one day. Saban's appetite for getting better never turned off, so after the clinic when other coaches would drink beers and blow off steam, he still had football on his mind. He'd corner a speaker, picking his brain for hours on techniques and schemes for any little piece of knowledge he could squirrel away.

Before Saban went to LSU, he did his due diligence. He knew his Michigan State program was on the rise so it didn't make sense to leave for anything other than an opportunity that got him closer to his long-term goals. He was skeptical at first about the job, asking his old Cleveland Browns coworker Chris Landry, an LSU graduate, "If it's such a great place, why do they keep firing coaches?" Landry connected Saban with former New York Giants head coach Bill Arnsparger, who told him that, of all the jobs he had in his long career, LSU was the best. That seemed to resonate with Saban, who respected the longtime NFL defensive coach who won an SEC Championship at LSU before leaving to become Florida's athletic director. He called veteran SEC offensive line coach Rick Trickett, whom he had worked with at West Virginia, and asked him what he thought of LSU. Referencing that the school had no real competition in talent-rich Louisiana, Trickett said he thought Saban could win a national championship there.

With that thought in the back of his head, when it came time to meet with LSU's leaders—school president Mark Emmert, AD Joe Dean, trustees Charlie Weems and Stanley Jacobs, and Tiger Foundation president Richard Gill—Saban wanted to know why LSU hadn't been more successful. With pages of handwritten yellow pad notes beside him, Saban referenced how many of the necessary ingredients seemed to be there, yet the results were missing. In the preceding ten seasons, LSU went through three coaches and suffered through a losing 50–58–1 record. Saban pressed the leaders on what was holding LSU back and whether those influential men were committed to remedying the issues.

"He had done his research and he saw we've got no competition in-state, we've got a great bed of talent for that reason, we've got a great recruiting radius, we have a wonderful history and a passionate fan base," says Weems, then chair of LSU's Board of Supervisors. "What we didn't have was a demonstrated commitment to excellence. Our facilities were old. Our academic support for student-athletes was poor. We just had not been willing to commit the resources, as some other schools had, to being a champion."

Before he agreed to come to LSU, he demanded promises from those LSU leaders that they were committed to making the football program as successful as it could be. He went into the situation with his eyes wide open and addressed his concerns on the front end before deciding. He also smartly realized he had leverage after a meandering LSU coaching search hadn't left many other options. Butch Davis, then Miami's coach, was LSU's initial number one choice, but he was candid that he wanted to go to the NFL and would prefer to stay at Miami until that came to fruition. Minnesota coach Glen Mason and Oregon State coach Dennis Erickson were two other options, though neither worked out.

"We were kind of coming down to the wire and we didn't have a lot of good options at the end," says Weems. "We weren't too excited by the prospects we had left when Gil Brandt got some indication from Nick he might be willing to leave Michigan State."

Once he agreed to come on board, there was a strong synergy of everyone pulling in the same direction now that they had properly identified the primary problems. That was an important piece of the puzzle for Saban, who never felt that synergy at Michigan State. He never believed the school was all in on giving him the necessary resources to be as successful as the program could be. Shortly after Saban arrived at Michigan State, he agreed to let *Sporting News* writer Terry Frei have a behind-the-scenes look at what it was like for a first-year coach in the Big Ten. The first day they met, Frei remembers walking with Saban across Michigan State's campus and the new head coach candidly discussing how the school had to show its commitment.

"This sounds ridiculous in this day and age but he said, 'We've got to get a computer lab,'" says Frei. "'We have to have computers for these guys. We have to give them help.'"

Saban would eventually get the Downtown Coaches Club to buy five desktop computers for his team, but some of his other demands didn't come as easily. He clashed with his MSU bosses over the investment in not only the program but in him, another factor in his decision to leave East Lansing. "If Michigan State had shown him any love at the time, he would have never left," Weems says. "He really was hurt that they hadn't. They just hadn't shown much appreciation."

After Saban arrived in Baton Rouge, he worked tirelessly to turn a sleeping giant into one of the most successful organizations in the country. He personally raised money to pay for upgrades to the SEC's worst facilities and counted on LSU president Mark Emmert, one of his favorite bosses, to deliver on his promises. Pete Jenkins, the defensive line coach on Saban's first LSU staff, told him he had previously worked for three LSU head coaches, including Arnsparger, and they all saw the need for facilities upgrades too. Jenkins said there were probably previously unfulfilled architect renderings of proposed upgrades still kicking around the building Saban could look at. "They wanted that building built," Saban told Jenkins. "I'm going to get that building built." Over time, the school built Saban's desired new football facilities, overhauled its academic program, and committed major money to upgrade every aspect of a football program that had long underachieved. And the results followed.

That first season featured the highs of beating three ranked schools and a low of losing to Alabama at Birmingham (UAB) at home, which prompted a wave of panic and overreaction across the state. What Saban did a week after losing to UAB might have been the spark the organization needed when LSU defeated No. 11 Tennessee. That win over a program only two seasons removed from winning a national championship was the proof of concept Saban needed as he pitched his program's bright future on the recruiting trail to sign the necessary talent to make that vision a reality. "There were a lot of four- and five-star guys in Louisiana and all of those guys were starting to see what was going on at LSU and the changes he was making," says Brandon Hurley, a member of Saban's first recruiting class. "It just snowballed that guys started to commit, talk to each other, and form this thing where we can really do something special in our home state, and this guy might be the guy to lead us to that." After the season ended, Saban signed the nation's No. 2 recruiting class, a talented group featuring future NFL pros offensive tackle Andrew Whitworth, defensive tackle Marcus Spears, receiver Michael Clayton, and running back Joseph Addai, among others.

In year two, Saban guided the Tigers to a 10–3 record that included an SEC Championship win over No. 2 Tennessee and a Sugar Bowl win against No. 7 Illinois. By year four, LSU was a national champion. "I always felt like LSU was a diamond in the rough, and he hit it at the right moment," says Trickett, who joined Saban's first LSU staff as offensive line coach. "Alabama was in disarray. Auburn had made the change with Terry [Bowden]. I think he hit it at about the right time."

Says Jenkins, "You got no idea what a good job he did here. I had been there for years, that place was so different when he inherited that place. That man worked day, night, didn't rest, didn't sleep. He was so driven. And he got the thing done."

After winning the national championship, Weems remembers going to an away game and being seated next to Terry Saban, Nick's wife. Weems asked Terry what she and her husband wanted after making it to the top of college football. What did they see as their future?

"Well," Terry said, "he can be the Bear Bryant of LSU."

Weems thought for a second and told her she was right. "He can stay here, win multiple championships, and have a statue to him here just like the Bear does at Alabama."

And there is a world where Saban never leaves LSU and builds college football's greatest dynasty in Baton Rouge instead of Tuscaloosa. But the

PICK WHERE YOU CAN WIN

siren call of the NFL proved to be too irresistible for Saban even if he had it all at LSU.

At the conclusion of every season, LSU officials had to hold their breaths and hope they could survive the off-season without losing their coach. Saban was very highly regarded in NFL circles after his time working with Belichick in the NFL. Bill Polian, who was then the Indianapolis Colts general manager, told Weems he had previously tried to hire Saban multiple times while recommending him for the LSU job. Saban believed he could have been an NFL head coach if he waited but instead left Cleveland to return to the college ranks with Michigan State. The allure of the NFL never dissipated, and the temptations only increased after having success in Baton Rouge.

Numerous NFL organizations were interested in Saban while he was at LSU, with the New York Giants and Chicago Bears being two of the most serious suitors. The Giants were very interested in hiring Saban, though they opted for Tom Coughlin when he didn't move fast enough for the position. A week after LSU won the national championship, Chicago Bears general manager Jerry Angelo flew down to Baton Rouge to woo Saban to the NFL and even stayed overnight at the Saban family house. Saban ultimately said no to Angelo, but the threat was always there.

"The pros had romanced him," Weems says. "We were fighting off some pro job every year. It was a nightmare."

After saying no to multiple NFL jobs, the one he couldn't turn down was the Miami Dolphins. Wayne Huizenga, the billionaire owner of the Dolphins, rolled out the red carpet and recruited Saban as hard as the LSU coach would go after a five-star recruit. Saban had just suffered through a disappointing 9–3 season following the title season, and something was appealing about taking over one of the NFL's premier franchises. In classic Saban fashion, though, the decision didn't come easily. For as decisive as he is in almost every aspect of his life, making career decisions was always challenging for him. He initially told his staff he wasn't taking the job, but Huizenga never gave up and spent days in Baton Rouge wooing the coach. Saban hemmed and hawed about what he should do, again consulting with friends and trusted confidants about the best path forward.

"I spent part of every day on the phone with Nick, usually more than once, talking about what he was doing, what he was thinking, all that kind of stuff," says Weems. "And finally, Huizenga just made him an offer he couldn't refuse."

Saban broke the news to his team in Orlando on Christmas. Saban went through his staff meeting ahead of a planned party like everything was normal, detailing the practice schedule for the following day ahead of LSU's bowl game against Iowa. It was business as usual. "The last thing he says to us is, 'Oh, by the way, about this Miami Dolphins deal, I have to take the job,' and starts telling us why," says LeRoy Ryals, the tight ends coach on that LSU staff. "He's kind of talking low. I look over at [wide receivers coach] Bobby Williams and Bobby says, 'He's gone; he's out of here.'"

Says Paris Hodges, an offensive lineman on that team, "I remember the air being let out of the team. It was a lot, man. It affected us. I don't think we were mentally prepared after hearing that."

Saban was now an NFL head coach. It was a dream come true for him, but it didn't take long to turn into a nightmare.

While Saban had plenty of NFL experience and in some ways may have idealized what the experience had been like, the game had changed during his time in college. Salaries had exploded, and the power shifted from the coaches to the players. At LSU, Saban could always use playing time as a carrot to get his players to buy into the mission, showing no qualms about benching a talented player if he didn't fall in line. He demanded their respect, and if they bucked his authority, he had myriad tools at his disposal to deal with the situation. In the NFL, the players made more money and often had more power than the coach. Saban couldn't bench a player making $15 million a year to send a message.

"If Nick could have been a head coach when NFL head coaches had the power, then he would have been a helluva NFL head coach," says Cris Dishman, who played for Saban with the Houston Oilers as part of his thirteen-year career. "Nick came in 2005, and the power of the head coaches had changed."

Saban complained to friends that he felt confined by the NFL system that rewarded the worst teams with top draft picks. At LSU, he could outwork the competition and recruit multiple future first-round draft picks every recruiting cycle. With the Dolphins, he got only one first-round pick, and the better his team performed on the field, the worse his team's chances of getting an impact player at the top of the draft. The power structure of the NFL was different, too, where he wouldn't always get his way though he negotiated for as much control as he could. Saban has famously claimed he wanted the Dolphins to sign Drew Brees only for the team's doctors to medically fail him after shoulder surgery, leading him to sign with the New Orleans Saints. The Dolphins instead acquired Daunte Culpepper, who played four games for the team while Brees went on to play fifteen seasons for the Saints and led them to a Super Bowl victory in 2010.

Saban went 9–7 his first season in Miami, and after acquiring Culpepper, some experts picked the Dolphins to go to the Super Bowl in 2006. Instead, the season started miserably for Miami as Culpepper got hurt early and the team lost six of its first seven games. As Miami trudged forward amid a disappointing season, the rumors of Saban returning to college football cranked up. After Alabama fired Mike Shula, the talk intensified amid reports he'd be offered the job. He infamously told reporters on December 21, "I guess I have to say it. I'm not going to be the Alabama coach"—words he'd soon live to regret.

Despite the public proclamations he wasn't leaving Miami, Weems heard through back channels that Saban would like to return to the college game, and if possible, return to LSU. "He would have come back to LSU if we could have taken him," he says. "But we had just hired Les Miles, Les was doing fine at the time and we wouldn't do that to someone we just hired anyway. I did everything I could to talk him out of that Alabama job, but I just couldn't do it."

After weeks of speculation, Saban officially agreed to become Alabama's next coach on January 3. He accepted the job knowing the media would crush him—they did—for reversing course so quickly after promising he wasn't going to take the Alabama job. *Miami Herald* columnist Dan Le Batard, one of many to lambast Saban, wrote, "The punctuation of the Nick Saban Error is greasy and greedy. You know what he was as Dolphins coach? A failure.

A loser. A gasbag." He knew he'd be painted as a failure for giving up as an NFL head coach after only two seasons and a 15–17 record. But Saban had to accept a hard truth: it was a mistake leaving LSU for the Miami Dolphins even if it felt like a dream job at the moment. He had to accept that while he was a brilliant football coach, his skills were best suited for college football and not the NFL. For a successful and hardworking individual like Saban, that had to have bruised his ego.

Similar to his experience coming to LSU, Saban was in a great position to ask Alabama for the things he needed on the forefront. The school was desperate for a winning coach and had already been turned down by South Carolina's Steve Spurrier and West Virginia's Rich Rodriguez over a coaching search that moved at a glacial pace. Mal Moore, then Alabama's athletic director, famously told Jimmy Sexton, Saban's agent, he was flying to Cuba if he didn't return back to Alabama with Saban in tow. To leave Miami, Saban could dictate what he needed to win and then say, "Get out of my way and let me do my thing."

The school pumped money into the football program and had it returned tenfold after Saban's success led to a boom in out-of-state applicants and national interest in the university. An expanded football building? Done. Redone practice fields? Of course. New weight room and meeting space? You got it. It ranged from big moves like buying and clearing out Greek fraternity houses near Bryant-Denny Stadium to make it the "front door of your university," according to former associate athletic director Jon Gilbert, to moving four tennis courts to create space to increase the football facility footprint. University leaders worked hard to make Saban's life easier in any way they could, through financial investment and meaningful gestures like making sure football players got parking spots close to the facilities.

"The alignment between campus and athletics is unlike any place I've ever been," says Gilbert, who spent seventeen years working in Alabama's athletic department. "There is 100 percent alignment."

The move to Alabama also allowed Saban to again deploy his most trusted advisor: his wife, Terry. It's hard to understate just how critical Terry has been to her husband's success as everything from a valued sounding board to his secret weapon in navigating social situations that might make the introverted Saban uncomfortable. Terry has a say in most everything her husband does, from offering opinions on critical staff hires to pushing him to get involved in specific community causes. "She's the one person on the planet who can change his mind about things when he may not want to change his mind," says longtime friend Todd Alles.

She's as valuable as any assistant coach Alabama has in recruiting, taking the responsibility of hosting social events and bonding with the parents of recruits in a way her husband can't. She handles so many things that allow Nick to focus so much of his energy on the organization. At Alabama, Terry Saban is vitally important to the program's success in a way she never could be with the Dolphins. Not only is the NFL far more impersonal than college football, but NFL players don't need a "den mother" or care to socialize with the head coach's wife, taking away some of Terry's biggest value. In Miami, she was just another person; in Tuscaloosa, she's the queen.

"If there is a Hall of Fame for coaches' wives, then she's running the show," says Rick Venturi, who got to know the Sabans well in Cleveland. "She has been a vital part of his career, his football team, his program. She's smart, she has a business sense, and I've always felt at all times she brought humanism to the program."

All the pieces came together to help Saban reach unprecedented levels of success at Alabama. Could he have had similar levels of success at other schools? Absolutely, but as Pinkel noted, the list of schools equipped to do so is likely smaller than you think. It's a reminder to all of us that it takes hard work to get to the top and the right situation to encourage it. That could mean creating the right situation yourself or joining an already established organization with a track record of investing the necessary resources in being successful.

We can fall prey to wanting to be a martyr, to suffer it out at an organization we know is poorly run and incapable of reaching its ceiling because it's the "right thing to do." We'll cast ourselves as just being loyal, celebrate it even, and suffer through indignities along the way. Yet you may never reach your potential if you're not in an environment that cultivates it. There's a saying people love to reference, "Bloom where you're planted." But as those of us without green thumbs know, if the soil isn't right and the plants don't get the right nutrients, they won't bloom.

Pat Perles, who has known Saban for more than thirty years, believes being in the right environment has been crucial to the man's seemingly inexhaustible energy and desire to be the best.

"I think if you told him to run something he didn't like doing, he would burn out at the same pace as you or I," Perles says. "I think he found the thing that not only keeps him alive, but it's the most joy outside of his family he could have."

Saban has a legendary work ethic, but he's human just like everyone else. He keeps humming along because he found a career he loved and later an organization well suited to meet his needs to help him achieve success. He doesn't wake up dreading the day ahead or struggling to make himself motivated, because he found the thing he's best at and the place that lets him flourish. You may be thinking, "I wish I was as fortunate as Saban to find that," but what have you done to achieve it? Saban worked tirelessly to put himself in a position to win, and when he reached that, he delivered big. Relying solely on talent can't be enough.

Delegation Is Good but Too Much Kills the Culture

While putting together Alabama's recruiting big board, the list that would determine which players to prioritize, Saban wanted a consensus.

He assembled all his assistant coaches and recruiting personnel into a meeting room to analyze the prospects and agree on who should be the top fifteen players on the board. At that point in the recruiting cycle, NCAA rules limited the program to only one call to a recruit per week, so they needed to prioritize and decide who should be calling the top targets. After a healthy back-and-forth discussion, the group came to a consensus on Alabama's top recruiting targets moving forward.

"Everybody agrees this is the top fifteen?" Saban asked. "OK, I'm calling those guys; you guys figure out who you're calling."

"And he got twelve of them," says Todd Alles.

The challenge any leader who manages a group of people faces is what to do yourself versus what you should delegate. Go too hands-on and you get accused of being a micromanager. Assign too many important tasks to deputies and you risk becoming out of touch with the day-to-day happenings of your company. It's such a delicate balance to maintain the culture that makes your organization special while delegating enough to make it as efficient as possible.

Saban does exceptionally well in prioritizing the necessary things to be directly involved with while delegating other, still important tasks to a group of people he trusts. We know by now that Saban is very good at finding the right people to populate his organization, giving him the confidence to delegate assignments. If you don't trust the people below you, that's when you can get in trouble by trying to do too much yourself and risk burnout and/or inefficient use of your time.

Take, for example, the recruiting prong of Alabama's organization, which has been well established as essential to the operation. When putting together that board of top targets, Saban gave all his key people an opportunity to influence which players were the most important for the organization's future success. After building a consensus so that everyone felt good about the strategy, Saban said as the leader of the organization, he was going to be directly involved in trying to get those players to come to Alabama. The assistant coaches would still have a role in those players' recruitment, but Saban's actions made it clear that if they decided these people are vital to the organization, he needed to be involved in the process.

That didn't mean Saban was getting in the weeds on all the details, though. He trusted his staff to do the initial evaluations, research the necessary facts about the recruits, and give him as much information to work with as possible before making his decisions. Saban perusing the internet to find fun facts about a recruit, as detailed in chapter two, wouldn't have been a good use of his time, so he trusts people like Trevor Hewett to do the job for him.

"The thing I always respected about Coach Saban is he controls every aspect of the program but he's not walking into the recruiting office and telling me what I need to do better," Hewett says. "He trusts his chain of command to do their job and to make sure those people under them are doing their job."

One of the unique aspects of college athletics is the academic component. Unlike professional sports, college coaches also have to worry about how their players perform in the classroom. Regardless of how good a player is, he can be ruled ineligible to play if he can't maintain a certain grade point average. Before Saban took over, LSU's football program struggled with academics, with multiple top players ruled ineligible under his predecessor. LSU had the worst graduation rate in the SEC, a grisly 40 percent, which made a hard job even harder. Knowing how it could impact the organization, Saban got directly involved in revamping the academic support programs and pushed LSU to invest more. It did in 2002 when it opened a $15 million, 54,000-square-foot academic center. LSU brought in Dr. Roger Grooters, a well-regarded academic support expert, to lead the new academic center. Grooters brought with him an academic points system built to root out issues before they become dire. Saban immediately got on board with the system.

Miss a class or skip a test? You lose a point. Lose too many points, and there are real ramifications. Every player starts at zero, but there are established intervention checkpoints if any player starts racking up too many negative points. At negative-three points, it prompted an academic discussion with the player's position coach to discuss the issues. If that didn't work and the struggles mounted to a negative-six, he'd have to go in front of the team's peer council and explain his actions, facing whatever punishment the council decided on. Finally, if none of that worked and he accumulated negative-nine points, it warranted an automatic suspension and a one-on-one meeting with Saban.

College classes could be challenging, and they didn't provide the same endorphins the players got from a good workout or practice. Students can feel overwhelmed and uncomfortable early in their college careers and start avoiding classes as a result, creating a self-fulfilling prophecy. The points system made it easy for everyone to know where they stood, what was expected of them, and the ramifications for not doing what was needed. "The points system forces them to deal with it so they can't avoid it," says Dr. Jim Rost, who served as associate director of LSU's Cox Academic Center. "Then they realize with all the support, and everything else that is coming, 'I can succeed at this.' You build that intrinsic motivation of getting better."

It wasn't a system full of empty threats, like a parent threatening to take away a child's video games but never actually following through. There was a team of people who roamed the campus performing classroom checks—Was a player on time? Did he sit in the first two rows as requested?—and regularly talked to the players' professors, tutors, and mentors, reporting all the information back to Saban.

"We had operatives on every corner," Rost says. "It was a very tight system that was completely built on information. We had quantitative and qualitative information in these reports. They were analogous to a CIA briefing—we had that much information on the kids."

Saban met with the program's academic advisors each Thursday to review the points system and discuss the team's academic performances, both good and bad, over the prior week. As with recruiting, Saban knew how important academics were to his team's success, so he invested great time and effort into understanding the specifics of all his players' academic situations. These weren't quick, cursory meetings—some lasted as long as three or four hours—and he required his assistant coaches to attend. Saban believed if a player wasn't doing what he needed to do in the classroom, it had a way of impacting his football performance, too. He was good at taking the good news with the bad, but one week while at LSU there was no good news to report. It was a no-good, very bad, horrible academic week for the Tigers, so there was nothing Grooters and Rost could do to soften the blow. Halfway through that academic meeting, a beet-red Saban stood up, threw his pen, and started letting his assistant coaches have it.

"We are practicing like shit," Saban said. "We are studying like shit. Why do you think we are ready to play?"

Saban's ire was aimed at the assistant coaches, and not the academic advisors, because they had already proved their value to him. It is easier to delegate a task when you trust a person to be competent and capable of doing it. Saban doesn't hand out that trust freely, but when you've earned it, he'll respect your perspective.

Rost learned that early in his time working at LSU with Saban when he got called into the head coach's office one day. He walked in to see a star player, who had been struggling academically, already seated. As soon as Rost sat down, Saban launched into an impassioned rant telling Rost he needed to get his facts straight about the player, who had questioned Rost's assessment of the situation. Without saying a word, Rost opened a folder and started sliding over paper after paper of documentation of what the player didn't actually do as he had claimed to his head coach. Saban read through all Rost's papers, turned to the player, and started going in on him.

"I had been there for maybe six months and from then on anything I said in one of those meetings was like law," Rost says. "Once I proved to him I could do that, I was just as welcomed and respected as any member of his coaching staff or conditioning staff. Everyone was a valued member of his team."

What Saban was so good at was making every member of his organization believe his job was critical to the overall success. That might be easy to do with the offensive coordinator making $3 million a year, but it gets a lot harder with an entry-level employee making $25,000 who is multiple layers removed from the top of the hierarchy. It is a form of empowering leadership, and when deployed correctly, it can be incredibly effective. Consider the scene described in chapter two when Saban asked for every employee to come to a meeting where he stressed the importance of recruiting to Alabama's potential success. Not only did it set clear expectations, but it was Saban's way of showing that everyone in the building, including the janitors and secretaries he mentioned in his speech, played an important role. When Saban can trust that everyone in the building knows and appreciates their importance in the pursuit of success, it makes it easier to delegate responsibilities and not worry about the culture eroding in the process.

"He treated everybody in that building as if their job would determine if we won a football game or not," says Louis LeBlanc, who was a graduate assistant in Saban's first year at Alabama. "It really gave you pride in what you were doing no matter your paycheck, no matter your title or the task. It made the whole machine run."

At Alabama, Saban empowered the program's academic advisors by stressing the importance of their work at every turn. With the professionalization of college football, it can be easy to push the players to take the easiest majors possible and use the tutors solely to get the players passing grades rather than help them on their academic journies. There have been numerous scandals within college athletics that show exactly that. But deep down Saban views himself as a teacher and wanted everyone to know, whether they were recruits, players, or employees, that this was a point of emphasis, not a box simply to be checked. He'd celebrate a player excelling academically both publicly and privately and took immense pride in Alabama placing at the top of the SEC in graduation rates and GPA. When a player was struggling, he'd seek to understand why, asking Lance Walker, the program's academic advisor for a decade, for as much information as possible, including potential solutions to remedy the situation. He didn't want his academic interactions with players to be only negative when things weren't going well, so he'd call up a player to his office just to congratulate him on a good test grade.

"You can say in a press conference academics are important, but when you see early on that first group of recruits he's meeting with and he's asking them about what they want to major in and 'How can I help you reach your goals academically?'" Walker says. "When you see it firsthand and see him having those conversations, it's real and it becomes something everyone buys into."

The teacher in Saban informs a lot of his leadership style. He is primarily a lead-by-example leader, someone who will show you through his work ethic and actions how he wants things done. He realizes, though, that if he's not doing a good job communicating and showing how he wants something done, it'll lead to a long-term inefficiency. No one wants to have to explain simple concepts over and over again, but if you don't teach them well in the first place, that's what will happen. So he works hard to teach his players and coaches how he wants things done with the hopes that they'll grasp the concepts and help others with them in the future. It goes back to being able to trust the people around you to delegate. That manifested itself in everything from big-picture strategy discussions down to how he'd draw his Xs and Os on the whiteboard.

It might seem frivolous but it was one of the things that most impressed L.C. Cole when he worked with Saban at Toledo. After witnessing other coaches draw lines and circles that were practically illegible, Cole marveled at how Saban drew plays on the board. "It's like he has a stencil the way he draws those circles," Cole says. "I would practice drawing circles and squares." It's such a minute detail in the grand scheme of things, but it highlighted the attention-to-detail work Saban put in to create an easily understandable delivery system for his players. As a football coach, Saban worked with coaches and players from all kinds of different academic backgrounds, including some who had learning deficiencies. It was important and worthwhile for him to get to that level of detail as a leader because it could impact his team's ability to grasp several different concepts. "When you're up there teaching, when he draws circles, he's precise," Cole says. "It makes it easy for the kids. He does a good job teaching kids with different learning issues."

It's an underrated component of leadership. There are many different ways to get someone to buy in, as detailed throughout this book, but being able to explain why they should is, at its core, teaching. The goal should be to communicate a concept in such an easily digestible way that it clicks for the recipient and he wants to follow you for more learning. Hall of Fame quarterback Brett Favre once told me one of the most challenging aspects of coaching for him was taking what he saw and translating that to a player who wasn't seeing the same things. He had to adjust his "gunslinger" mentality as a player while working as an offensive coordinator at a Mississippi high school. "I have to process in a real short amount of time what we can do, not what I can do," Favre told me at the time. It's a predicament a lot of naturally gifted people go through; knowing the right thing to do has only so much value if you can't convey it to the rest of your team. Like Favre, Saban can see things no one else can, but what makes him special is he knows how to deliver that information. Bill Sheridan, who would later win a Super Bowl as a New York Giants assistant, says Saban is a "genius" in how he boiled down complicated topics.

"He is without a doubt one of the best teachers I've ever been around," Sheridan says. "I learned so much from him, and I tried to emulate it after I left working with him. He is so elite as a teacher, super succinct verbiage, and when he talks, it paints a genuine picture for the kid in his mind. He never talked just to talk."

He demanded his assistant coaches adopt a similar mindset. If he felt like one of his coaches was taking a simple concept and making it complicated for the players, he'd squash the behavior fast. He set the standard for how he wanted it done and trusted his coaches to follow through, but if it wasn't happening, he had no qualms about intervening to ensure that his message wasn't lost down the chain of command.

Saban was also teaching everyone in his organization what it took to be successful through his daily actions. Butch Jones, who spent three seasons at Alabama, says Saban is the "pace car of Alabama football," setting the speed and temperament that everyone else in the organization has to follow. "He sets the pace, and his ability to manage and balance all the factors of being a head coach that go into the daily structure, the daily routine, and then the weekly and monthly routines is really remarkable," Jones says. It is unquestionably a challenging pace to keep up with, as Saban demands a relentless pursuit of perfection that not everyone is well suited to achieve. Saban's philosophy boils down to, "I'm not going to ask you to do anything more than I'm doing," though he was, of course, doing quite a lot. When Pat Perles worked with him at Toledo, he remembers one day coming to the realization that his boss was "outworking me, out-studying me, and out-recruiting me." That can be an intimidating discovery, but for Perles, it brought the best out of him.

"I better step my game up because there's no letdown in this dude," Perles says. "He appeals to my competitiveness because he's so hardworking and he's so good at what he teaches. It challenges me that I need to be a better teacher because I'm letting him down."

When the entire organization feels that way, it promotes a highly effective and efficient work environment. Sedrick Irvin, a running back on the 1998 Michigan State team that launched "The Process," saw that in practice when he joined Saban's 2008 staff as a graduate assistant after his professional football career ended. Saban made Irvin feel important, that his input was just as valuable as one of his coordinators even if he was one of the lowest-ranking members of the organization, but also challenged him to match the standard he set. Irvin saw what many who have come through a Saban-led organization have witnessed: such a genuine respect and admiration for Saban's work ethic that no one wanted to let him down. When you know the highest-paid person in the company is still working the hardest, that he hasn't let fame or money change him in any way, it sets a high standard that everyone wants to emulate. So they embraced the challenge of trying to maintain his pace even though every former assistant will tell you no one is going to work harder than Saban.

"[Saban's] job is to make sure his coaches are on his level, or if not at his level, working to his level," Irvin says. "Now you talk about working to be better than one of the greatest college coaches ever. If he's got everybody working like that and putting in the time like that, you're going to have a helluva coaching staff."

It helps that Saban has been successful everywhere he's been, so they know if they put in the work and try their best to keep up with him, they'll almost certainly be successful. Conversely, if there were never any payoff for all the hard work demanded at Alabama, it would be difficult for Saban to maintain organizational buy-in with the pace he's established. There are plenty of other coaches who demand a lot from their players and staff members, but when things don't go as planned, that's when morale issues start popping up. In chapter eleven, we'll detail Saban's emphasis on preparation, but one of the ways he's able to get his team to put in the hard work at practices consistently is because he's successfully convinced them of its importance to their goals and has the track record to prove it.

"To quote Coach Saban, 'The fun is in winning,'" says former Alabama offensive lineman David Blalock. "Practice isn't fun. No one likes practice—the coaches don't like practice—but the fun is in winning. It's in being successful. Everybody there understands that, and that's what you have to buy into."

There is always going to be one area Saban struggles to delegate, though it hasn't negatively impacted the organization. Coaching the defensive backs is Saban's first love, one that as a former college defensive back he's never been fully able to walk away from even as he's worked his way up the ranks to become a head coach. He likes to joke that he's just a defensive backs graduate assistant, but everyone in the organization knows the truth: he's the one really coaching the defensive backs. "Nick is always going to be around the DBs," says former NFL defensive back Harlon Barnett. "If you're his DBs coach, you're not really the DBs coach. Just go there and be ready to learn from the sensei. You do that, hang around him for a year or two and get what you need, and then you can go do your own thing."

You'll see him throwing balls a specific way at the defensive backs and directing them through drills at practices. When he was the Miami Dolphins head coach, Saban once stopped Cris Dishman, a thirteen-year NFL cornerback on a minority internship with the Dolphins, because he wasn't throwing the ball the way he wanted. Dishman was throwing the ball a bit casually to the cornerbacks when Saban told him there was almost no point in a game where a pass would come perfectly right to a cornerback, so why was he practicing it that way? Saban then personally demonstrated how he wanted it done, and as is usually the case, Dishman realized he was right about it.

"He's the best secondary coach that's ever lived," says Rick Venturi, a long-time NFL defensive coordinator. "There's no doubt about that. He shaped my views forever on how he approached the defensive backfield."

It helped that Saban was so effective and efficient in every other aspect of his job that he could do that without the overall product suffering. It was almost like a hobby for him, where he got to live out the thing that made him love football in the first place without neglecting other responsibilities in the process. Not everyone can do that as they move up the ladder and take on more and more responsibilities while moving away from the day-to-day happenings. But it's important to remember why you got into something in the first place, to remember how you would have wanted to be treated when you were the low man on the totem pole, and to remember how important it was to be delegated an important task from your boss.

Establishing a culture can be very challenging, and when you succeed at creating a good one, it's worth celebrating. If you want to stay successful, you'll have to work hard to maintain it. The formula can be different for each leader and organization, but a laissez-faire approach will rarely last over time. Being the leader who tries to do it all isn't advisable, but neither is being the one who does nothing. It can be tricky to find the right balance. Saban's approach boils down to working hard to stay involved with every level of his organization—he will always have his hands on the areas he deems most important—while still trusting his employees enough to give them the space to do their jobs. When you can feel comfortable doing that as a leader and the product doesn't suffer, you'll know you've established a quality culture.

CHAPTER 11

Preparation Is Everything

Still more than four hours before the game was scheduled to start, it was Mike Vollmar's time to shine.

As Saban's director of football operations, Vollmar was in charge of many of the football program's logistics—an area the attention-detailed Saban cared a lot about—but now it was time for him to present his research.

Vollmar had to offer in-depth reports on the things that Alabama couldn't control so that it could, well, control them to the best of its ability. Vollmar's report included detailed information on all of the referees and their tendencies over the last two years so Saban could offer specific instructions to his players. For instance, Vollmar would explain how often a back official called pass interference, information Saban would then take to his defensive backs to guide how aggressive they could be against opposing receivers.

He'd do the same for weather reports, eschewing the local weatherman for the National Oceanic and Atmospheric Administration (NOAA) to ensure the information was as accurate as possible. If it was going to rain, Saban wanted to know the expected outcome for every hour the game was played to inform his decisions. Vollmar would go over the stadium diagram for away games—where the opposing band and student sections were situated, where their traveling fans were, and so on—so everyone knew what to do in certain situations.

"If we go to overtime, we aren't going to start talking about it then and there," Vollmar says. "We're going to that end of the field based on the way things are laid out in the stadium. The detail that went into that stuff prior to even kicking the ball off was amazing."

Saban loves being prepared, constantly searching for any and every possible advantage he can find. He knows that the person with the most accurate information, and the best way to harness that information, will likely be successful. He's also learned the hard way what happens when you don't consider all the possibilities in your preparation.

Vollmar's weather and stadium layout report has its genesis from Saban's first head coaching job at Toledo. Against Central Michigan and down by one point late in the game, Saban sent out his kicker for a game-winning field goal attempt. After the kicker hit the ball, it floated in the air before hitting a wall of wind and stopping almost in midair. It was Saban's first loss as a head coach, a moment that stuck with him throughout his career.

"That's something I learned in that game: that the conditions do affect the strategy of how you play," Saban later told ESPN.

Years later as LSU's head coach, Saban used that experience to his advantage. Studying the weather patterns that day, he knew the wind would be blowing strong and in a certain direction, informing what side of the field he wanted to start the game. That decision paid off when Marcus Randall found Devery Henderson for a 74-yard Hail Mary touchdown to beat Kentucky at the last second, known as the "Bluegrass Miracle," benefiting from thirty-mile-per-hour winds in a favorable direction. Kentucky players were so sure they were going to win before the play they dumped a Gatorade jug on head coach Guy Morriss and oblivious Wildcats fans rushed the field before realizing what happened. Of course, Saban wasn't particularly pleased after that game even if the preparation had helped the Tigers get a fluky win. "We won the game but we didn't defeat the team," he said. "If you want to be happy with the results, I'm happy with the results. If you want to be happy with the process, I'm not."

Saban seemed to sense what could be coming when the Tigers got crushed the following week against Alabama, 31–0 Nearly twenty years later,

Saban still referenced that game as an example of what could happen when the good feeling of a win covered up the need to make changes. The players let their good feelings from a miraculous win mask their need to improve, a valuable lesson for everyone on the team.

"We were of the mindest, 'We just won that game, it was awesome, and look at us all on *SportsCenter*,'" says former LSU offensive lineman Brandon Hurley. "And not thinking, 'Man, we shouldn't have won that game—we were lucky to win and we need to never put ourselves in that position again because we didn't deserve to win.' The next week, we paid for it."

That Alabama loss taught Saban a valuable lesson, too: don't show scary movies the night before a big game. Saban has long made a team movie night a staple of his preparation, getting the team together on Friday nights to watch a movie. Over the years, he liked to show mostly motivational movies like *Red Tails* about the Tuskegee Airmen, *The Last Samurai*, and *Gladiator* to send a message to his team before a game. Before the Alabama game, Saban took his LSU team to see the horror film *The Ring*, which features mysterious deaths after watching a cursed videotape. The movie had an especially adverse effect on the team, with some players so disturbed by its contents they were unable to sleep that night.

"I remember him giving his pregame speech and using the girl with the hair in front of her that came out of the screen as part of the pregame speech," says former LSU offensive lineman Jimmy Courtenay. "He said, 'You need to scare the hell out of these people like that crazy bitch coming out of that screen last night.'

"I remember that because it was the first and last time we saw a scary movie, and he used it in his speech. We got our asses kicked. Several starters didn't go to sleep that night because of the movie we watched."

Saban's emphasis on preparation takes many different forms within his organization. It impacts the way Alabama recruits, how it practices, how it plays in the games, among many other aspects. Saban would often tell his staff, "I can handle good news and I can handle bad news, but I don't deal with surprises very well." The best way to never be caught off guard is to be prepared, a philosophy that flows through the organization. He keeps an eighteen-month master calendar that everyone in the organization is expected to follow. Saban's day is planned down to the minute, a dual desire for efficiency and structure to maximize his output and limit any last-minute surprises.

"He's the most amazing person at being able to control his reality every day," says former Alabama associate AD Doug Walker. "That's not a shot at his reality or saying he doesn't face anyone else's reality. He's in charge of what he's doing and where his organization is going, and he manages it extremely effectively."

During the football season, Saban and his staff work tirelessly through film review, meetings, and team practices to run through every possible outcome that could occur. He never wanted his team to be unprepared for a situation, whether that was on the field or in the locker room before the game. He taught his team what they should do with big issues like the clock not working or a rain delay as well as the minutiae of what to do when a shoestring breaks. Saban would guide "what if" meetings in the lead-up to games where his staff could throw out scenarios that could pop up and then debate what they should do. Todd Alles, who preceded Vollmar as director of football operations, remembers an Alabama assistant coach saying "the hay's in the barn" after a Thursday meeting, meaning they had done all the preparation they needed to do for that Saturday's game.

"Bullshit," Saban said, eyeing the assistant coach. "The hay's not in the barn. I'm still looking for ways to win the game when they're playing the National Anthem."

Saban looked for every possible advantage until the last minute, but the most important work happened in the days leading up to the game. Saban then determined what he wanted his team to do on Saturday and what he expected the opposing team to do in return. The best coaches can adjust during the game based on what they see, but it is still a huge advantage to know convincingly headed into a game what weaknesses are available to be attacked.

In the lead-up to the 2016 national championship game against Clemson, Saban and his staff noticed a Clemson tendency on kickoffs. The way Clemson lined up bunched up in a tight alignment led Saban and Bobby Williams, the team's special teams coach, to believe it could be exploited for an onside kick, if necessary. In the days before the game, Alabama practiced its onside kick play over and over again to limited success. Williams said Marlon Humphrey, who was expected to make a play on the ball, successfully recovered it 50 percent of the time in practice. Saban felt comfortable enough in what he saw on film to tell kicker Adam Griffith in the hotel before the game to be ready to do it.

With the game tied at twenty-four in the fourth quarter and Clemson quarterback Deshaun Watson carving up the Tide defense, Saban sensed he needed to do something big if Alabama was going to win the game. When he saw Clemson line up the way they had in his film review, he opted to go for an onside kick. He walked down to Williams and said, "Do it." Griffith kicked it perfectly, Humphrey recovered, and Alabama scored a touchdown two plays later when quarterback Jake Coker connected with tight end O.J. Howard for a 51-yard touchdown. After the successful onside kick, Saban cracked a rare smile, knowing his hours of studying had paid off in a big way. The game wasn't over at that moment—the two teams would trade touchdowns in a high-scoring fourth quarter—but it dramatically shifted the game for Alabama on its way to another national championship victory. All because of being prepared and using it to capitalize when needed.

"It's a gutsy call," then-defensive coordinator Kirby Smart said after the game. "High risk, high reward. That's what makes him a great coach."

Two years later, Smart learned what it felt like to be on the receiving end of a decision like that.

Tua Tagovailoa's game-winning touchdown pass to DeVonta Smith on 2nd-and-26 against Georgia might be the most famous play in Alabama's storied history. Winning a national championship on a walk-off touchdown is remarkable and storybook-like in itself, but doing so with a true freshman backup quarterback added an extra layer of improbability. Down 13–0 at halftime, Saban made what looked like a bold, if not slightly desperate, decision to bench Jalen Hurts in favor of Tagovailoa, who had never started a college game and played only sparingly that season. Hurts hadn't fared well in the first half, completing only three of eight passes for 21 yards, but he was 25–2 as Alabama's starter and came within a few seconds of winning a national championship the previous season. It would have been easy to stick with Hurts, to be beholden to his previous success. In the moment, it felt like Saban's gutsiest call as a head coach in the most significant moment possible, but when you peel back the curtain you realize, as with most things with Saban, it culminated from considerable discussion and consideration that took place long before kickoff.

Saban didn't make a spur-of-the-moment decision to insert Tagovailoa into the title game because he was losing. In fact, he had already strongly considered making the switch in previous games; he had just never pulled the trigger. "I remember hearing against both Auburn and Clemson that Saban over the headset was ready to pull [Hurts]," says Hunter Bryant, a tight end on that Alabama team. "I think everybody was ready to pull him, but Jalen would always make that one play, or the offense would stay alive long enough for it not to be a disaster."

Behind the scenes, even if Alabama was winning, there were signs that the offense was wobbly. Hurts had a terrific freshman season, guiding the Crimson Tide to a 14–1 record and title game appearance, and had no reason to question his standing as the team's returning starter when Tagovailoa, a five-star left-handed quarterback from Ewa Beach, Hawaii, landed in Tusca-loosa. Tagovailoa possessed physical abilities Hurts didn't, particularly as a passer, which became difficult to avoid during practices. Tagovailoa wowed his teammates and coaches with what he could do in practice against Ala-bama's stout defense. Those performances started to leak out to message boards and radio show discussions. Hurts not only saw what Tagovailoa was doing in practice each day, but now he was hearing about it outside his bub-ble too. As the noise got louder as the season went on, it impacted Hurts. "He lost his confidence," says CBS Sports analyst Gary Danielson. "I saw it every day in practice through that season—it was bad out there. He had lost his ability to really throw the football because he watched the hype, listened to the hype, and saw the way Tua was coming on."

When Hurts was sick with the flu ahead of Alabama's Sugar Bowl semifinal against Clemson, Tagovailoa got to practice with the first-team offense. His play in two practices has become the stuff of legend, with the true freshman quarterback completing 54 of 58 pass attempts, according to *The Athletic*. Saban and his offensive staff put together what was essentially a break-in-case-of-an-emergency plan against Clemson to play Tagovailoa should Alabama ever find itself in need of his superior passing abilities, but the moment never came. Alabama's defense overwhelmed Clemson, limiting the Tigers to two field goals and returning an interception for a touchdown to a 24–6 win. Alabama didn't need Hurts to do much to win the game, but Saban knew that might not be the case against Georgia.

Down 13–0 and with his offense unable to do much against the Bulldogs, Saban made the quarterback switch. There was a noticeable shift in the team's energy right away, says Bryant, when they realized Tagovailoa was going into the game. The left-handed quarterback cut Georgia's lead to 13–7 with a 6-yard touchdown pass to Henry Ruggs midway through the third quarter, and then rallied Alabama back from a 20–7 deficit when the Bulldogs scored a few minutes later. Even though Tagovailoa hadn't played much in actual games that season, he had the necessary confidence in his abilities after having success in practice against an Alabama defense that featured future NFL stars Minkah Fitzpatrick and Trevon Diggs. The team rallied around Tagovailoa's talent and infectious energy, setting up a furious comeback effort that sent the game to overtime.

After Georgia kicked a field goal to go up 23–20, Tagovailoa took a sack on his first offensive play, pushing Alabama back to the 41-yard line mere minutes after Tide kicker Andy Pappanastos missed a 36-yard field goal that would have won the game in regulation. Alabama didn't panic as offensive coordinator Brian Daboll called "Seattle," a four-verticals play, and Tagovailoa threw a perfect pass to an open Smith racing down the sideline to win the game. It felt miraculous in the moment, and no one could have anticipated ending the game in that fashion, but Tagovailoa's role in it came as no surprise to Saban or the rest of his staff. Inserting the true freshman into the game was a calculated decision, the result of hundreds of hours of watching Tagovailoa up close in practice and readying him for the big stage. The preparation is what gave Saban the confidence to make a big decision in a pressurized situation.

It's a point that sometimes gets forgotten or overlooked when remembering a triumphant moment. Alabama fans will always remember 2nd-and-26, but what Saban will remember is all the hard work preparing for that moment. Tagovailoa and Alabama officially won the championship on January 8, 2018, but they really won it in sweltering August practices and by trying to treat every weekday practice the same as the most important game. Being prepared is a mindset as much as it is a lifestyle. It takes a lot of work to be as organized and attention-to-detail proficient as Saban, skills he actively works not only to maintain but to improve every single day. It should be no surprise that the best-prepared people are usually the hardest workers, because they make a conscious decision to make the time investment, knowing it can directly correlate with success.

While at Toledo together, L.C. Cole remembers getting a call one morning from Saban. It was Christmas.

"What are you doing, L.C.?" Saban asked his running backs coach.

"Well, I'm here enjoying my first Christmas with my wife," Cole responded.

"You want to go watch some film?" Saban asked.

"My wife heard him and looked me right in the face," says Cole. "I said, 'I don't think so, Coach—you're going to make me get divorced.'"

The phone call left a deep impression on him. "Man, this guy is on perfection on Christmas Day. He's looking at film on Christmas."

It's an extreme example but illustrates the level of commitment Saban had even in his first head coaching job to be the best. He'd evolve as he got older and experienced more success, but the borderline obsession with working to be prepared will never leave him. It's why he and Bill Belichick, another film-obsessed coach, get along so well now, though Saban was known to grumble at times in Cleveland about how much work Belichick expected from his coaches. Saban struggled at times balancing the need to be properly prepared and the accompanying long hours it took to achieve that versus any semblance of a work-life balance. It's a challenge every leader grapples with at some point in assessing the line between an emphasis on preparation being a good thing versus a potential detriment.

When Harlon Barnett was part of Saban's title-winning LSU staff in 2003, he remembers his boss as hesitant to give the staff a couple of scheduled days off during a bye week. "There ain't nothing to do at home," Barnett remembers Saban saying. "We should be here. There ain't nothing to do at the house." Saban himself would later acknowledge he wasn't a good-enough father at times during his LSU tenure, opting to work late in the office rather than spend time with his family.

Those tendencies didn't suddenly disappear when he got to Alabama, either. There was more work to do, more factors to consider in the already lengthy preparation process. Saban threw himself into the work, and the rest of the organization noticed. No one wanted to leave before Saban, a downside to having a leader with a healthy appetite for long work hours. Sometimes staffers stayed late in their offices because they didn't want to leave before Saban, only to realize he had already left. "You could be there for another hour and not know he's gone," says Tyler Siskey, who was Alabama's director of player personnel for two seasons. "You'd be done with everything and you're just waiting for him to be done."

Siskey opted for a creative solution to the predicament. He started paying one member of the night cleaning crew to focus on one specific area from 9:00 p.m. until midnight that Saban would have to walk through on his way out of the building. When he saw Saban leave the building, he'd find Siskey to give him a heads-up. "We'd wait about ten minutes and go," Siskey says. "I took care of my guy."

As Saban aged, he realized even he had limits, and working anything more than fourteen or so hours a day had diminishing returns. He'd get in a little before 7:00 each morning and typically stay into the evening, but there was no sleeping in the office or hanging around just to prove a point. He'd work through lunch, with his wife, Terry, telling friends she'd have to remind him to take a bite of his salad when she visited him. Saban was doing everything to maximize his output in his working hours, always striving for peak efficiency. Saban's critics would argue his pace was still too grueling and created an environment devoid of fun. As one Alabama insider put it, "Just because Nick handles that grind so well doesn't mean everybody does, and in fact, most of them don't. There's an unintended brutality to it." But others who have been inside it say some of the criticism is overblown.

"I've worked for guys who are much greater grinders than Nick Saban is," says Vollmar, who worked with him at Michigan State and Alabama. "Does he work hard? Yes. Does he put in hours? Yes. But I feel Nick Saban is a very balanced individual, and that makes him so successful. I know he grinds at it as hard as any college coach in college football, but he's a family guy. He knows when you need to take a break. He's not one of those guys to grind the grind to say he's going to grind. If it can't be productive, I've never known him to do that."

That last part is more important than you might think. Darren Anderson, who played for Saban at Toledo before a seven-year NFL career, compares it to the sales world. A good salesperson, Anderson believes, won't work for a bad manager. It's the same in sports, where a high-level athlete won't stay motivated for a bad coach who wastes his time. Anderson saw it firsthand in his NFL career, where coaches would make it a point to hold meetings that stretched late into the night but weren't always a good use of time. Everyone could walk away saying they had worked a lot of hours that day, but no one could say they were efficient.

"If you're in a Saban program, you're going to work your ass off, and it's going to be fruitful," Anderson says. "You may not like it—you may hate it—but if you do what is part of the program and you buy in, you're going to have success. It would be nice to bottle that up and sell that so coaches knew how important it was. Coaches lose rooms." Saban doesn't hold a meeting just to say he did. He doesn't assign busywork to underlings just to check a few things off a list to look productive. If he was asking you to a meeting, he expected it to be worth not only your time but his. It made everyone more organized and better at managing their time, knowing that in a Saban meeting they better have their facts right and better be prepared to deliver them succinctly.

As a football coach, Saban spends a lot of time putting his team through very challenging practices to prepare for games. This serves two primary purposes: it limits surprises and can make the games almost seem easier by comparison. Remember the stories about how Saban is the greatest recruiter ever? That allows him to create intense competition in practice when even the backup players are former four- and five-star recruits who have a good shot at playing in the NFL one day. At Saban-led practices, there is no standing around, and everyone is going full speed, whether they are a starter or a walk-on who is unlikely to play. The ultimate goal was to feel as confident playing a backup in a game as a starter, and that meant he held everyone to the same standard in what he expected in practice. Saban drilled a specific mantra into his organization: "Don't practice until you can get it right. Practice until you can't get it wrong."

"Coach Saban makes practice entirely hard and very adverse for players," says former Alabama receiver Christion Jones. "When you get in a game, you've watched so much film. Coach Saban runs reps religiously to get guys to do it right. When a practice is so hard and so intense and high-energy, it gets to the point where you can't really mess up."

Saban is utilizing what psychologist Albert Bandura coined as self-efficacy theory. Self-efficacy, in its most basic terms, is a person's belief in his ability—a.k.a. confidence—to carry out an action. Bandura believed there were four primary components to building confidence:

1. Performance accomplishments
2. Vicarious experience
3. Verbal persuasion
4. Physiological information

How do those constructs work within Saban's preparation strategy? Performance accomplishments can be as simple as a player having success in a challenging practice, which boosts confidence for the upcoming game. Vicarious experience relates to building self-confidence through what you observe, which could be watching film before a big game or seeing your teammates also perform well in practice, making you feel more confident in the team's chances at success. Saban and the rest of his staff provide the verbal persuasion, whether through building a player up or pointing out that he can perform better if he does something different. Finally, it comes back to each member's physical and emotional state, which is why Saban and Co. employ nutritionists to make sure a player eats well, track a player's sleep to maximize that area, and incorporate other strategies so players have the right mindset heading into a situation.

During practice of a game week, Alabama's scout team would run through every play its opponent ran in a game over the last year. And if, for instance, that opposing school's defensive coordinator was at a different school the previous season, they'd look at everything he did there, too. "If there was a one in a million chance we could see that play," says a former player, "we were going to practice for it."

As a result, Jones says in his four years at Alabama he can remember only three instances during a game when the opposing team did something they hadn't seen before. Knowing there wouldn't be any surprises in a game gave players more confidence in their chances at succeeding. It also boosted their confidence in their leader, Saban, recognizing that he knew what he was talking about and there'd be a payoff to the time-intensive preparation tactics he put the entire organization through. When Saban found something in film review that could benefit the team or helped a player work on his craft during practice and it paid off in a game, it just further engendered confidence from his team. They were wholly bought in even though the practices could be miserable at times because they knew Saban was giving them the tools to be successful they wouldn't get anywhere else. The same was true for most aspects of Saban's approach: you knew it was going to be very difficult, but it would be worth it.

Cris Dishman can still remember when he found out he was going to start his first NFL game. In his first year with the Houston Oilers, a rookie Dishman was only two games into his NFL career when he got the good news he would start the next game. Starting an NFL game was a dream come true for the cornerback out of Nebraska, and the accomplishment overwhelmed him. He was so excited to start his first game, he didn't really read the scouting report Saban, his position coach, had prepared for the Oilers' game against the New York Jets.

It didn't go well.

Dishman was matched up against Wesley Walker, who burned him for two touchdowns on the way to the Jets crushing the Oilers, 45–3. Later, a dejected Dishman picked up the scouting report and his eyes got big. Saban had warned against falling victim to Walker's deceptively fast running style, in which he seemed to scoot down the field. Saban wrote that once the Jets got past the 40-yard line, they liked to throw a deep first pass to the left side, exactly how Walker scored a 50-yard touchdown.

"If I had read my scouting report that week, I would have seen all that," Dishman says. "I realized, 'Oh man, this stuff is actually good. It actually comes through.'"

And in a hectic and combative Oilers defensive backs room, Dishman became one of Saban's early converts.

The emphasis on being prepared is the backbone of the meritocracy Saban strives to maintain within his team. In his first meeting with his defensive backs in Houston, Saban told them, "The people who want to play, who want to start, are the people who perform on the practice field." Saban is very open about the fact that he'd rather play a well-prepared yet less talented player than a talented player who hasn't put in the work to learn the playbook. He wants to trust his players out on the field, and the ones who have shown a track record of being prepared are the ones who earn it. It's another way he scrapes away any hype or attitude a highly rated recruit might have coming into his organization, because no matter how good you think you are, Saban has no qualms about playing someone else if you don't put in the work.

"If you want to make a name for yourself at the University of Alabama, you've got to step up to the plate and step up to those standards, or you're going to get left behind," says former Alabama linebacker Keith Holcombe. "Just like all these five-stars who come in and you say, 'Oh, I wonder why he didn't pan out?' He wasn't there mentally the majority of the time."

The lesson, of course, is it doesn't matter how naturally gifted you are at something, it's what you do with those gifts. "If you don't know what you're doing with Coach Saban's system, you're done," says former Toledo safety

Tim Caffey. "I don't care how good you are. If you're making mental errors, it's a wrap. You won't see the field."

Caffey learned that the hard way at Toledo. As a former track star, Caffey had the athleticism and talent to start on the first team Saban guided as a head coach. But he didn't know the playbook as well as he should have and that showed on one fateful day in practice. Caffey had to cover his roommate, tight end Vince Marrow, who relished beating him after getting into an argument in their apartment the night before. After Marrow burned Caffey for a touchdown on a wheel route, Saban made them rerun the play. Same result.

"Hey, Caff, what did you do to piss him off? I thought he was your roommate," Saban asked. "If you mess this up one more time, we're going to send you on a one-way bus ticket back to Youngstown."

"Lo and behold, that's what I did. I messed it up," Caffey says. "That was it. [Saban said], 'Get him out of there and don't put him back in again.'"

Rather than complaining over the treatment, Caffey realized that he couldn't just rely on his natural abilities and needed to work harder. It made him appreciate Saban even more. He dedicated himself to learning the playbook better and became a starter his final two years at Toledo.

"You'll play for anybody like that because you know there's no hidden agenda, there's no politics involved," he says. "It's how you perform on and off the field. You can't be mad at a person who's giving you a fair shot and you don't hold up your end of the bargain."

The benefits of being prepared extend far beyond football practice. If you've ever interviewed for a job, you've had to prepare in some fashion. It's a stressful process that can be overwhelming for someone desperate to make a good impression. Saban opts for the heavy-research approach, and it's been incredibly beneficial to his career. He might be the greatest college football head coach now, but he wasn't the initial top choice for most of his early job opportunities. It took having a detailed plan and thoughtful interview questions to win over the people making the hires. Before he sat down for any prospective job, he did extensive research to be as well prepared as possible when he walked into the room. M. Peter McPherson, the former president of Michigan State, remembers Saban was "particularly well prepared for the interview, and that was his approach as the coach." Saban wasn't McPherson's initial top choice or even his second choice, but a face-to-face meeting won him over and convinced him that he was the right man to lead the Spartans' football team.

When LSU interviewed Saban to replace Gerry DiNardo, it was almost immediately unclear who was interviewing who, according to Charlie Weems, then chairman of LSU's Board of Supervisors.

"Nick had his own yellow pad with pages of notes and questions on it," Weems says. "He had really done his homework on LSU and on us. It was typical Nick Saban, as I came to learn—overprepared, knew exactly where the pressure points were and the things he needed to feel good about in order to make that kind of a career decision."

Similar to Michigan State, Saban wasn't the initial top choice. Seemingly hurting Saban's chances of getting in the mix for the LSU job was the resistance of one of the key decision-makers. Joe Dean, LSU's athletic director, told Weems he didn't think Saban would be a good fit at the school. He referenced when Saban's first Michigan State team badly lost to LSU in a bowl game in Shreveport as part of his rationale. "Don't you remember him from the Independence Bowl?" Dean said. "He's not our kind of guy." It took a strong pitch from Saban's agent, Jimmy Sexton, and endorsements from well-respected football figures to get Dean to agree to meet with him. Saban so thoroughly impressed the LSU search committee, including Dean, in his interview that he had a job offer before it even ended.

The Independence Bowl loss that worried Dean explained a downside to Saban's preparation emphasis: it was hard for him not to overprepare through practice. Saban was well regarded in the coaching community, but he had never actually won a bowl game when LSU hired him. "I remember him being pretty candid, saying he'd gotten his ass kicked in every bowl game at Michigan State, and that something had to change," former LSU assistant Derek Dooley told author Monte Burke. Saban successfully adjusted his late-season practice strategy to win three of his five bowl games at LSU, including the national championship in 2003. Still, the tendencies that led to defeat at MSU didn't altogether leave him.

If there is a critical flaw in the Alabama Death Star, it's how hard it has been for Saban to let go of the brutal practices he's used to establish his culture at every head coaching stop. Challenging practices were the backbone of how Saban prepared his team, and it was incredibly successful. No coach was better at having his team ready to play week one of the season, with the Crimson Tide winning every single season-opener in his first fifteen seasons, many of them against top-flight opponents. The issue that emerged over time was whether Saban had his team peaking at the wrong time, as the advent of the College Football Playoff prolonged the season. Saban's desire to get high-intensity repetitions in practice and lots of them became somewhat of a liability as the players wore down over the longer season. In the days leading up to Alabama's first playoff game against Ohio State on January 1, 2015, one assistant coach was alarmed by what he saw during practice. "Our guys can't move," the coach remembers thinking. "It's three days before the game, and we are still in pads." Saban brushed off concerns brought up to him about the preparation strategy.

Alabama held a 21–6 lead late in the first half against the Buckeyes before the wheels started coming off. Ohio State scored two quick touchdowns at the end of the half and then followed it up with the first two touchdowns of the second half. Ohio State looked like the fresher team, and never was that more evident than when no Alabama player could stop Ezekiel Elliott on an 85-yard touchdown in the fourth quarter that all but assured Ohio State's victory. To the former coach, it was the culmination of Saban stubbornly refusing to ease up his practices late in the season and paying the price for it. "That's why they are dead at the end of the year," the coach says. "They never lose at the beginning of the year; they lose at the end of the year."

Alabama's first playoff foray went badly, as Saban's program didn't adjust its approach the way it needed to be successful. If there was a benefit to the defeat, it made the coach more willing to embrace technology to prevent similar wear-downs in the future. Catapult Sports is an Australian-based company that developed a GPS product that can monitor acceleration, directional changes, and player workload. Alabama first started working with the company in the spring of 2014, but it gained momentum after the playoff loss to OSU. Staffers followed the daily data coming out of the 40 GPS units during practice to determine how a player performed relative to usual performance to guide whether that player needed to be doing more or less in practice. The more accumulated data, the easier it became to know when to take preventative measures to limit injuries and promote players being at their best at the optimal time.

Most importantly, it took the guesswork out of the decisions. No longer did the organization have to rely on an eye test or asking a player whether he was good to go. There was now quantitative evidence that everyone could reference to influence decisions on whether a player needed a break or a course correction. The day after each practice, Saban gets a report covering a wide range of information, including whether fatigue is causing any player performance decline, to inform his decisions for the next practice. It helped trainers like Jeff Allen know when a player was ready to come back from an injury, with the data sometimes going against their preconceived notions of an injury timetable. It influenced running back Kenyan Drake's rehabilitation after a gruesome ankle injury, who went on to play an important role in that 2016 national championship when he ran a career-best 22.05 miles per hour on a 95-yard kickoff-return touchdown. The moment was celebrated internally as proof the technology worked, and it was worth following. "This system really allows us late in the year to do the right thing with our players," Allen told AL.com, "and it has changed how we practiced late in the year."

Will Lowery, who played on the 2009 and 2011 title teams, heard from players and coaches how big a difference it made in guiding Saban's preparation tactics. "I know for a fact in the bowl games they've cut down greatly on how much they are demanding out of the guys physically when it gets to postseason play than how they did when I was there," he says.

Saban adjusted the preparation specifics after learning from a loss, but the core philosophy was still the same: the best-prepared organization was the most likely to be successful. The same applied to the best-prepared employee. It was an emphasis on attention to detail, meticulous planning, hard work, and consistency. The famous American inventor Ben Franklin said, "By failing to prepare, you are preparing to fail." Saban lives that mantra every day.

CHAPTER 12

Don't Waste a Failing

Burton Burns stood at the front of the room, a book in hand and a look on his face that was "as serious as a heart attack."

As one of Nick Saban's longest-tenured lieutenants, Burns gathered a group of players to discuss the worst loss of the Saban era at Alabama. Clemson dominated Alabama in almost every possible fashion in an embarrassing 44–16 loss for the Crimson Tide in the 2019 national championship game. Alabama played sloppily, the coaching staff looked outmatched against Clemson's, and even Saban made uncharacteristic coaching decisions seemingly out of desperation, such as a misguided faked field goal attempt in the third quarter while down 31–16. "Probably the worst game we played that year was in the championship game, myself included as the play-caller and on offense," says former Alabama offensive coordinator Mike Locksley.

The decisive defeat felt like a direct shot at the Alabama mystique. Never before had a Saban-led team played so poorly in such an important game. When the stunned Alabama players returned to Tuscaloosa, they were looking for answers. Was it time for the program to make changes to its approach after getting destroyed on the biggest stage possible? The players were embarrassed and wanted to know what Saban and Co. would do to make sure they never felt that way again.

Burns directly answered those questions.

"I'm holding how we do things," Burns began, "and we're not fucking changing a thing. If some of you have a problem with that, you can get off the team now."

"Everyone came in very down, like in an abyss," says wide receiver Mac Hereford. "We just made it to the national championship game and the whole school is like, 'Screw those guys.' We come in all down, and Coach Saban and Coach Burns just rip into our ass. It's like going to your parents for sympathy and you get the exact opposite."

When Saban and his staff assessed what went wrong during the 2018 season, they concluded that players and coaches weren't adhering to The Process rather than The Process no longer being good. There were distractions from coaches already making plans to leave the program after the season. Amid a perfect season full of lopsided victories to that point, player leaders bought into the hype and weren't holding each other accountable the way they were supposed to. Program insiders believe Saban knew in the lead-up to the national championship game that his team wasn't mentally ready for what awaited them. In the immediate aftermath of the game, Saban walked into a dour locker room and apologized to the team. "I failed you guys," Saban said, taking the blame for what he saw as the result of not being properly prepared for what awaited the Crimson Tide in California that night.

"That team against Clemson wasn't ready to play," says Corey Miller, a nine-year NFL veteran whose son Christian played on that team. "That team didn't have the focus, because some individuals were not focused on that game but focused more on themselves. There's no way they should have lost that game, but the way they lost—this team wasn't ready."

And thus began an important tone-setting within the Alabama program. Saban has a favorite saying he preaches to his players: "You never want to waste a failing." A loss requires introspection, a chance to evaluate what led to the failure, and an opportunity to formulate a plan to avoid it moving forward. The losses will always stick with Saban longer than the wins, a mentality that makes him do everything possible to avoid that feeling. One person who knows him well offered a dark description of the mindset that drives Saban, saying, "He lives his life looking into the abyss. A win is simply a step back. The joy of winning is less important than avoiding the tragedy of defeat."

What Saban excels at after a setback is knowing when to make the big change and when to double down on what he's already doing. He abhors doing things because "that's the way we've always done them," but he's also confident enough in his evaluation to know when to keep pushing a similar approach. The championship game loss in 2019 didn't prompt blowing up The Process; it demanded a recommitment to it.

How a leader handles a loss can be critical for how the organization rebounds. In poker, there's a phenomenon called going "on tilt." It typically refers to a poker player acting recklessly after losing a hand. When you lose something big—a game, a job, a large sum of money—you can react emotionally and make poor decisions. In poker, going on tilt can turn a bad moment into a disastrous night in a hurry.

Saban doesn't allow his emotions to overtake him after a loss. His critics have long referred to him as a robot, but where it really helps him is his ability to check his emotions to avoid saying or doing something he'd regret after a loss. There's rarely screaming or breaking clipboards when Alabama loses. He's much more likely to be angry after his team wins but plays poorly than after a loss. In the rare times the Crimson Tide comes up empty-handed, Saban is collected and analytical while evaluating why his organization didn't get its desired result. Everything is a teaching moment for Saban, so he'll immediately offer thoughts on why the team lost the game and explain what they need to do to move on.

"They scored here because of this; they sacked our quarterback because of this. It wasn't, 'We just got our ass kicked,'" says Bill Sheridan, who spent two seasons as Saban's linebackers coach at Michigan State. "He would never say anything as vague and general as that. He never coached like that; he never talked like that. There were never ambiguous comments. If he was saying something, it was pinpointed at a specific thing."

As detailed in chapter seven, Saban is intensely curious about human psychology and how to find the right ways to motivate his team. When you boil down his approach, it can be quite simple: After a win, he doesn't want his team to get complacent, so he finds things to keep pushing them. After a loss, he senses his team needs a pickup, and he usually doesn't want to make them feel worse. "He knows when to put the hammer down, but he knows when you've done the best you can," says former LSU assistant LeRoy Ryals. "He's going to make everyone understand the expectations and not have a sense of entitlement."

He also pushes a strategy he learned under George Perles at Michigan State: the twenty-four-hour rule.

The premise of the twenty-four-hour rule is simple though challenging to maintain. No matter how big a win or how bad a loss you experience, you get twenty-four hours to deal with it and then you have to move on. Now, of course, this rule wasn't created to deal with things like the death of a beloved family member or other life-changing events. No one is saying to move on that fast. But it is one of Saban's lessons most applicable to every aspect of life. Didn't get the promotion you wanted at work? You get twenty-four hours to wallow in it, and then you have to move on or risk it lingering and hurting any future chance you have of moving up in the organization. We'll dive deep into Saban's aversion to complacency in chapter sixteen, but the twenty-four-hour rule tries to prevent that, too. Celebrate a victory too long and someone else out there who is working harder than ever to win is going to surpass you. In sports, we call this the winner's hangover, when teams struggle to repeat as champions because of how much they enjoyed celebrating getting to the top. Won an award in your professional field? Great—you get twenty-four hours to live it up and then it's back to work if you want a shot at winning another.

Saban stresses the importance of the rule because he doesn't want anyone within his organization getting too high or too low off a single outcome. When he was at Michigan State, Saban told his players, "The biggest difference between winning and losing is the way the fans and media treat you."

"If you can get over that fact and stay in the middle of the road emotionally, at the end of this thing you're going to be so much better off," Michigan State tight end Josh Keur remembers Saban instructing his team.

When his teams do lose, Saban owns it publicly. In postgame press conferences with the media, Saban will be honest about why his team didn't win, but he works hard to avoid blaming his coaches and players. As the leader, the onus is always on him. That might seem like a basic concept, but you'd be surprised how many leaders like to shirk responsibility when times are tough. If you want the people below you to buy into your vision, how you respond during the bad times is even more important than when everything is going well. Shielding the rest of your team from the fallout of a negative result can go a long way to building goodwill and respect. Legendary Alabama coach Paul "Bear" Bryant once said, "If anything goes bad, I did it. If anything goes semi-good, we did it. If anything goes really good, then you did it. That's all it takes to get people to win football games for you."

"He's the first to take responsibility and say, 'I didn't do my job well enough and because of that we didn't win today,'" says David Blalock, who played at Alabama from 2008–2012. "He comes in, he's calm, and he says, 'We didn't do this and we have to go work on it.'"

Early on in Saban's Alabama tenure, two losses played significant roles in the team's journey to an eventual national championship in 2009. The first was an embarrassing loss to Louisiana Monroe in Saban's first season, the one most widely identified as the worst of his time at Alabama before the title game loss to Clemson. Louisiana Monroe entered the game as a 24.5-point underdog, a little-known school in west Louisiana scheduled as an easy win for Alabama before its big annual rivalry game against Auburn. Even during an up-and-down first season, everyone expected it to be an easy win for Alabama. The Tide raced out to an early 7–0 lead but lacked focus and committed multiple sloppy turnovers. ULM kept hanging around as the Tide struggled, leading to a tied 14–14 game headed into halftime, stunning the 92,138 Alabama fans in attendance. It only got worse for Alabama in the second half as the pressure started building that it could actually lose to a team no one gave a shot to win.

And it did. Alabama committed four turnovers, including two John Parker Wilson interceptions and a late Jimmy Johns fumble on ULM's 14-yard line to allow the Warhawks to preserve the shocking 21–14 upset. "Losing to Louisiana Monroe would be the worst loss," Wilson told me years ago. "There were ones that hurt more, but that was definitely a low point."

In the locker room after the game, one of Alabama's senior defensive leaders went on a profanity-laden tirade in front of the entire team and coaching staff. The player laid out all the reasons Alabama had just lost, including taking the opponent lightly, players breaking curfew, and not putting in the necessary film work because they didn't think Louisiana Monroe warranted it. "This is what happens," the player said. "You get your ass embarrassed."

Saban listened intently as the player emphatically let all his teammates have it. The Alabama coach asked him if he was finished, and when he said he was, it was Saban's turn to deliver the lesson.

"That's a great speech," Saban said as he addressed the team, "but it was about three days too late. You should have had the courage to say that on Tuesday or Wednesday when you saw this going on. Anybody can say it after the fact."

That loss served a long-term purpose for Alabama. It taught Alabama players they had to hold each other more accountable at all times and couldn't fall back on "I told you so" after the fact. Saban didn't want anyone to forget what happened in that game, so he broke his twenty-four-hour rule and had his staff post pictures and posters from that game throughout the football facility, including in the players' locker room. That loss highlighted problems apparent throughout the season, including a penchant for blowing games in the fourth quarter, and he wanted them to think about it all offseason. He wanted them to use it to fuel the drive and dedication it would take to be better moving forward.

"When stuff was out of line, it was getting addressed right then," says Antoine Caldwell, a team captain of the 2008 team. "There was no more after the fact or let things slide; we were addressing things immediately. And it makes a world of difference. When you draw a line in the sand, it permeates through the team."

Alabama players worked harder than ever in the Fourth Quarter Program to get ready for the upcoming season. The results started showing right away as Alabama knocked off No. 9 Clemson in the season-opener. Before a highly anticipated game against No. 3 Georgia, strength and conditioning coach Scott Cochran told the players Georgia was wearing black that night because they were headed to a funeral. Alabama won 41–30.

In just his second year at Alabama, Saban guided the Crimson Tide to a perfect 12–0 regular season record. Everything he had preached seemed to be working headed into a No. 1 vs. No. 2 showdown against Florida in the SEC Championship. The winner moved on to the national championship game. Alabama had the talent to compete with Florida and even had a fourth-quarter lead, but the veteran maturity of quarterback Tim Tebow and the Gators proved to be too much. Years later, when Caldwell asked Saban why he thought Alabama lost, the coach told him they were the better team but they didn't believe it yet. The loss was devastating for Alabama players who had invested so much into winning the SEC only to come up short. They stumbled into a Sugar Bowl against Utah with one former player joking that most of them were "still on Bourbon Street when the game kicked off." Utah crushed the Tide, 31–17, leading some outside the program to question just how legitimate Alabama's undefeated regular season was.

But that heartbreaking loss to Florida was an extra piece of motivation to power all the necessary off-season work to make sure it wouldn't happen again in 2009. After the SEC Championship loss, future Heisman Trophy winner Mark Ingram walked up to Caldwell and told him, "We are going to handle this next year. Don't even worry about it."

"I believed it one thousand percent," Caldwell says. "They were going to be back again and they were going to destroy them the next year."

"When we lost to Florida in the SEC Championship, I knew we were going to win a national championship the next year," says Blalock. "I can't explain it to you but I just knew. And we went out there, and we did it."

A year later, Alabama took care of business like Ingram promised and easily defeated Florida, 32–13, in an SEC Championship rematch on the path to a national championship.

Failure hurts, but it can be a great learning experience. Alabama needed losses like those against Louisiana Monroe and Florida to get everyone on board with the level of dedication and commitment required to become champions. Most of us don't get a chance to win a national championship, but the ability to rebound in the wake of a loss is applicable everywhere. When managing a group of people who just suffered a defeat, whether that's missing out on a big contract or not meeting expectations, remember that it serves as a great opportunity to redirect their sense of loss into a greater good. Saban has repeatedly talked about how much easier it is to get everyone's attention after a loss. It is human nature not to want to feel like a loser after a defeat, which is why people might be the most open to change or coaching in those immediate moments afterward. Take advantage of it.

"It's really making guys refocus, whether it was discipline, actions off the field, classroom. All of that is a buildup," says Christion Jones, who experienced only a handful of losses in his time at Alabama. "It's him trying to exploit that situation and letting people know, 'If we correct this, we won't be in this situation.' It's not about chewing guys out, it's all about moving forward. What are we going to do this week to eliminate the things that created a loss for ourselves last week?"

One of the rare losses Jones experienced at Alabama came on November 10, 2012, when Johnny Manziel and the Texas A&M Aggies traveled to Tuscaloosa. The two-loss Aggies went into the game ranked No. 15 in the country but were still nearly two-touchdown underdogs against Alabama. The outside world didn't give Texas A&M much of a shot, but it had two big things going for it: Manziel, who would go on to win the Heisman Trophy, and the timing of the game. A week earlier, in a rematch of the 2011 national championship game, No. 1 Alabama narrowly beat No. 5 LSU, 21–17, in Baton Rouge. Alabama won on a last-minute T. J. Yeldon touchdown after the Crimson Tide nearly blew a 14–3 halftime lead. The thrilling victory was one of the best games of the season, a result the team struggled to move past. "I could tell in practice and [Saban] knew it, too, even in warm-ups—these people are still thinking about last week," says former Alabama running back Ben Howell. "We had a big letdown because of that, and he knew it."

Texas A&M threw the gauntlet down from the get-go, building a 20–0 first-quarter lead it would never relinquish. Alabama had a spirited comeback attempt in the second half only to fall short in a 29–23 loss. Manziel accounted for 345 of Texas A&M's 418 offensive yards, plus two passing touchdowns, and overnight became the Heisman favorite. Recognizing it was a lack of effort and concentration rather than a lack of talent that resulted in the loss, Saban used the experience to galvanize his team.

"He made every senior stand up and say why this is not going to happen again," Howell says. "He had [captain] Barrett Jones stand up and say what he was going to do. He said, 'What are you going to do to make sure we don't lose again? What are you going to do personally?'"

The coverage of the loss mostly centered on what it meant for Alabama's national championship hopes. A *New York Times* headline said, "Error-Prone Alabama Seals Its Loss, and Maybe, Its Fate," while the Associated Press recap said the loss left Alabama with "badly bruised national championship hopes." Saban reminded his team they had been in this position before, including the previous season, and still found a way to win it all. Those comments, along with the seniors feeling the pressure to do more, accomplished what Saban intended. "When we came back that Sunday, you could tell it was a different team," Jones says. "Coach Saban wasn't flustered. Everybody was saying, 'From here on out all we can do is control what we can control.'" Alabama went on to win the remainder of its games that season on its way to another national championship, its third in four seasons.

That Alabama didn't win three consecutive national championships is the result of a play you can watch one hundred times and still marvel at how improbable it was. What happened at the end of the 2013 Iron Bowl will still be played in Alabama homes long after the rest of us have left this world. Known as the "Kick Six," it might be the most famous play in college football history. Alabama watched its national title hopes implode when Auburn's Chris Davis returned a missed Adam Griffith field goal 109 yards for a game-winning touchdown. Jones thinks Saban still has to have sleepless nights over that loss, while the Alabama head coach has said he'll never get over it.

Initially, the officials ruled the game was over and headed to overtime after a 23-yard T. J. Yeldon run took the ball to the 39-yard line. Saban immediately protested that there should be one second left on the clock, which referee Matt Austin later confirmed was true. Rather than go to overtime tied, Saban sent in backup kicker Griffith to attempt a 57-yard field goal. It was a risky move given Griffith had never tried a kick that long. The rest is Iron Bowl history.

As the last game of the regular season, everyone knew what the loss meant. There was no chance to bounce back and still compete for a national championship the way it had the previous two seasons after a loss. Auburn extinguished Alabama's chances at a three-peat, and the effect was immediate. By the time Saban made it to the locker room after Auburn fans swarmed the field, he saw a heartbroken group of players.

"You walk in and everyone is crying. Fifty percent crying and fifty percent tearing up," Jones says. "Coach Saban was in tears—he could barely talk. His face was red. Everyone was emotional; it was a funeral moment."

Situations like that prompt less direct action and more empathy. Sometimes you just need to let your team know you are hurting just as bad as they are. Once the team has had a chance to mourn the loss, that's when Saban steps back in and uses it as a learning lesson. Saban tells his team all the time that in life, you have to have perseverance. There will be obstacles that appear seemingly out of nowhere that you did nothing to create or deserve. Those obstacles can be frustrating, devastating, and debilitating, but if you can overcome them, it can be empowering. "You cannot have a great victory in life unless you can overcome adversity," Saban likes to say. "The adversity is what makes it a great victory."

Long before getting to Alabama, Saban overcame an obstacle many face at some point in their careers. He was fired. Saban will go down as the greatest college football coach ever, but even he has lost a job before. It happened only once but it taught him a valuable lesson that has powered much of his success.

An ambitious Saban worked hard to move his way up the ranks, jumping from Kent State to Syracuse to West Virginia as a young coach. It was then he felt like he had hit the big time when Ohio State offensive coordinator Glen Mason and defensive coordinator Dennis Fryzel vouched for him to get a job on Earle Bruce's staff in 1980. He was only twenty-eight years old and his career was now on the fast track as the college football power's new defensive backs coach. The Buckeyes opened the season as the nation's No. 1 team and started 9–1 before losing the last two games of the season to Michigan and Penn State. Saban was well regarded for recruiting and working with the team's young defensive backs, though he occasionally clashed with Bruce over which players to recruit and the best defensive secondary schemes to use. Bruce was resistant to change, believing if he kept doing what had previously led to success, the good times would never end. Saban saw the game was changing and that Ohio State needed to change with it, but didn't always convey that in the most respectful manner to his boss during staff meetings. Thinking you know more than your boss isn't an uncommon feeling, but years later Saban would tell friends it taught him to always respect the chain of command. "He told me that's when [he] learned the head coach is the head coach," says former Cleveland Browns scout Chris Landry. "You may think you're right and you may be right, but the head coach is the head coach. If you challenge that authority, it doesn't work."

Ohio State again went 9–3 the following season, but there was tension building after early-season losses to Florida State and Wisconsin. Bruce at one point banned his assistants from talking to the media only to find Fryzel speaking to reporters after an uninspiring Liberty Bowl win over Navy. An incensed Bruce quickly called for an early-morning meeting the following day and then fired his entire defensive staff. In a moment, a thirty-year-old Saban went from a coach on the rise to unemployed. "It never should have happened," Mason says. "He got caught up in friction between the head coach and another assistant coach and became collateral damage."

The experience of being fired had a profound effect on Saban. He wrote in his book it made him rethink making coaching his career, question his abilities, and think hard about whether the instability was worth it. "I had failed," Saban wrote. "I was devastated and humiliated."

He didn't wallow in that feeling long, though. He quickly connected with former WVU colleague Gary Tranquill, who was then Navy's head coach, and packed his bags for Maryland. It was a significant career drop for Saban, who went from recruiting the top players in the country to trying to find players willing to sign up for a service academy that came with mandatory service after graduation. The firing proved to be a blessing in disguise when

Saban got to know a veteran coach on Tranquill's staff named Steve Belichick. Through the elder Belichick, Saban met his son Bill, which birthed a close friendship between two of football's greatest coaches ever.

Saban would never again be fired after the Ohio State experience. It wasn't simply because of his prodigious talents, either. He hated the feeling he experienced when Bruce fired him, and he decided that he would never feel that way again, pushing an already-strong work ethic to new heights.

"In coaching you preach to your players all the time—and you better buy into it yourself—when you get knocked down you get up and go again," Mason says. "A lot of guys when they get to a place like Ohio State and get fired, you think, 'Oh man, what do I do now?' He landed on his feet because he's a real good coach, but initially he didn't land at another Ohio State. He got off the ground and went to work."

Of Saban's seven national championship–winning teams, only two made it through the season undefeated. Five teams that ended the season crowned as the best in the country suffered through a loss at some juncture in the season, rebounded from it, and emerged as champions. Five different times a champion team had to not only get past a loss, but find the value in it. For many of those championship teams, it was the loss that brought things into focus, that centered the organization on what needed to be accomplished to avoid suffering that fate again. It was a hard reset for everyone on what happens when there wasn't 100 percent buy-in, and prompted a change in behavior and mindset. Loss is inevitable, both professionally and personally, but it is up to each individual to choose how to respond to it. One of Saban's favorite sayings, one he uses whenever an obstacle pops up, is, "So what? Now what?" It made it less about what just happened and more about, "What are we going to do about it?" For Saban, that "now what?" offered a timely opportunity to grab his organization's attention to reestablish the necessary commitment for future success.

CHAPTER 13

Evaluate Yourself Constantly, Evolve When Necessary

The most famous coach in college football couldn't stop himself from getting fired up about what he saw happening in the game he loved.

Fresh off an Alabama win over Hugh Freeze's Ole Miss team, a reporter asked Saban what he thought about the no-huddle, spread offense trend starting to take over college football. He had thoughts—a lot of them, it turned out.

He thought the increased game tempo created player safety concerns because of the inability to swap players in between plays. The players couldn't get lined up correctly, Saban said, and that's "when guys have a much greater chance of getting hurt when they're not ready to play."

He recognized why coaches were doing it, noting it led to very high-scoring outputs and created "a tremendous advantage for the offense." Knowing the way the winds were blowing, Saban wanted to know if it was the right direction.

He wrapped up his comments with a question: "Is this what we want football to be?"

At the time, news coverage painted Saban's take as a grumpy coach complaining after his defense struggled to keep up with the high-powered offenses starting to populate the SEC. With hindsight, though, those comments were really a warning to the rest of college football. Saban didn't want football to head in that direction—he is a defensive-minded coach, after all—but he saw the advantages of playing that way.

Saban adopted the mindset of: I don't want to play this way, but if this is what you all want, I will do it better than you.

He'd go on to win his third national championship that season utilizing a defense-first, conservative-offense style. Then the transition began. It took only a few years for an Alabama offense famous for a ground-and-pound approach to become one of the most electrifying and high-scoring offenses in college football. When Saban won his first Alabama title in 2009, he had the nation's second-best defense (11.7 points per game) and the twenty-second-best offense (34.1 ppg). When he won his sixth title in 2020, he had the nation's second-best offense (48.5 ppg) and thirteenth-best defense (19.3 ppg). Saban won four national championships with one style, saw the game was changing, and adjusted on his way to winning three more titles in a completely different way.

"I grew up with the idea that you play good defense, you run the ball, you control vertical field position on special teams, you're going to win," Saban explained. "Whoever rushes the ball for the most yards is going to win the game. You're not going to win anything now doing that."

"Coach Saban has shown time and again that he is 100 percent never so set in his ways that he's unwilling to compromise the system to change it up to continue getting the best formula for success each given year," says former Alabama defensive back Will Lowery. "He continues to adapt his team, his program, his approach, his process around the game of college football because it's changing at a rapid pace between the rules and players, how recruiting is done and how the players are themselves."

One of the biggest misperceptions about Saban is he's a rigid man unwilling to change his ways. The truth is he's very rigid about certain things like The Process of not focusing on results in the pursuit of greatness, but he's willing to change other aspects of his strategy and coaching. He's constantly evaluating what he's doing and tweaking his approach whenever necessary to put his organization in the best spot to be successful. Sometimes that meant bringing in people like Lane Kiffin, armed with new ideas and perspectives to push the organization forward, as detailed in chapter five. Other times it meant changing how hard to push the team in practices before a big game so they were at their most ready, as we learned in chapter eleven. He was never so set in his ways that he was unwilling to evolve, especially if a better way of doing things presented itself.

"I think he says, 'How do I improve my methodology in making people better?'" says Pat Perles, who played for him at Michigan State and later coached with him at Toledo. "As a coach, how do I make my coaches better? Who do I need to talk to? Who do I need to read and study?"

It's one reason why he brings in consultants like The Pacific Institute and Trevor Moawad to help players with their mental conditioning. It's why he brings in famous speakers like Kobe Bryant, Mike Tyson, and Michael Jordan to talk to the organization about their approach and what it took to achieve the success they had. It's why he brings in people like John Underwood, who founded the Human Performance Project and taught the "Life of an Athlete" presentation. Saban's right-hand man, Ellis Ponder, booked Underwood to give a talk to the team about his research into sleep dynamics, positive leadership, and the daily commitment it takes to be successful. Underwood has worked with Navy SEALs, Olympians, and countless professional and collegiate sports organizations. As he addressed the Alabama players and coaches, he looked over and saw Saban in the first row, dutifully taking notes the entire hour-long speech. "He is a calm man, a thinker," Underwood says. "He is constantly looking for anything that can make his program better. He is not the typical big and loud football coach."

By the time Johnny Manziel and Texas A&M rolled into Tuscaloosa in 2012, Saban knew change was needed. Attending that game were Christian Miller, a four-star linebacker out of South Carolina, and his father, Corey, a nine-year NFL veteran. As they watched Manziel make his Heisman Trophy case in leading the Aggies to an upset win over Alabama, the Millers were struck by how badly Tide defensive players struggled to keep up with the speedy quarterback. Every linebacker Alabama started weighed at least 245 pounds, forty more than the younger Miller, who questioned his fit in the

Tide's defensive scheme at the time. After the game, Saban used the loss to answer Miller's concerns.

"We are transitioning to guys like you," Saban told Christian. "We need long, athletic, rangy guys who can play the run but also pass rush, can cover tight ends, and can be a buzz drop in the flats."

In his first few years at Alabama, Saban preferred big, strong linebackers like Rolando McClain and Dont'a Hightower. The NFL-trained coach recruited specialty players for specific situational defenses. He used a massive nose tackle at the center of his 3-4 base defense, guys like the 370-pound Terrence Cody, who delivered the "Rocky Block" to preserve a win over Tennessee in 2009. It became too challenging to substitute players when teams utilized no-huddle spread offenses. Alabama couldn't afford to play someone like Cody and risk him getting stuck out there. As the game shifted toward a basketball-on-grass style, Saban realized his defense needed to get faster and more athletic if it was going to slow down the A&M and Ole Miss offenses. The Tide needed players who could play every down on defense. It needed players like Miller and five-star linebacker Rashaan Evans.

Saban hired Ole Miss director of recruiting, Tyler Siskey, to help with the transition. The critical-factors sheet the organization relied on had to change as they looked for different types of players to fill spots all over the field—defensive line, linebacker, and defensive secondary. Alabama's recruiting process had to change, and it required hard work to accurately project out and acquire the new types of players it needed.

"The guys who were athletic enough, big enough, and physical enough to play linebacker in this league in that system were not playing linebacker in high school," Siskey says. "They were playing rush end, so you ran into an issue where you're trying to fight the instincts of the players."

Here's what's notable: Even after losing to Texas A&M, Alabama still went on to win the national championship that season. Saban didn't start shifting his defensive approach, especially in recruiting, after hitting rock bottom and having no choice but to change if he wanted to keep his job. He started the shift at the top of his industry, realizing if he wanted to keep hoisting that trophy above his head at the end of the season, he couldn't stay static.

"If you want to sit there and cry and mope that the rules have changed and you don't like it, you do that," says former Georgia head coach Mark Richt. "Or you can say, 'These are the rules, what can I do to succeed?' He has the ability to do that, to see it and make the change and have everybody on board to get it done as quickly as it needs to get done."

If that seems easy, there's a long list of businesses once on top of the world now out of business because they failed to react to industry changes. Blockbuster Video used to be one of the most powerful entertainment companies in the world but passed up on a chance to get in the streaming game, paving the path for Netflix. Blockbuster even had an opportunity to acquire Netflix for $50 million in 2000, but its leaders thought the online company's business model wasn't sustainable and basically laughed Netflix executives out of the room. A decade later, Blockbuster filed for bankruptcy and Netflix had a $10 billion market cap. By 2020, Netflix was worth more than $200 billion.

Quiznos brought innovation to the competitive sandwich market when it started toasting sandwiches. It was a hit, and the company exploded to 4,700 locations worldwide. But once competitors like Subway added the ability to do the same, Quiznos couldn't find the next thing to stay ahead of the curve and started hemorrhaging market share once Subway debuted the $5 footlong sandwich deal. Quiznos filed for bankruptcy in 2014.

It is much harder to make a change when things are going well than when they aren't. During a time NetApp was flourishing as a company, Tom Mendoza hired Harvard Business School professor John Kotter, whose leading change theory we explored in chapter one, to review the company's business model and efficiency. It was a rarity for Kotter, who worked with companies all over the world, and he told Mendoza that NetApp was one of only three successful companies to hire him when things were going well rather than declining. Kotter said that 80 percent of companies that set out to change fail, and the reason was they couldn't maintain a sense of urgency. Kotter explained that a sense of urgency is mostly built around a "burning platform"—essentially, 'If we don't immediately do this, our organization will fail.' That call to action can work for a period of time, but it won't last forever.

"It's not a sustainable reason for people to get up in the morning wanting to do something different," Mendoza says. "Eventually it'll get a little better and they'll say, 'Why do I need to keep doing this?' The alternative is that you change because you have a vision that what we can do is much more spectacular.

"Many companies get one idea and think, 'If we don't change anything, we'll be good forever.' That's never true. The world doesn't work like that; it doesn't sit still waiting for you."

With Saban, the change wasn't always about the recruits he pursued but the way he interacted with them. Some call it mellowing that comes with getting older and seeing your children have children of their own. And that likely played a role in Saban's outward demeanor softening ever so slightly. But it was also responding to the way the world was changing. Saban couldn't coach his 2020 Alabama team how he coached his 1990 Toledo team, because the people involved were different. They reacted differently to situations and expected more from their coaches.

In 2020, Saban oversaw a group of young, mostly Black, men who had to grapple with a tumultuous and traumatic summer after George Floyd was murdered in Minnesota. For most of his career, Saban stayed away from controversial topics. He's not going to endorse an Alabama politician, and outside of a few key issues close to his heart—the opioid crisis and suicide prevention, among a couple of others—he tries to stick to what he knows best. And yet there Saban was side by side with his players leading a Black Lives Matter march. It's hard to imagine a young Saban doing that, not because he didn't care, but because that outward showing wasn't expected back then.

Saban needed to evolve his style to connect with a new generation of players such as running back Najee Harris, who was often homesick at Alabama and clashed early with his head coach. Younger players like Harris not only needed to know more of the "why" behind Saban's decisions, but also expected him to be more than just a coach. When Harris and other players approached Saban in August to tell him about their plans to march, Saban reacted like a "proud father" that they proactively did it rather than wait for him to address it. His response and willingness to support the players in a cause that mattered a great deal to them had a considerable impact on the team, Harris explained in my employer AL.com's fantastic *Road to the Pros* documentary series.

"I feel like that's what really made us win this championship, to be so close," Harris said. "That's what made the team really gain trust in him and respect for Saban other than football. That's what really propelled it—when the issues happened and that's what really made us bond together as a team."

It can be a weird experience for former Saban players to see him now. They might catch an all-access feature on television and see him cracking jokes and smiling during a practice. The players who signed up to play for Saban in the early years can remember him smiling only once or twice a season, usually after a national championship win. Greg McElroy, the starting quarterback on Saban's first Alabama title team, says his relationship with his head coach was purely business. "Quid pro quo," McElroy says. "If I throw a touchdown, he likes me. If I throw an interception, he doesn't like me. That was all the relationship I wanted." It's a sentiment shared by plenty of others on those early Saban teams.

"If you walked in a hallway past Saban and he smiled at you, you might have been scared like he did something," says Paris Hodges, a member of LSU's 2003 title team. "He was going to walk into that meeting room with his no socks on with his shoes and look like he's coming out of a board meeting because that's how everything was treated. It was straight to business, man."

Christion Jones, who won two national championships (2011, 2012) as an Alabama receiver, believes Saban couldn't show a lighter side of himself early on. There was so much work to be done when he first arrived at Alabama, Jones says, that Saban had to maintain a certain outward demeanor to set the tone for how things needed to be done. Saban didn't want anyone getting the wrong impression he was trying to be their friend and would let things slip to maintain that relationship. "Once he set that standard, he had to hold that standard for about five, six years," Jones says. "I think he was smart enough to understand when to become the fun coach."

Those in the program around that time point to a tragic loss of a former player in 2015 as the impetus behind Saban's shift in showing more of his personality. Altee Tenpenny was a can't-miss prospect out of Little Rock, Arkansas, a U.S. Army All-American and one of the nation's top high school running backs. He arrived in Tuscaloosa as part of a star-studded 2013 recruiting class that included future NFL star running backs Derrick Henry and Alvin Kamara. Tenpenny had a big smile and an infectious personality, a young man people naturally gravitated toward and wanted to be around. He had that innate ability to connect with anyone and everyone around him, regardless of racial background or economic status.

Headed to Tuscaloosa as the top player from the state of Arkansas, Tenpenny struggled transitioning to college and the structure in place at Alabama. He didn't get a lot of playing time in a crowded running back room and got in trouble for a marijuana possession charge and for missing meetings. After the 2014 season, Tenpenny made the decision to transfer to UNLV despite Saban's best efforts to keep him at Alabama. Saban wasn't happy with some of Tenpenny's conduct, asking him to sign a contract promising to stay out of trouble, but he believed he could do it at Alabama. At his core, Saban always believed he could help a person within his organization.

Tenpenny lasted only a few months at UNLV before he was kicked off the team. He resurfaced at Nicholls State in Louisiana in August, where he again ran into trouble and never played a game before leaving the program in October. He packed up his things and began the long drive from Houma, Louisiana, back home to Little Rock. While driving on U.S. Highway 1 in Mississippi, Tenpenny is believed to have fallen asleep at the wheel and crashed his Dodge Charger. Tenpenny died from the injuries sustained from the one-car accident. He was only twenty years old.

The news of Tenpenny's death hit Saban and the team hard. Many of Alabama's players had kept in touch with Tenpenny, who stayed a great friend until the moment he died. A heart-stricken Saban addressed the team and said, "It's hard for me like I know it's hard for you guys. If there's anybody that needs help or wants to talk, please come see me, come talk to anybody on our staff." Days later, sensing his team was still profoundly affected by the situation, Saban made a small gesture that meant everything to the team. Saban could be very old-school, traditionalist in how he expected things to look, which meant he didn't like wild alternative uniforms, flashy clothing, and wasn't a fan of putting stickers on the back of helmets the way other programs did. But that week he announced to the team they would put number 28 stickers on the back of every helmet to honor Tenpenny.

"When he said we could put that 28 sticker on our helmet, it was like we all got drafted first-round," says former Alabama right tackle Dominick Jackson. "It meant the world. It was that piece of safe haven to finish through that we needed."

The loss of Tenpenny greatly impacted Saban. He felt guilty for not doing more, for not finding a way to save a young man who had so much promise ahead of him. Saban was always disappointed when it didn't work out with a player, often willing to give players second chances, and Tenpenny's death amplified all those usual feelings. Saban quietly paid for Tenpenny's funeral costs, a gesture the private Saban made far more often than anyone knew, but he recognized it needed to be more than that. Players on that team noticed Saban eased up more around them and became more willing to joke around. It was around that time Saban started using his famous "Deez Nuts" jokes more often around his players, a juvenile joke that showed a mischievous, fun side of Saban that his team loved. The guarded Saban brought down his walls, not all the way, but enough for players to see a softer side of him, which deepened the connection between coach and team.

"After Tenpenny died, he really became that nurturing father that 98 percent of us need, in all honesty, the ones who didn't have a father figure growing up and only had mentors or coaches," Jackson says. "When Tenpenny died, he had more jokes and was just more of a human. Not so much business and ball. For him to show that vulnerability and show his feelings to us—to let us into his natural him and not just coach—it says a lot about his character and who he is."

That next spring, Keith Holcombe was splitting time between football spring practice and playing baseball. Saban, a baseball fan, would walk up to Holcombe when he was stretching and ask him how he performed that weekend. In one instance, Holcombe had a particularly good weekend and informed Saban he had multiple hits including a double. Saban looked at him and said, "Gosh, I used to hit three dingers a week. They don't make them like they used to anymore. Man, you gotta be better," before walking away and laughing.

"As soon as we step off the field, or as soon as we step out of the football facility, he's the most personable guy you'll ever meet," Holcombe says. "He'll do absolutely anything for his players, you can sit down and talk about golf, talk about baseball. Coach Saban is one heck of a man."

Former Alabama tight end Hunter Bryant, who played on the team from 2014–2017, says the Tenpenny situation changed Saban to become "more joyful and more emotional." He noticed it his last two seasons at Alabama, when Saban told those teams they were two of his favorites he had ever coached. The Alabama head coach rarely, if ever, opened himself up like that to his teams early in his career. "He definitely softened and maybe it became more real the effect he had on these guys," Bryant says, "and the opportunity to build those relationships, and to really enjoy the powerful things he was doing with them."

When Saban got his first head coaching job at Toledo, he operated primarily off a one-size-fits-all manual. He wanted a fair and equitable system in which no one got special treatment and everyone was held to the same standard. He learned over time that wasn't the most effective strategy. Nearly every former player mentioned how Saban's best skill might be his ability to read people and determine the best way to motivate them. He learned that when he yelled at players, some would respond well to it and others would go in the tank. As he got older and more experienced, he became a master at reaching all the various personalities that came through his organization. He modified his approach to benefit each individual better.

Consider the story of punter JK Scott. He could be the best punter Alabama has ever had, but he was a bit of an unknown when he first arrived in Tuscaloosa. Alabama didn't spend as much time evaluating him as it would for a quarterback or offensive tackle, so there were questions about how good he was when he arrived on campus.

At Scott's first practice, Siskey remembers sidling up next to Saban to see what they had. Almost immediately, they felt great about their future punter. Scott was crushing the ball, launching punts high and long, a skill he would show off plenty in an Alabama uniform those next four years. But then Brendan Farrell, a special teams analyst, asked Scott to adjust how he was dropping the ball and the angles he was kicking it from. It was only his first practice, and Scott went along with his coach's advice. His results took a nosedive, though, as he mishit the ball over and over again using this new technique.

Saban had seen enough. He called over Farrell and told him, "Don't say another fucking word to him. You let him do whatever he wants to do."

On another day in Scott's first year at Alabama, Saban again walked up to his punter shanking the ball. He asked him what the problem was, and Scott said the backs of his hamstrings were too tight; he couldn't properly extend his kicking leg after a heavy lifting session in the weight room the previous day. Saban nodded and moved on to another section of the practice. Two hours later, Saban instructed Siskey to gather every coach for a meeting after practice and to make sure strength and conditioning coach Scott Cochran was in attendance.

"Ahh shit," Cochran said when he heard Saban was looking for him. He knew what was coming. Once everyone arrived, Saban launched into it.

"I don't care what it costs, go get whatever machine this kid wants," the Alabama head coach said. "[JK] doesn't have to lift weights with another freaking group the rest of his time he's here. Let him go lift whatever the hell he wants to do, send him off to the side, and get him whatever leg machine he wants."

After that meeting, Siskey says, "JK Scott ran that place."

There's something amusing about Saban allowing a punter of all players to get perceived special treatment, but it came from realizing that Scott needed a different set of tasks than an offensive lineman or linebacker. Forcing Scott to do the same thing as other positions just for the sake of equitability, especially the same weight training, would have been a mistake. Not only was it not going to help Scott to do that, but it was also actually detrimental to his chances of helping the team. If Saban insisted on doing it the way he always had, Scott would have been a less effective player.

Once you become successful, it gets even harder to change. Why mess with a good thing, right? It would have been easy for Saban to look down at his three championship rings in 2012 and plow forward with the style that won them. There was a part of him that wanted to, too. For as good as Saban was at making the necessary big changes to philosophies and strategies, it was still challenging for him. He readily questioned the need for evolution at times when Kiffin and analyst Eric Kiesau introduced no-huddle, faster-tempo offensive concepts.

"Why do I have to do this?" Saban asked Kiffin and Kiesau more than once. "I win twelve games a year, I win SEC championships, I win national championships. Why do I have to change?"

"I think it was really hard for Coach Saban at first," Kiesau says. "I think in the back of his mind he knew he had to change because the game was changing."

Had he never evolved, it likely would have kept working for a while, too. Alabama was getting outstanding players, and that wasn't going to change for the foreseeable future, or maybe ever, as long as Saban was there. But if Alabama refused to evolve, eventually innovative competitors would have surpassed it, and once that happens, it becomes tough to play catch-up. Instead, Saban adjusted on the fly, and Alabama never really suffered from drastically evolving the organization's offensive and defensive philosophies. In that transition period, Alabama was the Kick Six away from playing in the title game in 2013 and made it to the national semifinal in 2014.

Saban built a whole second run of Alabama success because not only did he recognize the game was changing, but he was willing to change with it. It went against what he philosophically believed in, but he was never so egotistical to put his preferences over helping the team. So Saban hired coaches like Kiffin, recruited players like Miller, and evolved. Not because he wanted to but because he realized he needed to. He pulled it off seamlessly because he was constantly evaluating whether his organization was reaching its potential and was always willing to evolve when it wasn't.

CHAPTER 14

Honesty Is Hard but Critical

S aban was upset. Very upset, one might say.

At a walk-through practice, one of Alabama's managers spotted the ball at the wrong spot. Everything during Alabama practices is scripted to the nth degree, so a variance sent Saban over the edge. He loudly and in no uncertain terms let the manager know he was upset about the mistake.

Alabama defensive back Will Lowery remembers watching it unfold and thinking it might have been unnecessary. "It was just the ball boy," Lowery says. "I felt bad for him. Give the guy a break."

The very next play, Lowery heard Saban yelling at someone the exact same way he had yelled at the manager. As Lowery looked over to see the recipient of Saban's ire, he saw offensive coordinator Jim McElwain. Saban was upset about something and let McElwain know in front of the whole team.

"You've got the ball boy and then you've got the assistant head coach, number two guy in the program, and if you didn't know whose name was who, you wouldn't have been able to tell the difference when he ripped their butts," Lowery says. "He ripped them the same way. Everybody is held accountable for their jobs with the exact same intensity."

"I thought when those moments happened, they were incredible moments not just for the program as a whole but for those players to see, 'This is the level of focus we're supposed to have in our practice, even the coaches,'" says Louis LeBlanc, a former Alabama GA.

Saban's style wasn't for everyone, but he never shied away from a confrontation if he felt it would benefit the organization. If you've ever had to tell an employee they aren't doing a good enough job, you know how hard that conversation can be. It's a skill that doesn't come naturally to all leaders, as plenty would prefer to be liked by their direct reports rather than pushing them to be their best. It can be uncomfortable having those difficult conversations or calling someone out who's not getting it done, but it's an important part of leadership.

Harvard psychologist J. Richard Hackman, the author of *Leading Teams: Setting the Stage for Great Performances*, believes the most effective leaders possess four essential components: they need to know some things, they need to know how to do some things, they need an above-average level of emotional maturity, and they need personal courage. When he studied what made the best leaders, he concluded that organizations can fall into the trap of "participation management," or trying to please everyone, and that the success came from establishing a clear, challenging direction that had real consequences for the organization.

With the personal courage component, Hackman writes, "Leadership involves moving a system from where it is now to some other, better place. That means that the leader must operate at the margins of what members presently like and want rather than at the center of the collective consensus. This requires challenging existing group norms and disrupting established routines, which can elicit anger and resistance. Leaders who behave courageously can make significant differences in how their teams operate but they may wind up paying a substantial personal toll in the bargain."

It's not easy to push people beyond what they believe they are capable of accomplishing. Saban wanted everyone within the organization—and the organization itself—to reach the apex of their potential and was going to push and prod every day to try to make that happen. If Saban saw someone making a mistake, he'd step in and correct it immediately. There was no letting things slide in practice because they occurred during practice and not a game. The small things mattered. Saban was fighting to hold on to the established standard every day, and letting little mistakes go was a surefire way for that standard to erode.

"Critique and praise all day long," says former Missouri coach Gary Pinkel, a college teammate of Saban's at Kent State. "Constant evaluation. Not bring a guy in every three months and talk to him. I'm talking daily, if something's not right, he's going to fix it. He's not going to wait three or four weeks."

Saban was aware that wouldn't work for everyone. He knew not everyone wanted to be pushed that hard, and it would lead to accusations of being a jerk, or worse. His style reminded former players and coaches of Chicago Bulls great Michael Jordan. In the multi-part documentary *The Last Dance*, an emotional Jordan talks about the toll of pushing his teammates to be their best. "When people see this, they're gonna say, 'Well, he wasn't a nice guy, he may have been a tyrant,'" Jordan says. "Well, that's because you never won anything. I wanted to win, but I wanted them to win and be a part of this as well."

That was Saban. He directly connected to that Jordan quote, telling one reporter, "Everybody wants to be comfortable, but you've got to get used to being uncomfortable if you're really going to be successful and you're really good. I could really relate to that because that's what we've always tried to get the players in our program to do. Some understand it, some don't."

"They think he's a tyrant, they think he's a bully, and he's everything but that," says Todd Alles, who has known Saban for more than forty years. "He's got a presentation that's got some rough edges, but Nick Saban the man loves those kids and he wants them to be successful so bad, maybe even more than some of their parents want them to be successful. He's more proud of what they do after they leave the program than when they are in the program."

Saban wasn't the kind of leader to freely tell his staff how much he loved them. He wasn't giving out big hugs to everyone who walked through the front door each day. He mellowed some over the years and became more emotional as the years passed, but his love language was really acts of service. He showed his love by giving each member of his organization the road map to success in life. Saban believed if he could do that, even if his system was arduous and could push you to the brink, they'd respect what he did for them in the long run. "His job was to get you better, to make you more money," says former Houston Oilers cornerback Cris Dishman. "Most coaches want to be your buddy and tell you what you want to hear. Nick is going to tell you what he sees and move on. He doesn't care that we aren't going to be the best of friends. He knows if he's truthful with you, you're going to be his friend."

"He was hard to play for, he was hard to coach for, and he was very demanding," says former LSU offensive lineman Brandon Hurley. "He's not the warmest, sweetest guy in the world, but he would never ask anybody to do something he wasn't willing to do in terms of putting in the work, preparation, and being super detail-oriented, leaving no stone unturned. He was the best at it, and he demanded that out of us."

There was a point to Saban's style: he was cranking up the pressure every day because he knew how tough it was outside the organization. If you couldn't handle Saban yelling at you in the low stakes of a practice, how would you handle the stress of a big game? If you didn't feel confident enough to push back against Saban in a meeting, how could he trust you to have the confidence to make a hard decision in a pressurized moment? Multiple former coaches and staffers referred to working for Saban as a "pressure cooker" that he cranked up daily. Saban would much rather accept the uncomfortableness of being the bad guy to have the tough conversations before the big event than have to console a group of people upset over a defeat. His words could be coarse and abrasive at times—former Alabama receivers coach Mike Groh says to succeed working under Saban, "You gotta be the alligator, not the onion"—but the end goal was always to make everyone better.

"If you're going to crumble over a little bit of words by a man that really cares and loves you, there's no way you can handle the criticism on TV and playing in front of five million people on TV or in front of one hundred thousand people screaming at the top of [their] lungs intoxicated and having fun," says former Alabama right tackle Dominick Jackson. "You can't be that soft in football, I promise you."

It also stoked the other side of the honesty coin. He needed the people around him to be honest in their opinions and assessments of everything from which players to recruit to the strategy for a big game. If his staff couldn't tell him when he was wrong, Saban knew he was in trouble. It's why he pushed and prodded his coaches—so they had the confidence to push back against the leader. As former NetApp president Tom Mendoza explained it to me, "If you live in an ivory tower and no one can talk to you, you better be real smart because they're only going to bring you information you want to hear, and you won't get better like that."

Saban's unrelenting approach can lead to some challenging moments along the way. There will be resistance to being pushed that hard all the time, as he experienced throughout his career. He accepted that being the leader often meant not being the most popular guy in the room. He wasn't letting anyone off the hook just so they'd like him better. While working together at Toledo, L.C. Cole remembers Saban addressing it head-on when going over film one day. Saban would tell his coaches that if they weren't coaching the behavior, they were letting it happen. And if the behavior continued, he had no problem stepping in to squash it. "If you don't want to do it, I'll do it. I'll be the bad guy," Saban told his staff. "I'm going to rip him and chew him out, and then you go to the store and get him some candy."

Hall of Fame coach Bill Parcells believed that being brutally honest with everyone in the organization was the only way to maximize potential. That philosophy no doubt influenced Saban through their shared connection to Bill Belichick, who worked for Parcells in three different NFL organizations. Parcells turned up the heat on Belichick, confronting him in ways that sometimes seemed over the top, but the unvarnished honesty shared between the coaches brought the best out of both as they teamed up for two Super Bowls with the New York Giants. In a *Harvard Business Review* piece titled "The Tough Work of Turning Around a Team," Parcells wrote, "You have to tell them the truth about their performance, you have to tell it to them face-to-face, and you have to tell it to them over and over again. Sometimes the truth will be painful, and sometimes saying it will lead to an uncomfortable confrontation. So be it. The only way to change people is to tell them in the clearest possible terms what they're doing wrong. And if they don't want to listen, they don't belong on the team."

During the football season, postgame film sessions Saban called "The Good, The Bad, and The Ugly" focused on honest, constructive criticism with no feelings spared in the process. Whether it was a win or loss, Saban used the sessions to show that all it took was a few moments here and there to impact the game's outcome. After a win, Saban drilled into players not to get complacent and pointed out all the areas that weren't perfect even in a successful outing. After a loss, it would be a way to build his team back up by showing them it wasn't about what the other team had done but about what they controlled: their own performance. "You walk out of that film meeting thinking, 'We didn't get beat, we obviously beat ourselves,'" says former Alabama tight end Hunter Bryant. "He shows you fifteen key plays that if one or two guys had done their jobs right, the game goes totally differently."

Saban abhorred selfish behavior, a topic he'd return to plenty in his Good, Bad, and Ugly sessions. Early on in his tenure at Alabama, Saban reached the "Ugly" stage of the review and pulled up a play where a player got an unnecessary unsportsmanlike conduct penalty on an extra-point kick late in the game with the outcome already decided. It infuriated Saban, who used that player's bad decision to send a message to the entire team. "That is the most selfish shit I've ever seen," Saban yelled. As some players chuckled while Saban ramped up, he yelled, "It's not about you, what about the team? What about everybody else?" It's what it always came down to for Saban, who wanted everyone in the organization pulling in the same direction together, putting aside selfish desires for the betterment of everyone. Whenever he saw a player or coach go astray from that organizational ethos, he never hesitated to step in and call them out.

If an employee is doing something against what you want, you either step in and correct it or you're letting it happen. There's no blaming it on the person or coming up with excuses for why the mistake happened. You either fix it immediately or do nothing and give up any claim you might have to be upset over it. If the behavior keeps happening after you step in to correct it, it makes it easier to make the hard decision to make a personnel change. You have to be willing to have uncomfortable conversations if you actually want everyone in the organization to reach their potential.

Saban is very honest and clear about his expectations to everyone who works within his organization. As you can gather, those expectations are quite high, but he's straightforward about it. In clear and concise language, he explains what their job responsibilities are and what success looks like. And then he holds everyone accountable for their responsibilities. It eliminates possible confusion about misguided instructions or what they're supposed to be doing daily. Organizations can struggle with efficiency, whether because of a messy hierarchy, changing priorities, or poor communication when employees don't know what they are supposed to be doing. Saban made sure that didn't happen. "You don't have to guess what he's thinking," says Michigan State assistant coach Harlon Barnett. "You've got to love that if you're a hard worker, a winner, and about your business. How he presents it sometimes you might not like, but at least you know. I know what he wants and I know where I stand and I love that about him."

When Barnett linked up with Saban at LSU in 2003, his boss used him to make a point with a team that would go on to win the national championship. Barnett had played for him at Michigan State and for the Cleveland Browns, and Saban would remind his young LSU players their new coach had it much worse than they did.

"He'd go off on a kid and say, 'Tell them, Harlon. I used to be worse than this,'" Barnett says. "And I'm thinking to myself, 'Man, you seem like the same dude to me.'"

Nearly twenty years later, in the lead-up to the 2022 national championship game, defensive coordinator Pete Golding was asked about Saban mellowing and dishing out less "ass chewings." "Absolutely not accurate," Golding said, maybe in part to make sure he didn't earn himself one. "Whatever you do here, Coach is going to make sure you do it to the best of your ability. You do it the way he sees fit, which I enjoy."

When players made mistakes in practices, Saban let their position coach know about it. It created a dynamic in which the players wanted to do their best because they didn't want their coaches getting yelled at for their mistakes. Former Michigan State defensive end Chris Smith thought it was "a genius thing he was doing and it was planned" when Saban went after an assistant coach for a player's mistake in front of him. It solidified a bond between assistant coach and player, a critical factor in getting organizational buy-in, as explained in chapter four. "You didn't want your position coach to look bad," Hurley says. "You spend a lot of time with those coaches so it's a closer relationship and you don't want to let them down."

"The players would bust their ass and try to do exactly what they were supposed to do to spare their position coaches the wrath," says Bill Sheridan, Saban's former linebackers coach at Michigan State. "The players rallied to that. It was all subconscious, no one ever talked about it, but the players tried to protect their position coaches because if they were screwing up, Nick was going to go after the coach."

It had a way of bringing the assistant coaches together, too. Sheridan says the Michigan State coaching staff relished that they had the right attitude and thick-enough skin to flourish in Saban's system. They knew there'd be no special treatment regardless of title and that everyone would have to bring their best to work each day if they didn't want to get called out. Many of them went on to do big things in the coaching realm, including Sheridan, who'd later serve as a defensive coordinator with the New York Giants and the Tampa Bay Buccaneers. When Sheridan was there, the staff included a future NFL head coach (Josh McDaniels), two future Power Five head coaches (Bobby Williams and Mark Dantonio), and a longtime Power Five defensive coordinator (Todd Grantham), among other coaches who'd go on to have success.

"We knew it was the best thing any of us had ever been around; we all thought, 'This is how you're supposed to do it,'" he says. "I guarantee you it was the measuring stick for every guy who left there and coaching at any other place, myself included, and it created incredible staff camaraderie and togetherness. What we were doing was at the top of the line in the profession—we knew that—and it created incredible staff camaraderie like nothing I've ever been around since."

Being a leader also means having the personal courage to be honest for the greater good, even if it upsets members of the organization. Saban experienced that in 2007 when zero Alabama players were taken in the NFL Draft, the first time that had happened since 1970. In the aftermath of that, stories popped up about how Saban was brutally honest to NFL teams about a group of players who didn't put in the hard work and were problems that season.

He directly addressed it with the team and told them he wasn't going to lie to NFL executives, because it would hurt the program in the long term. Saban wasn't going to risk his valued NFL relationships to hype up players who didn't deserve it. He wanted NFL general managers and scouts to trust his opinion when he went to the mat for players he loved. He also depended on those NFL executives to share honest feedback about his players—feedback he relies on to help advise his players on what to do—and he knew they would stop doing that if they felt like he'd hoodwinked them into taking a bad player. That approach is why Saban's opinion is gold to NFL people, who know he won't lie to them just to get a player drafted. It certainly helped in 2020 when he strongly vouched for defensive lineman Christian Barmore after "character concerns" popped up in reports about him. Perhaps it wasn't much of a surprise that old friend Bill Belichick ended up drafting Barmore.

Chicago Bears head coach Matt Eberflus, who played for Saban at Toledo, says it's the embodiment of the things Saban preached thirty years ago.

"He's been around football for so long, he knows that his word is everything to him," Eberflus says. "He's going to be honest and up front. That's what he taught us as players all those years ago. He said your word is everything and whatever you say, you better mean what you're saying. He still does that today.

"If you're going to give him a name or a couple of names, he'll give you an honest opinion on it. He's always done that."

Saban was willing to take the short-term organizational hit, knowing it would upset his team, because he knew it was the right thing to do in the long run. That isn't easy, but Saban could do it because he had a clear-eyed vision of the future and knew what needed to be prioritized. And, like everything at Alabama, it came back to recruiting. Alabama annually signs one of the best recruiting classes in college football for a multitude of reasons, but one is the proven track record of developing players for the NFL. They go hand in hand—the best players want to go to places that will prepare them for the NFL, and the highest-drafted players are frequently those same highly regarded recruits. Saban needs to be able to show recruits he can help get them to the NFL, and those long-serving relationships he has with key NFL personnel plays a big role in that. Through a combination of incredible talent and trust in how Saban prepares his players for the next level, NFL teams have turned to Alabama players year after year when it comes time to make a multimillion-dollar first-round commitment. From 2009 through the 2021 NFL Draft, thirty-nine Alabama players were taken in the first round, a stunning number that no rival coach or organization came close to matching. In fact, no college head coach in the history of the sport had ever had thirty-nine first-round picks before Saban accomplished it in 2021, when Alabama tied the record for most first-round picks in a single year with six. Not every Alabama draft pick has gone on to have tremendous success in the NFL, but NFL organizations largely know what they are getting when they draft one.

"If I'm a defensive coordinator in the NFL, you can send me every Alabama guy that Nick's ever coached," says Rick Venturi, who worked as a defensive coordinator for four different NFL organizations. "He's going to be pro-ready, he's playing pro schemes, and it's not that simplicity Friday-night stuff. You're getting a guy who can take coaching, because if he can't take coaching, he's going to be out of there. It doesn't matter if you're a five-star or a no-star when you're with Saban, you're going to get coached hard and you know it."

That hard-coaching component is predicated on honesty. Saban doesn't sugarcoat things for his players as he pushes them to be successful. He's very honest with them about what they need to work on to get better and will personally show them how to fix something not being executed properly. Recruiting is the lifeblood of Alabama football, but its ethos is getting the best out of the best. You have to put in the work to get the best people into your organization, but it doesn't end there. If you want to maximize their output, it takes holding them accountable through consistent, honest feedback.

Eberflus likens that whole process to gardening. We'll let him explain it.

"When you're building a football team, it's a lot like planting a garden," the Bears head coach says. "What's the environment, what's the soil? You've got to have great ingredients. His ingredients are his recruiting—he does an awesome job so he gets the best seeds he can get. He's the master at that. Once he brings them to Alabama, he's got the environment there, the soil, with everything from strength and conditioning to his schemes to his philosophies to his facilities. He cultivates those seeds, and, man, do they grow.

"He produces pro player after pro player after pro player. Is that talent? Yes, but what it also is, is development. He can develop them because he creates the environment for that. That's all done by the head football coach."

Being a leader is hard. Whether everything is going well or failing, the rest of the organization will look to you for answers. When Saban was asked, he'd always give an honest answer, regardless if it might ruffle some feathers. Alabama's environment, as Eberflus detailed, is built on that. It is built on consistent, honest feedback meant to make everyone in the organization better. It wasn't easy for Saban to do that, no matter how it looked from the outside, but it was imperative. To truly achieve something great as a leader, you must be willing to have the hard conversations, no matter how uncomfortable they might be.

CHAPTER 15

"Rat Poison" and Other Lessons from the Podium

I'm trying to get our players to listen to me instead of listening to you guys," a frustrated Saban snarled as he glared at a reporter.

Alabama had just beaten Texas A&M 27–19 in College Station on October 9, 2017, but not everything went according to plan. The Crimson Tide looked sloppy at times, not playing up to their potential. When a reporter asked about three offensive series struggles early in the game, Saban saw an opportunity to deliver a message to his team through the media.

"All the stuff you write about how good we are. All that stuff they hear on ESPN. It's like poison. It's like taking poison."

Saban paused for effect.

"Like rat poison."

The comments elicited some chuckles from the reporters, but everyone knew what he was doing. Saban might be the CEO of Alabama football, but unlike his counterparts at actual Fortune 500 companies who can largely hide from the media if desired, Saban must talk to the press after every big win or bad loss. Rather than complain about dealing with the media like other public leaders, Saban realized he could use the pulpit to his benefit. Every time he stepped behind a microphone there was an opportunity to send a message—to recruits, to fans, and, of course, to his team.

Rainer Sabin, who covered the Crimson Tide for AL.com, says not only did Saban's rat poison comments quickly spread like wildfire on social media, they reached their intended recipients. Alabama players started referencing it in interviews afterward, and even rival coaches like Lane Kiffin seemed to relish using it whenever given an opportunity. "It became part of the lexicon," Sabin says. "It was a thing for the rest of the season and beyond, where anytime anybody was overhyped, it was, 'I'm not going to succumb to the rat poison,' or, 'That's rat poison.'"

With how college football is covered, Saban knew he couldn't create a bubble where his players would never read or hear anyone talk about them as much as he wished he could. When you're consistently the number one team in the country, you will get lots of coverage from national media outlets such as ESPN to local ones like AL.com, which deploys a team of reporters to cover every latest happening within the program. That doesn't even account for all the attention players get on Twitter, Instagram, and other social media platforms that give fans direct access to tell their favorite players how great they are. Saban had to find a way to push back on that or risk his players getting too full of themselves and complacent.

So he meets them where they are. He knows that when he delivers a WWE-type rant about rat poison, it's going to be all over social media and TV and radio stations. When Saban was worried his players weren't committed to the necessary work or were overlooking an upcoming opponent, he'd use his press conferences to redirect their attention. He was giving them the same message privately but used the avenues available to him to get it in front of his team as often as possible. Saban once explained his approach as, "I think you guys use me sometimes to create a little news, so I'm just going to use you to create some news with our team."

"What he does through messaging is he reinforces ideas," Sabin says. "You can't just do a one-off message; it has to be reinforced. There's nothing better than getting it out to the media because what does the media do? They replay his messages over and over again."

There was no more apparent example of that than whenever Alabama played a Football Championship Subdivision (FCS) opponent in November.

Typically scheduled in between games against rivals LSU and Auburn, Alabama would play an opponent in a division below it that had no chance of beating it as a tune-up and a chance to avoid a taxing opponent before the Iron Bowl. While everyone knew why Alabama scheduled the game, Saban didn't want his team taking the opponent lightly. For the Wednesday press conference before the FCS game, Saban would walk into the room just looking for someone to allow him to go off. He'd wait for a question that in any way implied Alabama would easily win, and when some poor reporter took the bait, Saban delivered. Eventually, reporters learned his style, but that didn't stop his desire to use it as an opportunity to get his team to focus. In 2015, when Saban got a benign question about the FCS opponent having a quarterback who previously played at UAB, he realized it was time.

He launched into an impassioned speech saying he typically gets questions about whether a freshman would play against an FCS opponent, lamenting its implied assumption. He referenced a 2011 game against FCS opponent Georgia Southern that tallied more than 302 rushing yards against an Alabama team that went on to win a national championship with one of the nation's best defenses.

"I don't think we had a guy on that field that didn't play in the NFL, and about four or five of them were first-round draft picks," Saban said. "And I think that team won a national championship but I'm not sure. And they ran through our ass like shit through a tin horn, man. And we could not stop them. Could not stop them. Could not stop them because we could not get a look in practice. We couldn't practice it, right? And everybody said the same thing in that game. Y'all took a week off, this wasn't important, so it's not important to anybody else. It has to be important to the players and it has to be important to us."

He even worked in some advice about marriage within the rant, saying, "Everybody gets excited for the beginning of the season, and you get excited about getting married. But after you're married for a while, you've got to have a process to make it work. And no matter what happens, we need to have a process to make it happen in every game we play. Every game that we play. Can't assume anything."

He paused for a second before admitting what everyone in the room accustomed to covering Saban knew to be true.

"I don't even know what you asked me," he said. "I just wanted to say that."

His rant got national coverage, and it served its purpose: Alabama easily defeated its FCS opponent that week, Charleston Southern, 56–6.

Saban's propensity to use the podium to deliver high-energy speeches to his team can lead people to believe he's always one trigger away from losing his mind. And, let's be clear, there is no denying Saban is fiery and prone to energetic verbal outbursts if something is bothering him. When Saban starts rocking, whether at a podium or seated at a table, it is the telltale sign he's about to explode and everyone around him better hide for cover. But Saban's press conferences were almost always planned out and strategic, as he rarely, if ever, said anything unintentionally. It didn't matter what the setting was—it could be a press conference or a speech at a gala function. If Saban was giving public comments, he wanted to be prepared. He'd dutifully write his thoughts down on note cards beforehand and stick to the script. It was partly because Saban never wanted to be unprepared for anything and partly because he cared much more about his public image than he'd ever let on. "I think Nick's one of those guys that just wants to be appreciated," says former LSU trustee Charlie Weems, one of Saban's closest confidants in Baton Rouge. "He wants to be loved."

Saban didn't like the perception that he was a jerk prone to yelling and screaming at everyone in his vicinity—reporters, players, coaches, you name it. "I would come in and say to my wife, 'I'm not like that at all. Why do these guys say I'm that way?'" Saban told GQ in a piece titled "Nick Saban: Sympathy for the Devil." "And she would say, 'You ever watch yourself in a press conference?' You can blame the other guy for saying it, or you can look at yourself and say, 'I must have contributed to this.'"

Eventually, he realized he could use that media perception to his advantage. It was especially effective in recruiting, where players and parents walked into a meeting expecting one thing and experiencing something entirely different. It's how he's earned the reputation as the "Lord of the Living Room."

"You think you're about to talk to some tyrant who rips and roars and gets on everybody," says Tyler Siskey, Saban's right-hand recruiting man from 2013 to 2015. "But then when he talks to you, you're like, 'He's a normal person.' Automatically you think, 'Oh, he's being different with me. I like the guy.'"

That was Alan Evans' experience as he met Saban for the first time when Alabama was recruiting his five-star son Rashaan. "It blew me away because I wasn't expecting it," Evans says. "He's a totally different guy in person and away from the arena. He likes to have fun, and that's what makes these players fall in love with him. He's so different away from the stadium."

Away from the stadium, Evans saw a man who loved music and would gladly dance when hosting recruits and their families at his house. Saban was charismatic and easy to talk to in those recruiting settings away from the football stadium. Evan's other son, Alex, even captured a video of Saban dancing one night, and the video went viral, with fans in shock that the seemingly perpetually grumpy coach was even capable of moving his feet in rhythm to a song. The footage made real years of rumors and stories *BamaOnline* publisher Tim Watts had heard from parents but could never prove. "At the time, it was like folklore," he says. "I don't know how many times I heard a parent or a kid talk about how shocked they were that he did the Electric Slide."

Eventually, there was a purposeful strategy developed to show that side of Saban to the public more often. However, it took time for the coach to become willing to play ball. When he was still at LSU, ESPN showed up one day to do an all-access behind-the-scenes video feature on Saban's ascendant program. Saban knew the cameras were there and he knew they put a microphone on him, but it didn't change anything about his approach. Players on that team remember Saban as being annoyed he even had to deal with the visitors. "He might have been disgusted," former LSU offensive lineman Paris Hodges says about the experience. "He might have just been pissed off that they wanted him to put on a pony show, which he didn't. He did his job."

At Alabama, Saban still wasn't going to ease off the gas, but the people around him successfully sold him on the advantages of showing a different, friendlier side in national television and magazine features. They worked hard at building relationships with key people at ESPN they could trust to tell those stories. It led to stories like a 2016 piece at ESPN.com with the headline "Nick Saban Is Actually a Human Being. Honest." Like most things with Saban, what ultimately swayed him was recruiting.

"I don't think it's a secret that programs were coming out and using his personality against the program on the recruiting trail," says former Alabama quarterback Greg McElroy. "They would say, 'You're going to come out, you're going to go to Alabama, and you're going to have a miserable time.'"

Rivals painted Alabama as a no-fun, workaholic factory that players wouldn't enjoy even if they won lots of games. Emerging programs like Clemson played up a fun, family atmosphere complete with huge slides in its football facility, a direct contrast to the perceived environment at Alabama. That, coupled with Kirby Smart and Georgia stealing some of Alabama's recruiting momentum, led Saban and Alabama to again turn to ESPN to change the narrative. The result was a four-part all-access series in 2018 called *Training Days: Rolling with the Tide* that purported to show a different side of Alabama's football juggernaut. McElroy, now an ESPN commentator, says the evolution of Saban's public persona is "100 percent calculated. I don't think he does anything by accident."

The relationship with ESPN became so strong that Saban considered walking away from coaching to work for the television network. Before the 2013 season, Saban met with Nick Khan, a Creative Artists Agency agent who represented top media talents like Kirk Herbstreit and Skip Bayless. After the crushing end to the 2013 season in the famous Kick Six loss, Saban empowered Khan to reach out to ESPN with the message Saban was thinking about the next chapter in his career and considering whether media should be a part of that. Khan facilitated a meeting at the Langham Hotel in Pasadena, California, that January at which Saban, his agent Jimmy Sexton, and John Wildhack, then ESPN's executive vice president for acquisitions and programming, met to discuss what Saban working at ESPN could look like.

Saban zeroed in on a potential role with ESPN's flagship college sports program *College GameDay*. The Alabama head coach quizzed Wildhack on several topics about what life would be like at ESPN, from the weekly schedule to the organizational infrastructure to who led different parts of the operation. But the question that was the most important to Saban, one he repeated multiple times, was how working at ESPN would be like a team. Since he was nine years old, Saban had been part of a team and had repeatedly said the idea of not being part of one scared him to death. In that meeting, he made clear that if he was going to leave coaching, he wanted to feel still part of a team. Wildhack did his best to answer those questions, saying working on a production like *GameDay* was as close to being on an athletic team as you can get even if you weren't around everyone seven days a week, but left the meeting feeling Saban wasn't quite ready to make the jump.

"Not because we didn't have a good conversation and not because he wasn't intrigued by television, because he was intrigued and he was interested," Wildhack says. "If he wasn't interested, he never would have done it in the first place. But I also didn't think he was ready to step aside as being a head coach."

Later, Khan reached out to Wildhack and told him, "Coach is really appreciative of the meeting, found it to be very informative, and has a lot of respect for *GameDay* and ESPN, but at this point in his career, he still has a desire to coach."

It felt like an inflection point for Saban, who around that same time reportedly considered interest from Texas before agreeing to a contract extension at Alabama. Wildhack saw in Saban a man who was asking himself, "If it's not Alabama, what other options do I have?"

"You do your discovery, you gather as much information as you can, and then he makes the decision that he made," Wildhack says. "Turns out he made a pretty damn good decision."

That ESPN was considered a primary option didn't surprise Wildhack, who says Saban would have been "tremendous" and a "slam dunk" on *GameDay*. Not only did Saban quickly grasp the power of *GameDay* during their discussions, but Wildhack had already seen how well the Alabama coach understood the television component.

"Nick works and utilizes the media as well as any coach," he says. "He's very astute in how he uses the media to get his message out there and promote his program."

Players get used to Saban sending a message through the media, but it isn't always about working harder or focusing better. When he senses his team needs a boost, he'll gladly deliver it through journalists, knowing his players will see what he says. In 2015, after Alabama lost to Ole Miss at home, national media outlets, including *USA Today*, proclaimed the Crimson Tide dynasty finished. "Alabama's Dynasty Looks Like It's Over," blared *USA Today*'s headline. Alabama hadn't won a national championship since 2012, and with an early loss to the Rebels, Alabama's chances of even making it to another national championship game seemed in serious doubt. Perhaps sensing even his team might be thinking that too, Saban went on the offensive after a dominating win over Georgia, a rare game in which Alabama was the betting underdog. Speaking to reporters the following Monday, Saban let loose a passionate rant when asked about the perception of his team.

"I'm coaching and working for our players and our team for it to be as good as it can be," Saban said. "If that's not pleasing to somebody else, it's not pleasing to somebody else. I said before, I believe in our team. I do believe in our team and we're going to work hard to make our team better. And I hope our players respond the right way."

His voice rose as he started to crank up the intensity.

"And it's not going to be for you," he directed to the journalists assembled before him. "The fans, yes. Because if it was up to you, we're six-foot under already. We're dead and buried and gone. Gone."

Behind the scenes, Saban and Scott Cochran, the program's strength and conditioning coach, played up the "dynasty is dead" narrative with the players. Each Thursday, Cochran would show a motivational video to get the team fired up before its upcoming game. After the Ole Miss loss and all the ensuing negative coverage, Alabama coaches went back to that well over and over again. "They would pump that stuff through us all the time where it just fuels the fire," says former Alabama linebacker Keith Holcombe. "We knew what everybody was saying—it was, 'Alabama's over, they don't have it anymore, Saban's lost it, these guys can't change with the times.' We heard that, and we did not avoid it. We put it all in the locker rooms.

"It just added fuel to the fire we already had cooking."

It fueled Alabama to another national championship that season, indefinitely ending any "dynasty is over" talk. Saban's tactics hit home that season for an experienced Alabama team that wanted to leave no doubt after falling short of a championship the previous two seasons. There's broad appeal to Saban's approach: you defend your team publicly against criticism, and then stoke your team's motivation internally with it. It is a tried-and-true approach to use criticism or disrespect to motivate a group of people. Michael Jordan was famous for using perceived slights, sometimes fabricated ones, to power his relentless pursuit of success. Alabama occasionally did the same, such as before a national semifinal game against Washington in 2016. Undefeated Alabama was a 14-point favorite against the Huskies and a very popular pick to win the national championship that season. Without any real bulletin board material, Alabama took a page out of Jordan's book and just made it up. There were signs posted in player lockers that the national media thought Alabama was overconfident and that an unnamed Washington player said, "Somebody has to knock off Bama and that's going to be us." Those signs weren't based in reality, but they did the trick: Alabama beat Washington, 24–7. Alabama players even referenced the signs after the game as a source of motivation against the Huskies.

"Cochran was constantly pulling crap like that," says former Alabama tight end Hunter Bryant. "Guys loved it and ate it up, but later on I'd say, 'Wait a minute, no one from Washington is challenging Alabama. No one in the national media is picking Washington over Alabama, except maybe Danny Kanell.'"

You don't need national media coverage like Alabama utilized to tap into that feeling. It could be as simple as pointing out that some outside force doesn't believe you're capable of accomplishing something. Or that some competitor—and there's competition everywhere in life—thinks he's going to beat you. It might feel trite to rely on that, but there's a reason why it's such a successful approach, as Columbia University professor E. Tory Higgins, the director of the school's Motivation Science Center, once explained to the *Wall Street Journal*. Higgins believes disrespect might be the strongest motivator because of what it invokes inside of us.

"To be disrespected is extraordinarily dangerous because it's associated with being rejected," Higgins said. "If you're rejected from other groups, or even members of your group, your survival is threatened. Disrespect is very closely related to a survival threat, and that's why it's so motivating."

Saban's media approach taps into that, but it also insulates the organization from the pressures that come with playing college football at a big-time program. In the state of Alabama, there's nothing else that comes close to eliciting as much interest as Alabama football. The people of Alabama are used to being constantly reminded how poorly their state ranks in things like education, obesity, and wealth, but Alabama football is the pride of the state. It is the thing that allows them to beat their chests and say that in this one area, we aren't ranked last, we are the clear best. And with no major professional sports teams to siphon away interest, it always comes back to college football. It's not an exaggeration to say Crimson Tide football is discussed 365 days a year within the state. The moment that players arrive on Alabama's Tuscaloosa campus, they are celebrities.

There's a lot that comes with that, which is why Saban tries to shoulder the responsibilities. He enacted a "one voice" policy where he's the face of the program and parries away any arrows that may have been directed at an assistant coach or player. It's a strategy he learned from Bill Belichick with the Cleveland Browns and, funny enough, he initially resisted it, saying he would keep talking to reporters even after Belichick tried to stop him. He became a convert over time and set up a system that put the onus of the media responsibilities on himself to allow the rest of his program to focus on their assigned tasks. When Rick Trickett was with Saban at LSU, he quickly saw the value in that approach.

"They have talk shows down there twenty-four hours a day. They call kids out by name on the radio," says Trickett. "The pressure on the kids was so intense, and Nick did a great job of taking it off of them and putting it on himself. 'We are going to shoulder this thing and take the pressure off.'

He got rid of all the hearsay and rumors. Everything that came out of the program came from his mouth, and it was factual. It helped the players with setting their mindset that 'this guy has our back.' Everyone is on the same page."

While at LSU, Saban brought in media consultant Lisa LeMaster to guide his entire organization through an all-day session, a tradition he'd continue later at Alabama. After LeMaster left, Saban sent players to Dr. Tommy Karam, a senior instructor in the marketing department who taught classes on sports marketing and personal branding. Karam got his start working with LSU athletes when a young basketball player named Shaquille O'Neal knocked on his door one day and asked if he could help him with his inter-view skills. Facing a large contingent of journalists covering LSU football as a college athlete can be "terribly uncomfortable, intimidating," according to Karam, who worked to prepare the football players for what's to come. Saban always stressed to his team to not provide bulletin board material to the other team—he knew the motivational power of disrespect, after all—but it went beyond just what not to do. He recognized that no matter how good or bad things were going, the players could still face tough questions, and he wanted them to be ready for them. Saban stressed to his team that all it could take was one video snippet from an interview for fans and others to make a judg-ment call on not only the player but the entire team.

"Coach Saban wants them to be ready when that time comes," Karam says. "He knows who can be called up, and they know what their responsibil-ities are. He doesn't tell them what to say, which I think is wonderful, but he prepares them on how to think as they enter that setting."

It limited the chances for mixed messaging, too. Saban stressed to his coaches when they were putting together their weekly game plans that he was all about collaboration and debating the pros and cons of different strategies, but once they made a decision, he expected everyone to embrace it. He didn't want anyone detracting from the plan's viability by second-guessing or com-plaining about it before it was even enacted. It was a similar approach with public messaging in that Saban wanted everyone on the same page and stick-ing to the script. With a one-voice policy, Saban took on the responsibility to deliver the message he wanted out there and eliminated the possibility of an assistant publicly contradicting him, even if unintentionally. That policy came in handy when the media-friendly Kiffin was his offensive coordinator, given all the comments he made after leaving the program. As his protégés left to run their programs, many of them took with them his "one-voice policy," much to the chagrin of reporters everywhere.

Karam, who continued to work with LSU football coaches and players after Saban left, says how Saban manages every situation is really what makes him stand out.

"As good a coach as he is, I think his point of differentiation, in my eyes, are his management skills. I believe they are extraordinarily CEO-ish," Karam says. "I think part of that is, how do you control the message? He was really ahead of the time with the coach being the face of the team just like the big CEOs are now. He does it in a controlled way—simple message, very consistent, not too over the top—and it works really well."

As a leader, you have to use the tools at your disposal. Having to talk to the media multiple times a week during one's busiest stretch of the year would be a curse for some of us. No doubt, Saban probably privately felt that way at times, too. But he realized early on it was an important platform he couldn't avoid, so he might as well get the maximum value from it. It was always an opportunity to send a message, and he always wanted to choose his words in a way that resonated. Saban never stopped addressing his team in daily meetings—his media comments were simply a supplement, not the main course—but he knew as a leader you have to find alternative ways to reach your organization.

CHAPTER 16

Complacency Kills Future Success

After going through a host of wrong coaches, Alabama was now the nation's best team. Saban had guided the Crimson Tide back to the top of college football. The seventeen-year title drought was over.

But as confetti fell inside the Rose Bowl on January 7, 2010, Saban wasn't thinking about how happy he'd just made Alabama fans across the world. He couldn't help but focus on how poorly his team played at the end of the game. Sure, Alabama had just won a national championship, but it didn't play through the final whistle the way the players were taught.

Alabama built a 24–6 halftime lead only to watch it whittle down to 24–21 with six minutes left in the game. Alabama added two late touchdowns to secure a 37–21 title win, but Saban was thinking about how his team's sloppy play almost doomed it as the clock hit zero.

"He was pissed after that game," says offensive lineman David Blalock. "What team wins the national championship and they're not happy about it? He's got his standard, and if things aren't done to his standard, he doesn't let that go. He makes sure everybody knows it."

"He was not happy that we didn't play as well as we could have," adds offensive lineman Taylor Pharr. "He was truly upset that we didn't play as well as we could have."

In the victorious locker room after the game, Saban approached the younger players on the team set to return the following year and told them if they wanted to win another championship, it would require a higher level of commitment. What they did at the end of the game against Texas wouldn't cut it moving forward. "How many coaches would overlook any thought of that after you've won a national championship?" asks Pharr.

He delivered a similar message to his staff. The morning after the title game, Saban had Mike Vollmar, his director of football operations, hastily put together a meeting in the team hotel ballroom. Just hours after winning his first title at Alabama, Saban offered a short congratulations before lamenting that the program had fallen behind in recruiting and would need to deliver even more in the upcoming season if it wanted to stay on top.

Saban rattled off all the problems winning that national championship was going to cause. His biggest concern? Complacency.

A week later, Saban was back at Alabama celebrating the organization's national championship with a parade and packed crowd at Bryant-Denny Stadium. While everyone seemed to be relishing the celebration, Saban wanted everyone in the crowd—players, coaches, and fans—to know, "This is not the end. This is the beginning."

If there's one lesson to take away over all the others from Saban's successful approach, it is his total and complete aversion to complacency. One of Saban's favorite quotes that he preaches to his organization is "Complacency breeds a blatant disregard for doing what's right." So much of what he does daily is about fighting complacency within his organization. In many ways, it is a fight against human nature. He's doing everything he can, both personally and as a leader, to get everyone in the Alabama organization to keep fighting every day as if they hadn't just won a national championship.

"He's the most driven individual I've ever been around," says Jon Gilbert, who worked at Alabama for seventeen years. "I don't even know who number two is. He would enjoy a victory for about twenty minutes and then he would immediately focus on what was next."

The day after the 2010 national championship game, Gilbert, now the athletic director at East Carolina, bumped into an Alabama assistant coach. The assistant coach asked him whether they won the night before. A confused

Gilbert, unsure if the coach was joking or not, said of course. The coach explained you wouldn't have known that with how Saban was acting that day.

In that morning meeting with his staff, Saban told them they'd be out in California too long and needed to hit the ground running when they got back to Alabama. "We better get out on the road recruiting because we're behind from all the time we've spent out here," Saban said less than twelve hours after winning a national championship.

Gilbert told the assistant coach, "Did you tell him that we won the national championship last night and every recruit in the country was watching?"

The assistant replied, "Man, he didn't want to hear that. He wanted to make sure we hit the ground running when we got back."

After every big success, Saban finds a way to deliver a message that the work isn't over. After winning the 2017 national championship on one of college football's most famous plays—the 2nd-and-26 touchdown pass from Tua Tagovailoa to DeVonta Smith for the overtime win—Saban was in a state of euphoria when he told ESPN immediately afterward, "I've never been happier in my life." The next morning, though, Saban was already referencing his twenty-four-hour rule.

"If you're a competitor . . . in twenty-four hours, you probably need to move on," Saban said, "because there's another challenge and basically you created a target for yourself in the future in terms of people who want to beat you."

Later that day, he was already getting on staffers for not doing a good enough job in recruiting. It took less than a day for Saban to transition from "never been happier" to feeling his program was falling behind in recruiting and that the upcoming recruiting class wouldn't be up to snuff. It's familiar anxiety for Saban, who told a friend after the 2012 national championship, "That damn game cost me a week of recruiting," as recounted in a GQ story.

Tom Mendoza was at that national championship game. The former vice chairman of NetApp, a Fortune 500 company that specializes in data management, Mendoza is a big Notre Dame football fan and made the trek to Miami to watch Alabama easily beat his beloved Fighting Irish, 42–14. Saban's approach resonates with Mendoza, who got a similar lesson earlier in his career. While running sales at NetApp, Mendoza went into a board meeting expecting a parade after a successful quarter and, instead, had the most uncomfortable experience of his professional life. Don Valentine, the legendary founder of Sequoia Capital, was NetApp's chairman at the time and quizzed Mendoza on a number of topics he wasn't expecting. A stunned Mendoza walked out of the room upset—not only had he not been congratulated for his success, but he faced real pressure and pointed questions he couldn't answer from a man known as the grandfather of Silicon Valley venture capital. Sequoia Capital became famous for making big early bets on companies that became huge like Apple, Google, Oracle, YouTube, and PayPal, among many others.

Doug Leone, who'd later succeed Valentine at Sequoia Capital and become a billionaire venture capitalist, followed Mendoza out of the meeting. Leone asked Mendoza how Valentine treated him when NetApp was struggling. "He was extremely supportive," Mendoza said. Leone explained Valentine was challenging him for a reason.

"Get used to it because Don believes the killer of all great companies is complacency," Leone said.

"I adapted my leadership style right then to, when things are going well, I inject tension," Mendoza says. "When times are tough and people are struggling, I'm supportive. I think most people do it the completely opposite way."

That is Saban's approach in a nutshell. When things are going very well, he's going to try to bring the team down a peg. He'll go out of his way to point out things that weren't perfect to snuff out any sense of comfort. Conversely, as detailed in chapter twelve, when Alabama loses a game, Saban focuses on turning it into a positive and building the team back up. Saban learned early in his Alabama tenure if complacency sets in within an organization, it'll overpower talent.

Some still believe the 2010 Alabama team is one of the most talented Saban has ever had. The Crimson Tide returned most of its top stars like receiver Julio Jones, running back Mark Ingram, linebacker Dont'a Hightower, safety Mark Barron, and defensive lineman Marcell Dareus—all future NFL first-round picks—along with a host of returning starters such as quarterback Greg McElroy and offensive guard Barrett Jones. On paper, Alabama was the most talented team in the country and as the preseason No. 1 team, a popular pick to repeat as national champions. But with that came considerable pressure. Alabama was no longer a program trying to get over the hump; it was the king of the sport with a host of usurpers looking to overthrow it.

"We didn't know how to handle success," says former Alabama defensive back Will Lowery. "We didn't know how to sustain it. It was really tough to figure out how to handle being the champion. We didn't do it well. We weren't focused. We thought we were so good we were just going to show up and win every game."

Despite having a roster full of future NFL stars, Alabama stumbled to a 10–3 record, the worst record of Saban's time in Tuscaloosa after his initial 7–6 season. The trouble started early in the season when South Carolina stunned No. 1 Alabama, ending a nineteen-game winning streak. Leading the way was South Carolina's maverick quarterback Stephen Garcia, who had the best game of his career against the Crimson Tide. Garcia says he played with a "reckless abandon" and a confidence that the Gamecocks were good enough to beat Alabama that day. South Carolina wasn't scared and took advantage of an Alabama team that wasn't prepared to get every opponent's best shot.

"They do beat the hell out of teams often and they deserve to be feared a little bit, but that's not my mentality. It never has been and it never will be," Garcia says. "You are who your quarterback is and who your head coach is, and Coach Spurrier's ultra-confident and I'm ultra-confident, no matter if we are getting our ass beat or beating someone's ass. We are going to put it on you as much as possible."

Later that season, Alabama suffered close losses to LSU and Auburn to knock it out of national championship contention and into the Capital One Bowl. The loss against Auburn, known to fans as the "Camback" after Cam Newton's second-half heroics, was particularly tough for that team to swallow after being up 24–0 at halftime. Auburn went on to win the national championship that season, and Saban flew out to Pasadena to appear on ESPN's coverage of the game. Saban faced such a barrage of flak from Auburn fans at the game, still relishing the comeback win, that in his first team meeting back in Tuscaloosa he told his team, "We're going to beat their ass next year. They're all talking about this, but at the end of the day they're Auburn, and we're still Alabama." Alabama beat Auburn, 42–14, that following season on its way to the second national championship of the Saban era.

Going from winning a national championship to being unable to close out opponents in 2010 was an illustration of something Saban harped on with his teams throughout his career. At Michigan State, he would tell his players, "It's a slippery pole from the penthouse to the shit house." By the time he won big at Alabama, he had cleaned up the message, though its meaning was similar. "It's not hard to get to the top," Saban would tell his staff. "It's maintaining at the top."

There are a lot of college coaches around the country who would quibble with that first point—it is, in fact, very hard to get to the top—but complacency is real. In the last thirty years of college football, no one has been able to do what Alabama has under Saban. There have been multiple programs able to achieve multiple national championships in a certain period, but none has sustained it for as long as Alabama.

Nebraska won three titles in a pre-playoff era four-year span (1994–1997) before coach Tom Osborne retired. Led by Urban Meyer and Tim Tebow, Florida won back-to-back titles in 2007 and 2008 before the bottom fell out in 2010, prompting Meyer to retire. (He would come out of retirement to win another title at Ohio State in 2014.) USC was the Alabama of the early 2000s, winning consecutive titles in 2003 (shared with Saban's LSU team) and 2004 and finishing in the Associated Press top five in seven consecutive seasons until Pete Carroll left for the NFL in 2010.

What separates Alabama from many of the so-called dynasties before it is that there has been no drop-off. In Saban's first fourteen years at Alabama, he produced more NFL first-round picks (44) than games his team lost (23). He won national championships with a defense-first mindset, and then he won championships with an offense that averaged more than 45 points per game. Alabama didn't experience the slips the other schools faced when their coaches left because, despite being the game's most-decorated and highest-paid coach, Saban dug deeper and deeper even as he reached an age that prompted many of his peers to retire. The boy who grew up in a West Virginia coal-mining town wasn't going to let a $10 million salary and everything it could buy distract him from the work needed to justify it.

"He's still the same guy I've always known," says Senator Joe Manchin (W.Va.), who has known Saban since the coach was five years old. "There's no change at all. I call him Brother Saban—Brother has been the same since he was playing Pop Warner football. He's still the same hardworking person, very loyal, and he's a lifelong friend. I respect that and value that more than anything else."

Rick Trickett knows how rare that is. The longtime offensive line coach was one of Jimbo Fisher's top deputies in Tallahassee as Florida State made its effort to topple Alabama as college football's top program. Florida State beat out Alabama for quarterback Jameis Winston, who would win the Heisman Trophy, and rode him to a national championship win in 2013 over Auburn. The Seminoles were a popular pick to repeat as champions, finished the season undefeated, and made the inaugural College Football Playoff as the No. 2 seed. Facing a Marcus Mariota–led Oregon Ducks team, Florida State headed into halftime down 18–13 after a late turnover led to a touchdown. What happened in the second half was stunning, as Florida State had four third-quarter turnovers, Oregon at one point had thirty-nine consecutive points, and the Ducks rolled to a 59–20 win. "We should have beat their ass," Trickett says. "We had a good enough team to, but we weren't dialed in."

"The most unselfish football team I've ever been around in my career was the 2013 team that won a national championship," he says. "And the most selfish football team I've ever been around was the 2014 team. It was all about me and that."

One way Saban fights back against complacency? He convinces himself he's taking over a new organization every year. Players say he seems to enjoy winning a title for, at most, forty-eight hours before it's as if he deletes those memories from his brain and moves on to the next challenge. And with players and staff leaving in considerable numbers after each season, he treats it like a whole new team. It helps him eliminate the pressure of trying to top the previous year's accomplishments and instead lets him focus on achieving success with a new group of people. In his mind, he's taking on a new job without having to actually move or switch organizations.

After a championship, Saban will let his team enjoy it for about two weeks before it's back to work. When the players return to the football facility, there is no reminiscing about how fun it was to win it all. Mac Hereford, a receiver on the 2017 title team, says if you didn't have the actual memories to prove otherwise, you'd have no idea the program just won a national championship.

"We have our first meeting back [after the championship] and he'll say, 'I'm proud of what that team did, but this is a completely new team,'" Hereford says. "'There's not the same guys you all had last year; we have new guys coming in. This is a new team; this is a different group. Y'all can't claim that.'"

It's Saban's way of getting around one of the biggest challenges both individuals and organizations face after achieving success: How do I keep it going once I reach the top? It's why Saban harps so much on focusing on The Process rather than simply the results. If you are results-obsessed, it can be hard to move on once you achieve them. Saban has experienced that firsthand.

Saban won his first national championship in 2003 at LSU, a result that put him in rarefied air in college football history. He delivered on promises he made when he took the job and finally helped LSU capitalize on its long-untapped potential. But after the game, LSU trustee Charlie Weems remembers walking back to the head coach's locker room to congratulate and celebrate with his friend. In a mostly empty locker room, Weems found a slack-jawed Saban sitting on a chair by himself. He asked him what was wrong.

Saban looked at him and said, "What am I going to do now?"

"He wasn't thrilled, although I know he was inside, of course, about having won the national championship," says Weems. "The dominant emotion for him when the locker room cleared out was worrying how he was going to follow it up. 'What am I going to do next?'"

LeRoy Ryals joined Saban's staff as tight ends coach a month after LSU won the national championship. In his first staff meeting, Saban let his assistant coaches have it over what he thought was poor coaching in his Fourth Quarter Program. "He was getting on some details about wall runs and 'we have to coach it better.' " Ryals says. "I thought, 'Whoa,' because I saw a different person then. He let them have it about wall runs."

"One of the reasons why Coach [Saban] and Alabama have been able to sustain this success that they've been able to enjoy since 2009 is because the pressure's always on," says former Alabama receivers coach Mike Groh, who was part of three title teams under Saban. "It's never about what happened yesterday, it's all about what's going on today and anticipating what's going to happen tomorrow. He's not impressed with anything that's been done. It's always about what we have to do to do it over again."

There's a price to pay with this mindset. You can be accused of not enjoying the experience, not smelling the roses, or any other cliché you want to use. But if you want to be the best, this is what it takes. It takes a refusal to get too excited about one accomplishment, because the process never stops. There's always more work to be done, there are always more hurdles to be overcome, always some new opponent looking to take you down.

"Someday he's going to look back and say, 'Maybe I didn't appreciate it enough,' because he wouldn't let himself," says Gary Pinkel, a Hall of Fame coach who played with Saban at Kent State. "But that's a good thing. In this business, you exhale and you lose two games.

"You win, you get back to work in the office, and you demand the same level of excellence that you did the first day you got there when those players had no idea what kind of program he was going to run."

McElroy, the starting quarterback on Saban's first Alabama title team, knows all about that. When Saban was going around the locker room after winning the national championship telling players their effort wasn't good enough, McElroy says, "For a lot of us it went in one ear, out the other. 'Coach, we just won, c'mon, we get it.' " But like Saban, he found himself quickly trying to turn the page to get ready for what was next. It's a feeling McElroy believes is instilled in you when you play for Saban and one he's found hard to shake since entering the post-college real world. He jokes about spending hours looking at bigger houses on Zillow even though he loves the house he's in now.

"The level of satisfaction, it never, ever, ever hits you," McElroy says. "Even when we won the national championship, we didn't even celebrate it. We were happy and it was amazing, but we just felt like we did what we were supposed to do. It was almost as if we checked that box, what's next?

"That's something, in some ways, that's been detrimental because that constant thirst for something more can force you to not appreciate the moment. I know I've dealt with that. There's always something you're striving for and sometimes you can't sit back and enjoy where you're at in life because there has to be some level of constant improvement."

There are many reasons why Saban has achieved so much success over his career, but his reaction to the success itself is a significant one. As he stockpiled national championships, he never let it impact what he demanded from himself every day. He didn't get a big ego, he didn't consider himself too good to do certain tasks now that he was a famous coach, and he never eased on the brakes of anyone else in the organization who might not have his same resolve against complacency. He knew that if he ever eased up, if he ever allowed himself to be impressed with the accomplishments, that's when the fall would come. As Saban once explained, "Success is not a continuum; it's momentary. Just because you had success last year doesn't mean you're going to have success next year." To avoid complacency, it takes not only believing that but living like that every single day. Even after winning seven national championships, Saban never believes success is guaranteed—and it's why he keeps having more of it.

CHAPTER 17

Be True to Yourself

W e've been conditioned to expect our leaders to deliver the big, rousing speech to fire up their team ahead of a critical moment. In movies and television, the leader gives the perfect inspirational speech in the perfect moment, leading to a successful outcome.

In football, we've come to expect speeches like "Win one for the Gipper" in *Knute Rockne: All-American* and Al Pacino's "inch-by-inch" speech in *Any Given Sunday*. They make for great cinematic moments, and some leaders opt for that style, but that's not who Saban is. It wouldn't come naturally to him to deliver a fiery speech like Pacino or to punch himself in the face to fire his team up before a game the way his SEC counterpart Ed Orgeron did at LSU. "Most people think leadership is 'I'm gonna stand up in front of the group, and I'm gonna give this great speech, and that's being a leader,'" Saban said. "But really, you're trying to influence people on a daily basis to do things that would allow them to be successful or to buy into the culture better."

Instead, Saban chooses to use those precious moments before a game or during halftime of a game to give his team as much useful information as he can before they return to the field. It's quick, to-the-point, and meant to give his team an advantage rather than try to fire them up artificially. "Once you figure out what he's telling you isn't a Tony Robbins 'go, go, go' thing, it's, 'This is going to help us win the game,' you recognize it as bars of gold," says Pat Perles, who played for Saban at Michigan State before working with him at Toledo. "If I'm a player, that's better than any 'rah, rah, rah' speech because that speech isn't going to mean shit as a guy hits me in the face the next play."

We've all been conditioned to believe something. We're taught through our entertainment to our upbringing to society that we need to be certain things. We see people held up as role models or as visionaries, and we try to emulate them regardless of whether it fits our personality and values. Apple founder Steve Jobs wearing the same outfit every day wasn't what made him successful. It was simply an outward representation of a desire to be as efficient as possible. And yet, for a time, every new Silicon Valley inventor seemed to try to copy that approach, as if wearing the same type of clothes is what propelled Apple to become one of the world's most valuable companies. Saban has some Jobsesque quirks in eating the same thing for breakfast (a cup or two of coffee and two Little Debbie oatmeal cream pies) and lunch (iceberg lettuce salad with tomatoes and slices of turkey) every day for the similar reason of eliminating a decision in order to be more efficient. "He's one of those guys who has to have his eggs on the left side, his phone on the right side, and the A/C has to be the same temperature," says former Michigan State running back Sedrick Irvin. "He's precise with everything."

Eating the same thing for lunch isn't what makes Saban great, however, and shouldn't feel like some prerequisite while considering which leadership principles to adopt for yourself. There can be a desire when reading leadership and self-help books to do things precisely the way the subject does, but that might not be what is best for you. During his 1993 ESPY speech, former North Carolina State basketball coach Jim Valvano told the story of being a twenty-one-year-old rookie head coach and addressing his Rutgers team for the first time. Idolizing former Green Bay Packers coach Vince Lombardi, Valvano decided to do exactly what Lombardi wrote in his book when he talked to his team. Lombardi wrote he arrived just a few minutes before kick-off and paced around the room before saying, "Gentlemen, we will be successful this year if you can focus on three things and three things only. Your family, your religion, and the Green Bay Packers."

"I said, 'That's beautiful,'" Valvano said. "I'm going to do that. Your family, your religion, and Rutgers basketball. That's it. I had it."

Valvano humorously explained that he unfortunately followed Lombardi's approach a little too closely and told his Rutgers freshmen team the exact

Lombardi quote by accident. There was only one Vince Lombardi, just like there was only one Jim Valvano, and over time Valvano found an approach that suited him best, which resulted in a national championship.

Saban wasn't one to pace around a locker room like Lombardi, because he typically tried to be as calm as possible before a big game, knowing his team would feed off his energy. He was nervous himself, admitting he got butterflies before every game, but he believed if his team sensed his nervousness and saw him pacing around the locker room on edge, they might adopt it and come out playing tight. Or even worse in Saban's eyes, they'd come out too fired up to start the game and exert too much emotional energy too soon, leading to careless mistakes. It was all about how they finished, not how they started, and burning too hot, too soon could be detrimental. So Saban usually swallowed down any nerves he might have and presented himself as a calm, fully-in-control leader.

That's not to say Saban has never embraced the emotional and given a powerful pregame speech. He picks and chooses the very rare moment when he needs to alter his usual approach. "Seeing that fire in him is so unusual it lights a fire in you," says former Alabama linebacker Alex Benson. "Saban knows when to ramp it up."

He did that before a 2008 road game against LSU, the first time Saban returned to Baton Rouge since leaving the school for the NFL. The LSU fan base didn't take too kindly to Saban quickly reemerging in the SEC after his brief NFL stint, and loudly let him know when Alabama team buses pulled up to Tiger Stadium. "There were fans rocking the bus and the bus was going side to side," says former Alabama offensive lineman Antoine Caldwell. "It was insane. They were yelling at us and Nick, throwing bottles and really taking it personal." Saban told his team that everyone was making the game about him, but it was really about them. He said it had been a long time since Alabama could say it was a better team than LSU, but on this day, they were, and they needed to go out there and prove it.

A fired-up Saban then told his team, "You play fast, you play strong, you go out there and dominate the guy you're playing against and make his ass quit. That's our trademark. That's our MO as a team. That's what people know us as." Players described the atmosphere in the locker room after that speech as electric, and Alabama went on to win the game.

Former Toledo safety Tim Caffey says Saban had one memorable speech during his lone season as the Rockets' head coach, and it was about his dog. Before an important conference game, he told his team that as a kid his next-door neighbor's dog would often come over to his yard and mark his territory. The neighbor's dog, bigger than Saban's dog, would come over every day to do his business while Saban's dog sat in the house barking loudly at the window at the sight of another dog marking his territory in his yard. Until one day, Saban's little dog had seen enough.

"My dog ran over there and took back his yard," Saban told the team. "What's the moral of the story, guys? Don't let anyone come piss in your yard."

The best leaders take different concepts and philosophies they've picked up throughout their lives and morph them to fit their style. Simply trying to replicate exactly what someone else is doing is often a recipe for failure (more on that later). Saban has four primary influences on his leadership and management styles: his father, his college coach (Don James), and two former bosses (Bill Belichick and George Perles). It'd be inaccurate to say only those four men shaped his perspective, as Saban was on a never-ending journey to get better, but he took the most from those four. Saban has been compared to all of them as he progressed in his career, especially Belichick, but he's his own man. He didn't try to copy the style of one of his mentors whole cloth, because it wouldn't have been authentic and he wouldn't have been able to enact it convincingly while running his organization.

Start with Belichick, whom Saban has cited as having the most significant professional influence on him. Saban has repeatedly referenced how impactful Belichick's "Do your job" mantra was on him, and it has become a core tenet in his successful Process. He lays out very clear job responsibilities and expectations for everyone in the organization, a skill he traces back to his time working for Belichick in Cleveland.

Just as Saban will go down as college football's greatest coach, Belichick has a strong argument as the NFL's best coach. He built the NFL's greatest modern dynasty, winning six Super Bowl titles from a span of 2001 to 2018 with the New England Patriots. Long before both made their cases as the greatest ever, they paired up in Cleveland as a first-time head coach and defensive coordinator. Belichick was fresh off a Super Bowl as the New York Giants' defensive coordinator and convinced Saban to leave Toledo after one season to run his defense. "Both guys were the same in the sense of the way of life of football, and that is to be totally thorough, cutting-edge football, no stone left unturned and to drive a team and keep everybody accountable," says Rick Venturi, who joined the two as the Browns' secondary coach in 1994. "I'm a privileged guy to have sat in between those guys for seventeen weeks and put those game plans together. They were egoless at that time; nobody had really established themselves. We were just trying to win football games."

Saban and Belichick are considered by some almost to be twins, but Venturi saw plenty of practical differences in how the two defensive gurus operated. Saban was a "high volume guy" who liked to have multiple calls and checks in his game plan to be ready for any situation. He was more aggressive by nature and liked man-to-man press coverage in the secondary. Belichick was more about coming up with the best one call for any situation and always wanted to take away the one or two things the opposing team did best. If the Pittsburgh Steelers had a star running back, Belichick wanted a game plan that neutralized the player and made them win elsewhere. How both delivered the information could be a stark contrast. Saban was fiery, having no qualms about yelling to make his point, while Belichick was more likely to drop a sarcastic remark to point out something he didn't like. Harlon Barnett, who played for both in Cleveland, says Saban would go from "0 to 60" when he saw something he didn't like. "How does this man not lose his voice as much as he yells and screams?" Barnett says. "I'd be like, 'Man, don't get a heart attack, Nick. We need you around here, dog. Don't be yelling too much.' But that's just who he is, and he's not going to change."

Interestingly, Saban was less likely to do that yelling and screaming during an actual game. That's not to say it doesn't happen—there is a graveyard of broken headsets somewhere from when Saban has lost his cool during games—but it served less of a purpose in his mind than in the lead-up to a game. During practice, he'd try to crank up the pressure to see how people reacted. There was less of a need for that during a game, with Saban once claiming the only times he did were purposeful and "tension relief."

"He is a master game manager," Venturi says. "He'd be volatile all week, yelling and screaming and slamming doors, but when you got to Sunday, he could run that game. He did it very methodically and never lost it unless he did it for effect."

From Perles, Saban learned how to develop player leaders, the twenty-four-hour rule, and the Fourth Quarter Program. Perles was a talented recruiter and defensive mind who gave Saban his first chance to be a defensive coordinator and the responsibilities that came with it. He learned from watching how Perles managed his relationships and treated everyone in the organization. "I think what Nick saw in my father was whether it was Carl Banks or whatever great leader he had, take him one-on-one and challenge him in the leadership part, in the offseason part, in the lifestyle choices," says Pat Perles. The elder Perles would often say, "Organization is the key to success. Plan your work, work your plan," a motto easily recognizable in Saban's system.

Saban first developed those organizational skills playing and later working for Don James at Kent State. James might be best known for being the man who convinced Saban to become a college coach, but he's also a Hall of Fame coach who won a national championship at Washington. James stressed attention to detail and being consistent no matter the circumstances, principles Saban readily adopted. Consider this story from Gary Pinkel, another James disciple, and see if it sounds familiar.

"Coach James just got beat by Army or something—we played awful and got beat by twenty-five or thirty points," Pinkel says. "And then two weeks later we beat [U]SC, the number one team in the country. If you went into the Sunday meeting afterward, you would not know the difference. We just went in and went to work, did our jobs, and kept going."

Saban combined the physical attributes Belichick wanted in players with the mental attributes James taught him to look for to build out his recruiting strategy. The critical-factors sheet was a hybrid of the two worlds and served

Saban well as he consistently signed the top-ranked recruiting classes in the country.

Saban has found a way to blend all those influences into a style that is natural and works best for him. His acolytes haven't always found the same right formula. Since first becoming a head coach in 1989, Saban has built an extensive and impressive coaching tree that includes former Michigan State coach Mark Dantonio, Texas A&M coach Jimbo Fisher, and Georgia coach Kirby Smart. At the start of the 2020 season, five SEC schools employed former Saban assistants, a trend *Sports Illustrated* once labeled the "Sabanization of college football." That trend has produced highs like Smart winning a national championship in 2022 at Georgia using an exact replica of Saban's Process to the lows of the failed Derek Dooley experiment at Tennessee.

No discussion of the Saban coaching tree would be complete without discussing a statistic that appeared any time Saban coached a game against one of his former assistants. Until the 2021 season, Saban had a perfect record against his former assistants. Before Fisher finally beat Saban on October 9, 2021, the Alabama head coach had a 24–0 record against the men who once worked for him. He often won by large margins, too, with a cumulative score of 1,060–459, good for an average score of 42–18.

Smart, the most Saban-like of the disciples, used Saban's blueprint to win a national championship. Smart followed Saban from LSU to Miami to Alabama, where he spent eight seasons as his defensive coordinator. He paid close attention to how and why things worked at Alabama before taking that exact formula to Georgia, where he built a program capable of rivaling Alabama's recruiting behemoth. "We literally implemented everything Alabama did, from the weekly schedule with the coaches to the practice schedule to the weight room program to whatever," former Georgia assistant Shane Beamer told ESPN. "It was identical. He didn't have to say, 'This is what Alabama did.' You knew it. A lot of stuff we used even had the Alabama logo on it and was copy and pasted with the Georgia logo on it."

It took five tries before Smart could finally beat Saban with his own strategy. Smart guided Georgia to the national championship game in 2017, a brutal heartbreak for Bulldogs fans when Alabama's Tua Tagovailoa threw a game-winning touchdown pass in overtime. The following year, Smart's Bull-dogs built a 28–14 lead in the third quarter before backup Alabama quarter-back Jalen Hurts led a furious comeback effort to win, capped off by a 15-yard touchdown run with a little more than a minute remaining in the game. Saban beat Smart in consecutive years in the same venue (Mercedes-Benz Stadium), featuring a quarterback change in the second half of each. In those first two losses to Saban, Smart seemed to be pressing too hard to beat him.

"They think they can outsmart him," says former Alabama State head coach L.C. Cole, another branch in the Saban coaching tree. "They do dumb things. Kirby Smart thought he was going to trick Coach Saban on a fake punt. You aren't going to beat him like that. You're not going to trick him."

Smart broke through in 2022 when his Georgia Bulldogs beat Saban's Crimson Tide, 33–18, in the College Football Playoff national champion-ship at Lucas Oil Stadium in Indianapolis. That Georgia team, led by a stout defensive front and powerful running game, looked and played like one of Saban's early title teams in Tuscaloosa. It led to a powerful moment after the game ended, when a smiling Saban congratulated his former assistant on winning it all. The relationship between the two became strained in the years after Smart left for Georgia. Those inside the Alabama organization believed Smart took the program's recruiting evaluations and used them against his mentor. Smart told mutual recruits where they stood on Alabama's recruit-ing board and used anything that could be considered negative in Alabama's evaluations to hurt the Tide's standing with specific recruits. It was a ruthless maneuver in the pursuit of success—as was Georgia's public battle with Ala-bama over transfer defensive back Maurice Smith—that upset people back in Tuscaloosa. But after Smart won it all, it felt like when a little brother finally found a way to beat the older one. Across from him, Saban saw a man whom he had groomed and developed from a young graduate assistant at LSU to one of college football's best coaches. Saban wanted to beat Smart, there is zero doubt about that, but at seventy years old and with his legacy already well established, Saban seemed truly happy for Smart in that moment, whether out of begrudging respect or pride that someone who truly understood his Process utilized it to tremendous success elsewhere.

"There's a certain level of satisfaction that says, 'I've done more than just win titles,'" says Chris Landry, who has known Saban for thirty years. "'Look, I'm having an influence on other people,' and you don't think that way when you're forty-two."

Out of all the Saban assistants, Smart, Fisher, and Billy Napier had the most success after leaving the organization and faithfully following The Process. They made their tweaks along the way, but they had success in a way that felt true to their personalities. The issues seemed to occur more when an assistant tried to copy Saban without actually committing to it. Throughout this book, there have been numerous stories about the hard work Saban personally does and how he expects everyone in his organization to try to match his pace. That's a challenging endeavor, to put it mildly.

"You see a lot of his assistants get head jobs and they try to act like Nick Saban, but they can't," says Kentucky associate head coach Vince Marrow. "Nobody can act like him. He is who he is, and there will never be another like him. Trust me."

Before Marrow competed against Saban in the SEC, he was part of his first team at Toledo. Saban knew the Marrow family well after unsuccessfully recruiting Vince's two older brothers while he was a Michigan State assistant coach. While still a Houston Oilers assistant coach, Saban bumped into Vince's brother Brad one day and told him he had just gotten the Toledo job. He inquired about the younger Marrow, who had multiple football scholarship offers out of high school but initially decided to pursue a college basketball path. Knowing what kind of athlete he was coming out of high school, Saban told Brad that he had a scholarship for Vince if he was interested.

"He probably saved my life when he gave me a scholarship to Toledo," Marrow says. "I was playing college basketball, got in a little trouble, and was out of school when out of the blue he tells my brother he got the head coaching job at Toledo. Hadn't seen me in three years and gave me a scholarship.

"I don't know what path I would have been on. I'm always forever indebted to Coach Saban."

Since playing for Saban at Toledo, Marrow has become one of the best recruiters in college football. As Kentucky's recruiting coordinator, he successfully recruited future NFL players like Lynn Bowden Jr. and Benny Snell to Kentucky, helping a traditional SEC bottom-dweller punch above its weight in recruiting. He occasionally has to recruit against Saban, a weird occurrence he likens to looking across a table and having to face off against "the Godfather." When people ask him why he's such a good recruiter, he talks about his ability to relate to people of all backgrounds to find a common connection. It's a skill he says he learned from watching Saban recruit his older brothers.

"Nick Saban can go into the hardest part of the inner city and capture that house and capture that community," he says. "People knew he was real; there was nothing fake about him. My dad loved him. My dad was a hard-core man—he didn't take to many people, especially white people—and he loved Coach Saban. That's why I think I am who I am today."

Saban can be awkward and introverted at times, but he's always been comfortable around people of all racial and socioeconomic backgrounds. As a kid growing up in West Virginia in the 1950s, Saban's best friend was Kerry Marbury, a Black football player from a neighboring town. Cole says Saban was always at ease and relaxed when he went into a Black player's home and would quickly find a way to charm everyone. "You see him doing the two-step; how many coaches in America can you see them be that easygoing? It's like he's part of the family."

Says former LSU assistant LeRoy Ryals, "I've seen him go into an African American house and eat fried chicken and collard greens that mama cooked. And then he goes into an Italian house and eats spaghetti. He can adapt. It's natural; he's not putting on a front."

Saban isn't the perfect leader. There is no such thing. He makes mistakes, does things that upset people, and fails like the rest of us. But he's found a style that works for him, that gives him the best chance of consistently being successful and helping everyone in his organization grow. It's a style molded from growing up in West Virginia, playing for Don James, and working for George Perles and Bill Belichick. Even after achieving tremendous success, he is still on a never-ending journey to get better and learn new, different ways to reach his players.

As a leader, you must find what works best for you. We could all stand to gain from taking a few things Saban does and adding them to our daily efforts. But that's really what it's about—taking the things that best apply to who we are and what we're trying to accomplish, rather than simply closing this book and acting identically to Saban. Be true to yourself, develop the "process" that works best for you, and become the leader you need to be.

CHAPTER 18

Applying Saban's Lessons Beyond Football

O n April 27, 2011, the deadliest tornado in Alabama state history leveled the city of Tuscaloosa, leaving a path of death and destruction in its wake. The devastating tornado killed 53 citizens and created more than $2 billion worth of damage. In a matter of minutes, a city and a community were forever changed. When surveying the damage, President Barack Obama said, "I've never seen devastation like this." It was a call to action for Nick Saban, who had focused more on building a football powerhouse than getting to know Tuscaloosa's residents his first few years there. His football program was directly impacted when long snapper Carson Tinker was badly injured and his girlfriend, Ashley Harrison, was killed.

Saban called an emergency team meeting the next morning to make sure everyone was safe and to discuss what to do. With the help of sports psychologist Kevin Elko, Saban offered a phrase to guide his grieving team in those uncertain days after the tornado hit: "I'm not looking for blessing to come to my life; I'm looking to be a blessing in someone's life." Saban told his team they needed to support their fans the way their fans always support them.

"This city has lost everything but the most valuable thing you can give them is your time and your presence in spending time with them," Saban told his team. "You can cut checks and make donations, but the most valuable thing any of us could give is our time."

Saban and his wife, Terry, bought hundreds of gift cards and handed them out to impacted residents. They committed to funding what has become eighteen houses—one for each Alabama national championship—through the local Habitat for Humanity. But, more than anything, he listened. He listened to people who had lost everything in an instant. Doing so taught him a meaningful lesson that sometimes it wasn't about the grand gesture. It made him reconsider his role in the community, and how much it meant to people just to talk to him. Terry Saban told people it was the first time her husband stopped thinking about football since he started playing as a ten-year-old. He realized it wasn't about offering inspiring words, though he did to many people, or trying to fix everything with one big check. It was about being there and showing through your actions how much you care. "We spent $1.1 million in two days, and the only thing people ever say is, 'I saw Coach at this place,'" Saban told one interviewer. Elko told me years ago it turned Saban into more of a "we" person, who recognized the important role he had as a leader in Alabama beyond the football field.

"He really got out there in the community after that and really focused on spending time with people and just being there," says former Alabama lineman David Blalock. "And I think that meant a lot to people."

Saban's presence has meant a lot to many people, from strangers he helped after a devastating tornado to players he saw every day for five years. He has changed so many people's lives in so many different ways over the years, both in big and small ways.

As part of my reporting process for this book, I talked to lots of former players, coaches, friends, acquaintances, and others who have been in Saban's orbit through the years. In my conversations with them, I asked them about the practical ways they still use Saban's lessons in their professional and personal lives today. They told me Saban quotes they still reference daily. They remembered little teaching moments with Saban they use with their children now. They referenced how Saban's influence still impacts them today.

Consider this a bonus chapter of sorts of the real-world examples of Saban's philosophies in practice. It's meant to give you a few more examples from those who know Saban well that might help you incorporate some aspect of Saban's leadership style into your life.

Harlon Barnett, former Michigan State cornerback; now Michigan State defensive backs coach

"A lot of my base drills are what he does and has done. My foundation is Nick and then whatever I've learned on my own by playing the sport, playing the position, and in coaching. Even when I was doing the broadcasting thing, I was coaching high school football at my high school in Cincinnati, Ohio. I was coaching high school ball for five years before I got into college ball. He would run the DB meetings and what I did was take notes on how he presented, how he said things. You can know something, but how to present it is another thing. That's why I think a lot of professional athletes can't necessarily go right into coaching, because they know what they want and what it looks like but don't know how to say it or present it. I got a lot of my presentation stuff from Nick on how he coached them on press technique, all those types of things."

Alex Benson, former Alabama linebacker; now a commercial real estate broker

"The 'So what? Now what?' he talks about a lot—that happened, so what, now what—I think that's what I use most day-to-day. No matter what happens—like, so what, now what? Don't dwell on it, learn from it, but you've got to move on, and you've always got to be looking forward. So what, we won—now what? You've got twenty-four hours to celebrate but so what, now what? That's the thing I took away the most was that mindset.

In the real world, dealing with non-football-related everyday stuff, you see so many people get bogged down because something happened. They can't shake it off and move on. That's the main thing I apply, and I can see if that person could just shake that off and move on to what's next, [it] would help them a lot."

David Blalock, former Alabama offensive lineman; now a retail workforce specialist

"Within quick reach of me there's this quote that he used to preach all the time talking about choices where he says young people all think they have this illusion of choice, like I can do whatever I want to do. 'You have a younger generation now that doesn't always get told no, they don't always get told this is exactly how you have to do it, so they have this illusion that they have all these choices. But the fact of the matter is, if you want to be good, you really don't have a lot of choices, because it takes what it takes.' That mantra is something that stays with me and stands out. You don't have any choices. There's really only one choice, and it takes what it takes and you do what you have to do to be successful. That all ties into being disciplined, being focused, and really being able to grind when it gets hard."

Hunter Bryant, former Alabama tight end; now an asset management analyst

"I'm with a company that's acquiring and managing office buildings, basically. There are times my boss, he'll give me an underwrite for a building where I know and he knows we're not going to buy the building. But he expects every detail to be spot on and done right. It gives me these Saban-esque feelings where I'm doing the underwrite like I'm about to present to our CEO and my future with the company almost depends on it. That's my mindset and that's what's expected. It feels very similar to when we'd play, like, Mississippi State. With Mississippi State every year the narrative was this team always plays us hard, we're always asleep, we're never ready for this team."

Tim Caffey, former Toledo safety; now president of Selah Homes

"There's nothing in life you can't compare to football. Consistency. Always doing it right the first time, in practice doing it right. In home-building, I tell my foremen that all the time. We have to practice doing the right thing because when we don't, we lose money. Period. We have a fumble in the field, that meant someone forgot a cabinet space or did that—there's so many things that go on in construction. I remember one guy asking me, 'Tim, how do you keep your costs down?' I said, 'You see this sheet right here? That's the cost sheet.' He said,

'OK, everybody does that,' but mine's on a percentage. If I lose here, I have to gain here. It's telling me everywhere I may lose. If I'm $200 over, I've got to pick up that $200 somewhere else. That's consistency. Knowing when something was wrong, and fixing it immediately."

L.C. Cole, former Toledo running backs coach; now a high school coach

"When I became the head coach at Tennessee State University, I came in and did the same things he taught me when I was at Toledo and we ended up winning a championship over there. He taught me that when you give someone responsibilities, all you have to do is you check around them, and if they do their responsibilities and stay on top of things, you're going to be all right."

Jimmy Courtenay, former LSU offensive lineman; now an attorney at JJC Law

"It wasn't rosy on Monday mornings, even if we won the game. You went through the bad plays, win or lose, talked about it, and then you moved on. By the afternoon, it's on to the next game. I try to do that in my personal life; I try to do that in work life. I tell my staff, 'Look, if there's an issue that happens, you need to come tell me, we will deal with it right then and there, and then we'll move on.' We cannot live concerned about this incident for days; we have other things to do. Let's deal with it. If we can fix it, then fix it; and if we can't fix it, let's do what we need to do to deal with it and then we need to push forward. We cannot get lost in that. The production level just drops if you can't move past something that happens. And I think that's all from football."

Matt Eberflus, former Toledo linebacker; now Chicago Bears head coach

"I've learned to define roles for everybody. This is what Coach Saban did for coaches. For each individual coach, everybody knows what their role is; for each individual player on a given play, [they know] what their role is. Not only in terms of execution, but what it takes mentally and physically how we're going to play the game. He made that very clear for us. He had ways to measure it. He would say, 'What does running to the football mean?' 'What [does] getting off a block mean—what does that look like?' He would love to teach the techniques and the fundamentals of the individual positions."

Mike Groh, former Alabama receivers coach; now Indianapolis Colts receivers coach

"One thing I talk to players about all the time is just playing with a relentless competitive attitude, dominate your opponent, one play at a time. For sixty minutes, each play has a life span of its own. Just to be able to do that, each and every day, and in control of your own self-determination. You go out there with that kind of mindset to get better each and every day, then you will. If you eliminate the clutter and just focus on the process and not the results, you'll end up getting there faster."

Trevor Hewett, former Alabama recruiting staffer; now assistant general manager for McConnell Hospitality Group

"The biggest thing with Coach is everyone knowing what their role is, and what their job is, and what their expectations are in that job. There is one leader, there is one voice, and I have my orders and my job is to execute my orders. If you want people to do their job, they have to know what their job is. I knew exactly what my job was every single day I went into that office. I didn't have to do anybody else's job; I didn't have to worry if anybody was doing their job. My job was to do this and everybody was going to do their job. Because if they don't, they don't last."

Paris Hodges, former LSU offensive lineman; now an athletic coordinator

"He would talk to us and it was no rah-rah, it was stoic. It was calm and his presence was that. One thing that I got from him that I tell my guys all the time—[Saban] would always tell us to treat this like a business meeting. You prepare for your business meeting prior to and throughout the week because when you get to your meeting and you have to take or be physical, you already know what to expect because you've done your homework."

Keith Holcombe, former Alabama linebacker; now a sawmill manager

"I feel like if I'm sitting down, I'm doing something wrong. I'm always trying to look for something to do because the mindset at Bama is there's always something to do. That drive, that itch, be excellent at that. I'm demanding so much out of myself, it gets rolled over, it gets noticed."

Josh Keur, former Michigan State tight end; now a human services case manager

"He taught us not to get too high or low because one game and there you are back on the bottom rung. So I apply that every day in my work because I can see myself in the fact we all, in a lot of cases, are one emergency away from dealing with situations like my clients do where they're having a housing crisis or they lost a job and now they can't pay their bills. I use it with my kids. It's just teaching them, in my opinion, to stay the course and be humble and realize it's a slippery pole here in life that we're all holding on to. And even when you feel like you're at the top, you can quickly be back down at the bottom. So you have to keep that perspective."

Louis LeBlanc, former Alabama graduate assistant; now a high school football coach

"I've kind of molded his mantra that every play has a life of its own. I talk to the guys about being present in the moment, be where your feet are, and every play matters. I try to rephrase what he said any number of ways I can so that it connects. Every single play matters, and then I've got to forget this play when it's over and get ready for the next one, good or bad. I've got to get rid of it—it's not going to help me win the next one.

My big tagline that I tell everybody is I'm trying to use football to build better men. What a great segue into teaching these young men that how can you be the father you need to be if you're taking problems from work home and neglecting your kids just because you're pissed off? How can I be the coworker I'm supposed to be if all I can think about is how great I was last year and I'm getting screwed now because I'm not getting the big opportunities I need? How can I be who I was made to be if all I can think about is the person I was six seconds ago or six years ago? Good or bad. I'm a firm believer that we can't outperform our own self-identity. Saban really modeled—what's your self-identity? If it's locked in the past, what are you right now? What are you going to do right now?"

Will Lowery, former Alabama defensive back; now a real estate developer

"I think our minds are wired similarly. He's pretty straightforward in that he's got a task in front of him, to get the best football program he can put on the field *each season. He's got it dialed down to a very fine process on how to do that, and he is hell-bent and relentless in his pursuit of excellence and doing it to the best of his ability. I'm the same way. Right now, I run a real estate development company for a small private equity group here on the Gulf Coast, and I'm trying to apply it every single day. I'm trying to build this. I'm not to the point where he's just got it down to this fine science—we are still trying to get it figured out. We are trying to fine-tune those processes and dial in on exactly how to get there every day, and try to back that into a system, a process that you can record down and hand somebody and teach and replicate and grow and scale."*

Vince Marrow, former Toledo tight end; now Kentucky tight ends coach

"If you look at the recruiting success I've had, I learned a lot from Nick Saban and the drive and how you don't take anything lightly. You recruit as hard as you can and never take a break in recruiting. He never takes a break."

Greg McElroy, former Alabama quarterback; now an ESPN broadcaster

"The biggest thing I use every day is—every day, I compete against myself. That, I think, is something that is ingrained in who you are, but it is cultivated in that environment. I'm naturally a competitive person. If you are not competing with who you were yesterday, you're wasting your time. You are constantly competing either against somebody else or competing against yourself. I want to be a better broadcaster today, I want to be a better dad today, I want to be a better husband today than I was yesterday. That's not always going to be the case, but from one day to the next, I'm either going up or I'm going down. I'm not going to be the same. I think that's something the program teaches you: Are you going to be better or are you going to be worse? Because you're not going to be the same."

Taylor Pharr, former Alabama offensive lineman; now an attorney at Pharr & Goree

"You always think back to the twenty-four hours of, 'Hey, let me go sleep on this and think about how I want to do this or respond,' versus acting on emotion. You want to be emotional, but you don't want to get to the point where your

emotions drain your energy to the point you can't make a good decision. I use that every day. When we settle a case, we'll enjoy it for twenty-four hours and then we have other cases to work on. You try to always move forward."

Chris Smith, former Michigan State defensive lineman; now a high school teacher and football coach

"I think the main thing is accountability. The thing I still use with my team today is being accountable to each other, doing their jobs, and trusting that their teammates are going to be doing their jobs. I think that's a big thing. Coach Saban brought in these production charts and he would show which players are actually productive on the field and which ones weren't, and they didn't always line up with what the media had out there. So I really like the production charts. I really preached discipline with my kids in getting to class on time, not being idiots in the hallways, acting responsible off the field, being accountable to the football program and to your teammates. Those are all things that I picked up."

Lance Walker, former Alabama academic advisor; now athletic director at Hewitt-Trussville High School

"He said high achievers don't like ordinary people; ordinary people don't like high achievers. I think about that a lot in what I do now. Particularly when you're trying to hire people and have all the right people in your school and in your organization. I take so much that I saw from him into what I do now in my athletic director position in terms of hiring the right people, in terms of organization, in terms of trying to set the tone, in terms of having clear communication, attention to detail, hard work. There are so many things that come along where I think, 'How would Coach Saban handle this situation?'"

Acknowledgments

Nick Saban didn't participate in the writing of this book, but he certainly served as the inspiration for it. Writing a book has always been a bucket list item for me, but I never knew when—or if—I'd ever get a chance to do so. That you have this book in your hands right now, written during a pandemic, no less, is a credit to a lot of people.

Thank you:

To my parents, Bob and Kathie, and my siblings, Caitlin and Will, for their immeasurable support over the years in allowing me to pursue my dreams.

To Matt Holt, Katie Dickman, Mallory Hyde, Brigid Pearson, Michael Fedison, and everyone else at BenBella Books, for wanting to publish this book and shepherding it along the way. Matt made this experience as seamless as possible, and we should all be so lucky to have an editor like Katie, who offered such helpful, constructive feedback throughout the process.

To my friend David Magee, who was an early believer in this idea and deserves as much credit as anyone for turning a Jersey-born Maryland graduate into an SEC football expert.

To my bosses at Alabama Media Group: Izzy Gould, Kelly Ann Scott, and Tom Bates—for allowing me to pursue this project and continuing to support my childhood dream of writing about sports. I never imagined I'd cover Alabama sports, let alone doing so now for eight years, and it's a credit to their leadership and belief in me. Michelle Holmes, Bob Sims, KA Turner, Roy Johnson, and Elizabeth Hoekenga Whitmire have also helped me grow as a journalist at AL.com.

To every person willing to talk to me for this book, both those who gave on-the-record interviews and those who provided helpful information on background. This book wouldn't be what it is without them being willing to spend time sharing with me the impact Nick Saban made on their lives.

To my friends John Archibald, Paul Finebaum, and Rainer Sabin for their guidance and helpful suggestions to improve the book after reading early drafts of chapters. They made this book better.

To my fellow journalists Alex Scarborough, Joseph Goodman, Justin Yurkanin, Matt Zenitz, Michael Casagrande, Mike Rodak, and Ross Dellenger, for listening to me talk about this book for far too long and still offering valuable suggestions on how to improve it.

To Dr. Kathryn Bartol and Maj. Jordan Terry, who patiently explained leadership principles to me that helped shape this book.

To my PML crew: Kevin Roak, Peter Tartaglione, Chris Colaitis, Kenny Voshell, Matt Clementson, Scott Gilson, Josh Saxe, Steve Blaney, Tom Snyder, and Chris Hidalgo for all their encouragement throughout the writing of this book. These men are my brothers, who have celebrated the good times with me and pulled me through the bad ones.

Index

A

academics, 25, 118–122

accountability, 14, 24, 53, 102, 152

acts of service, 173

Addai, Joseph, 110

affirmations, 89

African Americans, 164–165

Alabama (state)

    football's popularity in, 192

    Saban's role in, 218

Alabama, University of, 4. *See also* Tuscaloosa

    conditions at, 14

    environment at, 114–116

    loss to, 130

    Moore, 20, 114

    offense, 58–59

    possibility of Saban leaving, 188–189

    previous coaches. *see* Bryant, Paul; Shula, Mike

    resources at, 105, 114

    Saban hired at, 113–114

    Saban's arrival at, 19

    Saban's record at, 53–54, 91, 153, 199. *see also* national championships

    2010 team, 198–200

Alabama at Birmingham (UAB), 109, 185

alcohol, 10

AL.com, 165, 184

Allen, Jeff, 145

Alles, Todd, 19, 26, 28, 85, 117, 132, 173

ambition, 106

analysts, 74–75, 77, 82, 83–84

Anderson, Darren, 2, 10, 138

Anderson, Joel, 11, 12

Anderson, Keaton, 96, 103

Angelo, Jerry, 111

Ansley, Derrick, 63

Applewhite, Major, 75

Arenas, Javier, 31

Arnsparger, Bill, 107, 109

ass chewings, 5, 60, 61, 177

assistant coaches, 50–53, 67–68. *See also* staff

    distressed assets, 73–84

    former, Saban's record against, 211

    relationships between, 178

    relationships with players, 177–178

    replacing, 62

Auburn University, 37, 185. *See also* Iron Bowl
    losses to, 155–156, 188, 199–200
Austin, Matt, 155

B
ball boy, 171
Bandura, Albert, 139
Banks, Carl, 210
Banks, Jeff, 63
Barmore, Christian, 179
Barnett, Derek, 73
Barnett, Harlon, 55, 92, 126, 137, 177, 209, 219
Barron, Mark, 32, 47, 198
Bayless, Skip, 188
Beamer, Shane, 211
Belichick, Bill, 4, 12, 23, 66, 85, 106–107, 111, 136, 158, 179, 192, 208–209, 210, 214
Belichick, Steve, 106–107, 158
Belichick & Saban: The Art of Coaching, 106
beliefs, limiting, 89
Benson, Alex, 15, 43, 88–89, 207, 219
Black Lives Matter, 164–165
Blalock, David, 44, 53, 125, 151, 195, 218, 220
blame, 150–151, 176
Blockbuster Video, 163
Bluegrass Miracle, 130
bonuses, recruiting and, 28
boosters, 28
Bowden, Terry, 110
Brady, Tom, 66

Brandt, Gil, 108
Brees, Drew, 113
Broyles Award, 77
Bruce, Earle, 156, 157
Bryant, Hunter, 61, 82, 134, 135, 168, 176, 191, 220
Bryant, Kobe, 161
Bryant, Paul "Bear", 1, 151
bully, Saban perceived as, 173. *See also* personality, Saban's; style, Saban's
Burke, Monte, 143
Burns, Burton, 52, 55, 62, 63, 147–148
Burress, Plaxico, 87
buy-in, 16, 140, 141–142, 177
buyouts, 73, 75

C
Caffey, Tim, 7, 10, 12, 141–142, 208, 220–221
Caldwell, Antoine, 15, 16, 47, 49, 87, 152, 153, 207
Captain Class, The (Walker), 44–45
captains, 43–47, 48, 55, 87
Carroll, Pete, 88
Casher, Josh, 95
Catapult Sports, 145
Center for American Progress, 62
change, 7–17. *See also* no huddle
    adapting to, 159–170
    adapting to players' needs, 168–169
    buy-in and, 16
    leading, 8, 9, 163
    no huddle, 58–59, 159–160, 162, 170

recruiting and, 164

resistance to, 15–16, 17, 157, 163

during successful periods,
163–164, 170

character, evaluating, 25–26

Charleston Southern University, 186

Chicago Bears, 17. *See also* Eberflus,
Matt

Clayton, Michael, 110

cleaning crew, 19, 137

Clemson University, 54, 68, 132–133,
134–135, 147, 149, 188

Cleveland Browns, 4, 12, 23, 106, 136,
192

clutter, 96, 100, 102. *See also* outside
factors

coaches, failed, 77. *See also* analysts;
distressed assets

Cochran, Scott, 15, 52–53, 55, 62,
96–97, 152, 169, 190, 191

Cody, Terrence, 162

Coker, Jake, 133

Cole, L.C., 9, 11, 122, 136, 175, 212,
221

College Football Playoff, 144

Columbia University, 191

commitment, 22, 136

community, Saban's role in, 218

competitive culture, 35, 37, 39

complacency, 150, 176, 195–204

resisting, 201–204

success and, 196–201

twenty-four-hour rule and, 197

computers, 109

conditioning. *See* strength and
conditioning

conduct. *See* discipline

confidence, 139, 175

confrontation, 11, 172. *See also* honesty

consistency, 15. *See also* continuity;
turnover

continuity, 12, 64. *See also* consistency;
turnover

copycat effect, 62

coronavirus, 28, 80, 98

Coughlin, Tom, 111

courage, personal, 172, 178

Courtenay, Jimmy, 102, 131, 221

coverage. *See* media

COVID-19, 28, 80, 98

Creative Artists Agency (CAA), 64, 65,
188. *See also* Sexton, Jimmy

Cristobal, Mario, 62

criticism/disrespect, 173, 175, 191. *See
also* honesty

Cromartie, Antonio, 83

Crum, Dick, 4

Culpepper, Daunte, 113

culture

changing, 7, 10, 11, 13. *see also*
change

competitive, 35, 39

delegation and, 117–127

establishing, 17, 126

hiring and, 81

D

Daboll, Brian, 63, 135

dancing, 187

Danielson, Gary, 82, 134

Dantonio, Mark, 178, 211

Dareus, Marcell, 198

Davis, Al, 57–58

Davis, Bo, 63, 65

Davis, Butch, 108

Davis, Chris, 155

Dawsey, Lawrence, 83

Dean, Joe, 107, 143

defensive backs, 125–126

delegation, 117–127

depth chart, 40

de-recruitment process, 34

detail, attention to, 129

Dickerson, Landon, 55

Diggs, Trevon, 135

DiNardo, Gerry, 143

disappointment, 91

discipline, 11, 36, 47, 49–50, 53, 91,
    166. *See also* outside factors

Dishman, Cris, 11, 112, 126, 140–141,
    174

disrespect/criticism, 173, 175, 191. *See
    also* honesty

distractions, 101. *See also* outside
    factors

distressed assets, 73–84

diversity, Saban's comfort with, 214

Dooley, Derek, 73, 143, 211

Downtown Coaches Club, 109

Drake, Kenyan, 145

Dunbar, Karl, 63

dynasties, 200. *See also* success

E

Eberflus, Matt, 8–9, 17, 179, 180–181,
    221

efficiency, 177

ego, 82, 204

Elko, Kevin, 87, 217, 218

Elliott, Ezekiel, 144

Emerson, Ralph Waldo, 94

Emmert, Mark, 107, 109

emotion, 168. *See also* personality,
    Saban's

employees, 19, 20, 121, 137. *See also*
    assistant coaches; staff

Enos, Dan, 68

Erickson, Dennis, 108

ESPN, 187–190

evaluation, constant, 159–170, 173. *See
    also* change

Evans, Alan, 36, 101, 187

Evans, Alex, 187

Evans, Chenavis, 101

Evans, Rashaan, 36–37, 101, 162, 187

evolution. *See* change; evaluation,
    constant

excuses, 21, 176

expectations, 8, 15, 19–20, 67–68, 176,
    208

F

failure, 146–158. *See also* losses

fans, 150, 184

Farrell, Brendan, 169

Fast and Slow theory, 60

father figure, Saban as, 167

Favre, Brett, 123

FCS (Football Championship Subdivision) opponents, 184–186
Fedora, Larry, 84
feedback. *See* criticism/disrespect; honesty
film, 136
Fisher, Jimbo, 64, 80, 83, 201, 211, 213
Fitzpatrick, Minkah, 135
Flood, Kyle, 63, 81
Florida, University of, 153, 200
Florida Atlantic University, 61
Florida State University, 28, 201
Floyd, George, 164
focus, 101. *See also* outside factors
Football Championship Subdivision (FCS) opponents, 184–186
40 GPS, 145
foundation, establishing, 17
Fourth Quarter Program, 12, 15, 29, 52, 152, 202–203, 210
4th and Goal Every Day (Savage), 90
fraternities, 102
Freeze, Hugh, 65
Frei, Terry, 109
Fryzel, Dennis, 156, 157
Fulmer, Phil, 73
future, 37, 93

G
game management, 210
Garcia, Stephen, 199
Gattis, Josh, 68
Georgia, University of, 133–136, 211–212
Georgia Southern University, 185

Gilbert, Jon, 19, 114, 196–197
Gill, Richard, 107
Glanville, Jerry, 4, 11
goals, 90
Golding, Pete, 65, 177
Good, Bad, and Ugly sessions, 175–176
graduate assistants, 76, 82, 84. *See also* staff
Graham, Shayne, 84
Grantham, Todd, 178
Griffith, Adam, 133, 155–156
Groh, Al, 75
Groh, Mike, 64, 68, 75–76, 80, 84, 174, 203, 222
Grooters, Roger, 119, 120
guiding coalition, 9

H
Habitat for Humanity, 218
Hackman, J. Richard, 172
Haden, Pat, 57
Harris, Najee, 83, 164–165
Harrison, Ashley, 217
Harvard Business School, 8, 163
health, Saban's, 95–98
Heisman Trophy
    Henry, 52, 59
    Ingram, 50, 52, 153
    DeVonta Smith, 24
    Young, 34
Henderson, Devery, 130
Henry, Derrick, 52, 59, 166
Herbstreit, Kirk, 188
Hereford, Mac, 47, 54, 96, 148, 202

Hewett, Trevor, 23, 29, 32, 40–41, 85, 95, 118, 222

Higgins, E. Tory, 191–192

Hightower, Dont'a, 46, 162, 198

Hill, Renaldo, 86

hiring, 78–79. *See also* staff

Hodges, Paris, 35–36, 74, 102, 112, 165, 222

Holcombe, Keith, 53, 55, 141, 167–168, 190, 222

honesty, 171–181

Houston Oilers, 4, 11, 140–141, 174

How Good Do You Want to Be? (Saban), 2

Howard, O.J., 133

Howell, Ben, 43, 49, 154–155

Huff, Charles, 63

Huizenga, Wayne, 111

Human Performance Project, 161

humbleness, 82

Humphrey, Marlon, 133

Hurd, Jalen, 73

Hurley, Brandon, 110, 131, 174, 178

Hurts, Jalen, 38, 133–134, 212

I

illness, 96–97

IMG, 87

influences, Saban's, 208–211

Ingram, Mark, 50, 52, 153, 198

innovations, 83. *See also* analysts

integrity. *See* self, staying true to

intensity, 10, 29

interns, 77

Iron Bowl, 185

loss in, 155–156, 188, 199–200

2013, 155–156

2020, 80, 98

2021, 199–200

Irvin, Sedrick, 124–125, 206

J

Jackson, Dominick, 59, 167, 174

Jacobs, Stanley, 107

Jagr, Jaromir, 87

James, Don, 3, 208, 210, 214

janitors, 19, 137

Jenkins, Pete, 67, 80, 99, 109

job interviews, 142–143

job loss, 156–158

job security, recruiting and, 28

Johns, Jimmy, 151

Jones, Barrett, 155, 199

Jones, Butch, 73, 80, 82–83, 124

Jones, Christion, 60, 139, 140, 154, 165

Jones, Quintorris "Julio," 31, 32–33, 35, 47–48

Jones, Mac, 38–39, 55

Jordan, Michael, 161, 173, 191

K

Kahneman, Daniel, 60

Kamara, Alvin, 73, 166

Karam, Tommy, 193, 194

Keitel, Harvey, 80

Kennedy, Billy, 40

Kent State University, 3, 4

Kentucky, University of, 130, 213–214

Keur, Josh, 12, 13, 48, 52, 95, 150, 223

Key, Brent, 68

Khan, Nick, 188

Kick Six, 155–156, 188

Kiesau, Eric, 58–59, 170

Kiffin, Lane, 57–62, 65, 66, 68, 73, 78, 79, 80, 82, 95–96, 161, 170, 184, 194

King, Martin Luther, Jr., 93

Kotter, John, 8, 9, 163

Kuligowski, Craig, 68

Kwon, Andy, 82, 83

L

Lambert, Jack, 3, 45

Lambert Award, 45

Landry, Chris, 107, 157, 212–213

language, Saban's, 10, 15–16

Last Dance, The (documentary), 173

Le Batard, Dan, 113

leader. *See also* assistant coaches
    meaning of, 48
    qualities of, 172

leaders, player, 151–152
    captains, 43–47, 48, 55, 87
    developing, 49
    discipline and, 49–50
    importance of, 54–55
    peer leadership council, 48–50
    preparing, 48

Leading Change (Kotter), 8

Leading Teams (Hackman), 172

Leatherwood, Alex, 55

LeBlanc, Louis, 22, 31, 66, 121, 171, 223

LeMaster, Lisa, 193

Leone, Doug, 198

Linehan, Scott, 84

liquidated damages, 75

Locksley, Mike, 38, 39, 68, 77–78, 147

logistics, 129

Lombardi, Vince, 206–207

losses. *See also* failure
    to Auburn, 155–156, 188, 199–200
    to Florida, 153
    learning from, 130–131, 146. *see also* preparation
    to Louisiana Monroe, 151–152, 153
    by LSU, 130
    to LSU, 199
    media after, 190
    to South Carolina, 199
    to Texas A&M, 154, 161, 162
    in 2019 championship game, 148
    twenty-four-hour rule and, 150, 152

Louisiana Monroe, University of, 151–152, 153

Louisiana State University (LSU), 14
    academics at, 119
    Bluegrass Miracle, 130
    bowl games at, 143
    coach turnover at, 107, 108
    ESPN program on, 187
    loss by, 130
    loss to, 199
    media and, 192–193
    Miles, 32
    national championship and, 3, 4, 55, 74, 102, 144, 177, 200, 202
    preparation at, 137
    reception at, 207–208

recruiting and, 32, 35–36
resources at, 105, 107–108, 109
Saban's interview at, 143
staff at, 69
love language, 173
Lowery, Will, 47, 100, 145, 160, 171, 199, 223–224
loyalty, 14, 66
Lupoi, Tosh, 68, 77

M

Maloney, Frank, 3
Malzahn, Gus, 75
management style. *See* style, Saban's
managers, 51, 171
Manchin, Joe, 201
Mannie, Ken, 7–8, 12, 13, 15
Manziel, Johnny, 154, 161
Mariota, Marcus, 201
market inefficiency, 75, 83
marriage, advice about, 185
Marrone, Doug, 81
Marrow, Brad, 213
Marrow, Brian, 27
Marrow, Duane, 27
Marrow, Vince, 27, 142, 213–214, 224
Mason, Glen, 4, 22, 62, 70, 108, 156, 157, 158
McClain, Rolando, 43–47, 162
McDaniels, Josh, 178
McElroy, Greg, 31, 46, 50, 165, 188, 199, 203–204, 224
McElwain, Jim, 76, 171
McNeil, John, 88
media, 150, 183–194

after losses, 190
AL.com, 165, 184
LSU and, 192–193
negative coverage, 5, 190
one-voice policy, 192, 193, 194–195
perceptions of Saban in, 186–188
positive coverage, 5
preparation for press conferences, 186
pressure from, 174, 192–193
recruiting and, 186–188
sending message through, 183–184, 190
mediocrity, 9
Medved, Ron, 89–90
Mendoza, Tom, 163–164, 175, 197–198
mental clutter, 101. *See also* outside factors
mental conditioning, 87, 161
mental makeup, 29
meritocracy, 35, 141–142. *See also* opportunity
Meyer, Urban, 200
Miami Dolphins, 4, 14, 111–114, 126
Michigan, University of, 105–106
Michigan State University (MSU), 3, 12–14, 106, 107
The Process at, 86
recruiting at, 27
resources at, 108–109
Saban's decision to leave, 109
Saban's record at, 86, 105–106, 143
staff at, 51–52, 68–70
middle management, 51

Miles, Les, 32

Miller, Christian, 93, 148, 161–162, 170

Miller, Corey, 93, 148, 161

mindset, 85, 89. *See also* Process, The

mistakes, honesty about, 177

Moawad, Trevor, 87, 161

Mollick, Ethan, 51

Moore, Mal, 20, 114

motivation, 149, 150, 152, 168, 191, 197, 205–207, 210. *See also* potential, maximizing

movie nights, 131

Mullen, Dan, 64

Muschamp, Will, 83–84

N

Napier, Billy, 40, 62, 76–77, 213

national championships, 54

    Auburn's, 199–200

    Clemson's, 68, 147, 149

    at LSU, 3, 4, 55, 74, 102, 144, 177, 200, 202–204

    staff turnover after, 63

    2009, 33, 46, 90, 151, 153, 160, 195–197

    2012, 162

    2015, 59, 61, 63, 190, 191

    2016, 132–133, 145

    2017, 38, 63, 68, 136, 197, 211

    2020, 1, 4, 53, 55, 63, 160

    undefeated seasons and, 158

    won by former assistants, 211, 212

Navy, 3, 106, 107, 157

NCAA, 21, 52, 74, 117

Nebraska, University of, 200

NetApp, 163–164, 175, 197–198

Netflix, 163

New England Patriots, 66

news coverage. *See* media

Newton, Cam, 199

NFL. *See also individual teams*

    coaches in, 17

    former Alabama players in, 4

    former head coaches, 81

    head coaches' power in, 112

    power structure of, 113

    Saban's career in, 4, 11, 111–114. *see also* Cleveland Browns; Houston Oilers; Miami Dolphins

    Saban's relationship with, 178–180

NFL Draft, 33, 113, 178–180, 200

no huddle, 58–59, 159–160, 162, 170

Noll, Chuck, 3

Nussmeier, Doug, 58

O

Oakland Raiders, 57

Obama, Barack, 217

obedience, 11

O'Brien, Bill, 66, 81

offense, 58–59

Ohio State University, 3, 86, 144, 156–158, 200

Ole Miss, 67

O'Neal, Shaquille, 193

one-voice policy, 192, 193, 194–195

opioid crisis, 164

opportunity. *See also* meritocracy

    vs. promises, 34–39, 41

recruiting and, 32–33
Oregon, University of, 201
organization. *See* employees; staff
Orgeron, Ed, 205
outcome-driven strategy, 90
outside factors, 95–103. *See also* clutter;
  COVID-19; discipline
overpreparation, 143

P
P3 Insights, 36
Pacific Institute, The, 88–90, 161
Panciera, Mark, 88, 89
Pappanastos, Andy, 135
Parcells, Bill, 175
participation management, 172
peer leadership council, 48–50
perfection, 92
Perles, George, 3, 12–14, 15, 27, 106,
  107, 150, 208, 210, 214
Perles, Pat, 25, 116, 124, 161, 205, 210
personality, Saban's, 5, 165–168, 173,
  186–188, 209. *See also* ass chewings
Peterson, Julian, 87
Pharr, Taylor, 14, 50, 91–92, 195,
  224–225
Pinkel, Gary, 3, 105, 115, 173, 203, 210
play, focus on, 86, 93
play calls, 59, 66
players, Saban's relationship with,
  164–168
playoffs, 144
Ponder, Ellis, 161
potential, maximizing, 175, 176, 180.
  See also motivation

practices, 11, 125, 138–140, 143, 171,
  174, 177
praise, 173
preferential treatment, 15, 168–169
preparation, 129–146
  benefits beyond football, 142
  meritocracy and, 141–142
  movie nights, 131
  organization and, 131–132
  overpreparation, 143
  playoffs and, 144
  practices and, 138–140
  for press conferences, 186
  productivity and, 137–138
  scouting reports, 140–141
  technology and, 144–145
  work-life balance and, 136–138
press. *See* media
pressure, 33, 174, 192–193
Price, Mike, 14
pride, 93
priorities, 118, 179
proactive, being, 106
Process, The, 64, 85–94
  devotion to, 160
  failure to follow, 148
  influences on, 208
  outside factors and, 100
  recommitment to, 149
  used by former assistants, 211–213
process thinking, 86
productivity, 137–138
promises, vs. opportunity, 34–39, 41
Pruitt, Jeremy, 63, 65
Pujols, Albert, 28

Pulp Fiction, 80
punishments. *See* discipline
PX2, 88

Q
Quiznos, 163

R
Randall, Marcus, 130
rankings, recruiting, 28–29
rat poison comments, 183–184
record, Saban's, 1. *See also* national
   championships
      before Alabama, 14
      at Alabama, 53–54, 91, 199
      at LSU, 109–110, 111
      at Miami Dolphins, 113
      at Michigan State, 86, 105–106,
         143
      at Toledo, 12
      undefeated seasons, 158
recruiting, 19–29, 66
      appearance and, 19–20
      bonuses and, 28
      change and, 162, 164
      competition in, 39–41
      during COVID-19 pandemic, 100
      delegation and, 118
      de-recruitment process, 34
      evaluating character, 25–26
      evaluating mental makeup, 29
      expectations and, 19–20
      focus on, 20
      interaction with players and, 164
      of Julio Jones, 32–33
      by Kentucky, 213–214
      by Locksley, 78
      at LSU, 35–36
      by Lupoi, 77
      media and, 186–188
      at Michigan State, 27
      in Mobile region, 31–32
      NCAA and, 21, 117
      negative, 39–41
      opportunity vs. promises in,
         32–33, 34–39, 41
      in-person evaluations, 28
      relationship with NFL and,
         179–181
      Terry Saban and, 115
      Saban rule, 21
      Saban sheets, 24
      Saban's approach to, 23
      Saban's comfort with diversity and,
         214
      Saban's health and, 97–98
      Shula's, 14
      staff turnover and, 64, 68
      success and, 24–25
      summer camps, 29, 33–34
      transfers and, 34
recruiting rankings, 28–29
recruiting weekends, 26–27
rehabilitation, 80. *See also* distressed
   assets
relationships, 51, 52–53, 106–107
reporters. *See* media
resilience, 103
resistance, to change, 15–16, 17, 157,
   163

responsibility, 151, 208. *See also* accountability; expectations; standards

results, 11

results-oriented strategy, 90, 92

Rhoads, Paul, 84

Richardson, Antowaine, 88

Richt, Mark, 77, 84, 163

rigidity, 60

Road to the Pros (documentary), 165

Rodriguez, Rich, 114

Rosen, Lionel "Lonny", 85, 86, 87, 105

Rost, Jim, 119, 120–121

Ruggs, Henry, 135

Ryals, LeRoy, 20, 112, 149–150, 202, 214

S

Saban, Nick
    background of, 1–2, 3, 214
    career before Alabama, 3–4
    career decisions, 64
    parents of, 3. *see also* Saban, Nick, Sr.
    wife of. *see* Saban, Terry

Saban, Nick, Sr., 1, 3, 208

Saban, Terry, 3, 20, 64, 110, 114–115, 137, 218

Sabin, Rainer, 184

salary
    buyouts, 73
    Saban's, 201

sales, 138

Sarkisian, Steve, 58, 60, 63, 78–80, 82, 84

Savage, Phil, 90

Scott, JK, 168–169

Scott, Karl, 63

scouting reports, 140–141

SEC Championship, 153

SEC Player of the Year, 38

second chances, 79, 167. *See also* distressed assets; Kiffin, Lane; Sarkisian, Steve

secretaries, 20

self, staying true to, 205–215. *See also* Process, The; style, Saban's

self-efficacy theory, 139

self-evaluation, 158–170. *See also* change

selfishness, 176, 201

self-talk, 88, 94

sense of urgency, 8, 163

Sequoia Capital, 198

service, acts of, 173

Sexton, Jimmy, 58, 64–66, 114, 143, 188

Shannon, Randy, 84

Sheridan, Bill, 21, 123, 149, 178

Shula, Mike, 14, 15, 31, 32, 113

Shurmur, Pat, 51

sickness, 96–97

Sims, Blake, 58

Siskey, Tyler, 22, 29, 67, 70, 137, 168–169, 187

Smart, Kirby, 53, 61, 63, 64, 84, 133, 188, 211, 213

Smith, Andre, 31

Smith, Chris, 13, 14, 177, 225

Smith, DeVonta, 23–24, 54, 55, 133–136, 197

Smith, Maurice, 212

Smithmier, Ken, 36, 59–60

social media, 57, 184

South Carolina University, 199

Spears, Marcus, 110

speeches, pregame, 205–207

Sports Illustrated, 80

sports psychology, 87. *See also* Process,
   The

Spurrier, Steve, 114

stadium layout report, 129–130

staff. *See also* assistant coaches; hiring;
   turnover; *individual staff members*
     at Alabama, 19
     analysts, 74–75, 77, 82, 83–84
     distressed assets, 73–84
     expectations for, 19
     former NFL head coaches, 81
     graduate assistants, 76, 82, 84
     hired away, 62–63
     honesty from, 174–175
     media and, 194
     relationships between, 178
     Saban's relationship with, 173
     Sexton and, 58, 64–66
     trust of, 121

standards, 9, 12, 66, 92, 124, 168–169,
   172

Stoops, Bob, 90

strength and conditioning, 15
     coaches, 12
     Cochran, 15, 52–53, 55, 62, 96–97,
       152, 169, 190, 191
     Fourth Quarter Program, 12, 15,
       29, 52, 152, 202–203, 210

Mannie, 7–8
     at Michigan State, 12–13
     recruiting and, 29
     at Toledo, 7–8
     winter, 8–9, 11

Strong, Charlie, 75, 98

style, Saban's, 173. *See also* personality,
   Saban's; Process, The; self, staying
   true to
     applying beyond football, 219–225
     copied by former assistants,
       211–213
     purpose of, 174
     turnover and, 68–70

success
     change and, 163–164, 170
     complacency and, 196–201
     good feelings from, 131
     long-term, 92
     middle managers and, 51
     recruiting and, 24–25
     2010 Alabama team and, 198–200

suicide prevention, 164

summer camps, 29

Summers, Tyson, 84

Swinney, Dabo, 76

Syracuse, 3

system. *See* Process, The

T

Tagovailoa, Tua, 38, 39, 54, 133–136,
   197, 211

teacher, Saban as, 122–123

team, building, 19. *See also* recruiting;
   staff

Tebow, Tim, 153, 200
Tedford, Jeff, 58
television money, 75
Tennessee, University of, 73. *See also*
    Jones, Butch; Kiffin, Lane
Tenpenny, Altee, 166–167, 168
Terry, Jordan, 16
Texas A&M, 154, 161, 162
Thompson, Lance, 32, 33, 60
Tice, Lou, 88
time wasting, 138
Tinker, Carson, 217
Toledo, University of, 4, 7–12, 25, 57,
    130, 142
tornadoes (2011), 217–218
Training Days: Rolling with the Tide,
    188
Tranquill, Gary, 157
transfers, 34, 52, 166–167, 212
Trickett, Rick, 28, 66, 99, 107, 192–193,
    201
Troy State University, 39
trust, 120, 180
Tucker, Mel, 62, 63
turnover, 57–70, 148. *See also* assistant
    coaches; staff
        after championships, 63
        continuity and, 12
        cost of replacing staff, 62
        loss to Clemson and, 68
        at LSU, 107, 108
        The Process and, 92
        Saban's management style and,
            68–70
        Sexton and, 65
    value in, 70
Tuscaloosa, 217–218
twenty-four-hour rule, 150, 152, 197,
    210
tyrant, Saban perceived as, 173. *See also*
    personality, Saban's; style, Saban's
Tyson, Mike, 161

U

UAB (Alabama at Birmingham), 109,
    185
undefeated seasons, 158
Underwood, John, 161
urgency, sense of, 8, 163
USC, 200

V

Valentine, Don, 198
Valvano, Jim, 206–207
Venturi, Rick, 91, 100–101, 115, 126,
    180, 209, 210
victories. *See* success
Villanova University, 24–25
violence, 50
vision, 10, 11, 179
Vollmar, Mike, 105, 129, 138, 196

W

Walker, Herschel, 38
Walker, Lance, 122, 225
Walker, Sam, 44–45, 48
Walker, Wesley, 141
Walsh, Bill, 107
Washington, University of, 191
Watson, Deshaun, 133

Watts, Tim, 32, 187
weather, 129, 130
Weems, Charlie, 65, 107, 108, 110, 112,
   113, 143, 186, 202
Weis, Charlie, 58, 75
West Virginia (state), 3, 214
West Virginia University, 106
White, Enai, 40
Whitworth, Andrew, 110
Wildhack, John, 188–190
Williams, Bobby, 51–52, 69–70, 112,
   132–133, 178
Williams, Dan, 10–11
Willis, James, 46

Wilson, John Parker, 151
winner's hangover, 150. *See also*
   complacency
wins, 131, 150. *See also* success
Winston, Jameis, 201
wives, coaches', 115. *See also* Saban,
   Terry
work-life balance, 136–138
Wright, Jay, 24–25

Y

Yeldon, T. J., 154, 155
Young, Bryce, 34

About the Author

John Talty is the senior sports editor and SEC Insider for Alabama Media Group, which includes AL.com, *The Birmingham News*, *The Press-Register*, and *The Huntsville Times*. He has also written for *Men's Journal*, *Slate*, and *Athlon Sports*, among other publications. Talty attended the University of Maryland. He grew up in Lincroft, New Jersey, and currently lives in Birmingham, Alabama.